D1765039

Sustainable Marketing of Cultural and Heritage Tourism

Cultural attractions play an important role in tourism at all levels, and draw huge numbers of tourists interested in heritage and the arts. Cultural heritage tourism has positive economic and social impacts but can also have negative impacts on communities and regions. This book draws together and links ideas of tourism from sustainable marketing perspectives and embeds it within a heritage management setting. Through a discussion and analysis of existing literature and practices, this book aims to propose a marketing strategy framework grounded in sustainable principles that can be used to maintain and preserve the authenticity of cultural heritage for future generations, whilst appealing to the suppliers, the regulators, and the consumers.

This book first explains the dynamics of cultural heritage with its authenticity underpinnings, marketing, and tourism, and proposes a strategic praxis drawn from core sustainable principles. This is followed by a pragmatic examination of the proposed framework from the shaper's (provider's) perspective. The material presented is not merely an agglomeration of documented secondary research, but the theoretical concepts are grounded in empirical research and interactive discussions with students and the travel and tourism industry. A variety of heritage institutions across the globe are used as starting points to test the applicability of the proposed paradigm: these include museums, historic house museums, heritage hotels/resorts, festivals, and heritage merchandise.

Sustainable Marketing of Cultural and Heritage Tourism is a timely offering to a growing and vibrant area of research; what is most pertinent is that it is a thorough and fresh take on the topic with primary research included. It will find a place in student materials for a variety of courses and it should be read by practicing academics and researchers.

Deepak Chhabra is Assistant Professor of Community Resources and Development at Arizona State University, USA.

Routledge Critical Studies in Tourism, Business and Management

Series editors: Tim Coles, University of Exeter, UK
and Michael Hall, University of Canterbury, New Zealand.

This ground-breaking monograph series deals directly with theoretical and conceptual issues at the interface between business, management and tourism studies. It incorporates research-generated, highly specialized cutting-edge studies of new and emergent themes, such as knowledge management and innovation, that affect the future business and management of tourism. The books in this series are conceptually challenging, empirically rigorous creative, and, above all, capable of driving current thinking and unfolding debate in the business and management of tourism. This monograph series will appeal to researchers, academics and practitioners in the fields of tourism, business and management, and the social sciences.

The *Routledge Critical Studies in Tourism, Business and Management* monograph series builds on core concepts explored in the corresponding **Routledge International Studies of Tourism, Business and Management** book series. Series editors: Tim Coles, University of Exeter, UK and Michael Hall, University of Canterbury, New Zealand.

Books in the series offer upper-level undergraduates and masters students, comprehensive, thought-provoking yet accessible books that combine essential theory and international best practice on issues in the business and management of tourism such as HRM, entrepreneurship, service quality management, leadership, CSR, strategy, operations, branding and marketing.

Published titles:

International Business and Tourism (2008)
Tim Coles & Michael Hall

Commercial Homes in Tourism: an international perspective (2009)
Paul Lynch, Alison J. McIntosh & Hazel Tucker (eds)

Sustainable Marketing of Cultural and Heritage Tourism
Deepak Chhabra

Economics of Sustainable Tourism (2010)
Fabio Cerina, Anil Markandya & Michael McAleer (eds)

Sustainable Marketing of Cultural and Heritage Tourism

Deepak Chhabra

LONDON AND NEW YORK

First published 2010
by Routledge
2 Park Square, Milton Park, Abingdon, Oxon, OX14 4RN

Simultaneously published in the USA and Canada
by Routledge
270 Madison Avenue, New York, NY 10016

Routledge is an imprint of the Taylor & Francis Group, an informa business

© 2010 Deepak Chhabra

Typeset in Times New Roman by Swales & Willis Ltd, Exeter, Devon
Printed and bound in Great Britain by CPI Antony Rowe, Chippenham, Wiltshire

British Library Cataloguing in Publication Data
A catalogue record for this book is available from the British Library

Library of Congress Cataloging-in-Publication Data
    Chhabra, Deepak, 1963-
    Sustainable marketing of cultural and heritage tourism / Deepack Chhabra.
    p. cm. — (Routledge critical studies in tourism, business and management)
    1. Heritage tourism. 2. Tourism—Marketing. 3. Sustainable development.
    4. Cultural property—Repatriation. I. Title.
    G156.5.H47C48 2010
    910.68'8—dc22
    2009038587

ISBN 13: 978–0–415–77704–9 (hbk)
ISBN 13: 978–0–203–85541–6 (ebk)

ISBN 10: 0–415–77704–6 (hbk)
ISBN 10: 0–203–85541–8 (ebk)

Contents

List of Illustrations

Figures

Plates

Tables

Boxes

Preface

Heritage tourism has become one of the most popular forms of tourism. Countries across the world have welcomed it as an instrument of economic development and advocacy of local culture and heritage. Heritage scholars often describe heritage as "contemporary use of the past" (Ashworth 2003). This definition encompasses both tangible and intangible elements of the cultural/heritage environment. Heritage tourism, in fact, occupies a forefront position in the global tourism industry because it involves millions of visitors every year who travel to visit a variety of heritage attractions and sites (Timothy and Boyd 2006). Because heritage resources are finite, there has emerged a parallel need to develop strategic marketing plans to ensure cultural and heritage sustainability. This form of sustainability requires "collaboration between tourism and cultural heritage management sectors along with the support for both by the host community as a basis" (du Cros 2009: 94). Contemporary documented literature also points to a growing need for corporate social responsibility which implies an ongoing commitment toward the use of sustainable practices, engagement with local communities, and development of brands which facilitate a dialogue between the organization's workforce, community, and the local heritage (Parsons and Maclaran 2009). Also, being advocated is a crucial need to plan and develop a sustainable marketing portfolio so that sustainable guidelines are implemented at the grass roots level. Balancing heritage consumption and conservation is not an easy task, not only at the organizational level but also at the individual level.

'Sustainable marketing' is a hybrid and paradoxical term. Hence sustainable marketing of heritage tourism is a complex notion as it aims to marry three dynamic disciplines: sustainability, marketing, and heritage. It is also a relatively new phenomenon with a meager body of work to carry the concept forward, conceptually and in application.

Cultural heritage, marketing, and tourism are three broad terms which if blended together in the clay of sustainability can produce a blue print for a strategic plan that is able to offer a breathing space to ongoing cultural discourses across several decades. Literature has often referred to heritage, tourism, and marketing as byproducts of the corporate world, focusing on monetization (permeation of money into the social fabric of the contemporary society). This book indicates that all three can be operated in a responsible and sustainable manner if meshed together with an objective to sustain and preserve cultural heritage in the long run.

The underlying justification for producing this book is the need for the heritage industry to formulate a proactive rather than a reactive consensual plan that can appeal to the suppliers, the regulators, and the consumers of the heritage tourism industry within a sustainability framework. Of the limited body of work that is available on cultural heritage marketing, exploration of a unified and harmonious blend of authenticity, conservation, commodification, civic engagement, and economic viability is remiss. Through the discussion and analysis of existing literature and existing practices in the heritage industry, this book aims to propose a marketing strategy framework grounded in sustainable principles for the cultural/heritage industry. This framework encompasses various components crucial for marketing and strategic planning to succeed in a sustainable manner.

The chapters in this volume suggest that sustainable marketing of heritage tourism and its application, although an arduous task, is not an impossible one. Range of success can be accomplished if knowledge, training, and public sector support in the form of regulations and tax breaks are available. The material presented is not merely an agglomeration of documented secondary research, but the theoretical concepts are grounded in empirical research and interactive discussions with students and the travel and tourism industry. A variety of heritage institutions across the globe are used as starting points to test the applicability of the proposed paradigm. These include museums, historic house museums, heritage hotels/resorts, festivals, and heritage merchandise.

Heritage tourism management needs to adapt to the changing world around it, and as competition grows apace and financial resources become scarce, traditional non-profit heritage institutions are required to perform often polarized tripartite functions of providing entertainment to the mass audience, and promoting civic engagement, and original function as custodians of both tangible and intangible heritage. Overall, the topics are designed to keep both academic and practitioner audience abreast of contemporary trends in sustainable marketing and heritage tourism. Given the orientation of much of this volume, the concluding chapter aims to help contextualize heritage tourism marketing within the broader framework of the non-heritage marketing environment. Important inferences are drawn from general marketing literature.

Structure of the book

This book is divided into two parts. The first part explains the dynamics of heritage tourism, marketing, and sustainability and proposes a strategic praxis drawn from core sustainable principles. Also, the pragmatics of the proposed portfolio is presented from the shaper's (provider's) perspective. The second half of the book is structured around the conceptual model illustrated in Figure 2.1. This is deliberate as the model profiles the author's conceptualization of sustainable marketing of heritage tourism and each chapter in the second half of the book offers an insight into the applicability test of the model.

Chapter 1 develops conceptual material on heritage and heritage tourism based on the documentation of numerous discursive accounts. It also identifies recurrent themes in marketing and provides a discursive view of the contemporary trends in heritage tourism marketing. Chapter 2 discusses a blueprint for sustainable tourism development. Issues, associated with the sustainable development of heritage tourism, are uncovered. Also, examined are sustainable heritage tourism marketing models from documented literature. Chapter 3 provides an extensive description of various elements that are required to formulate a sustainable heritage tourism marketing model. It begins with the marketing mix and then follows a description of numerous factors that are likely to influence the marketing mix. In closing, the crucial features of sustainability are examined which are later embedded into the proposed strategic sustainable heritage tourism marketing model. Chapter 4 describes the function and issues associated with contemporary museums before turning to examine the degree to which sustainable marketing is pursued by four unique museums. Chapter 5 focuses on historic house museums. It begins first by reviewing the core purpose of various organizations across the world entrusted with the task of promoting the conservation and public use of historic houses. Next, classifications of historic houses are given followed by an examination of multifaceted challenges posing a barrier to the successful and sustainable use of historic museums. The chapter ends with an illustration of the marketing strategies employed by four historic houses situated in four different countries of the world. Chapter 6 offers an interesting insight into the marketing strategies pursued by four unique hotels or resorts situated in different parts of the world and critiques them using the proposed sustainable marketing model. Chapter 7 examines three unique and popular heritage festivals and offers a discourse into the marketing strategies employed by the festival organizers. Chapter 8 begins by nesting heritage buying within the broader context of the tourism shopping phenomena. Next, is provided an overview of research studies on souvenirs and other categories of heritage merchandise. This is followed by an insight into the marketing strategies pursued by suppliers of three unique types of heritage merchandise Kashmiri shawls, Canadian Totems, and Scottish tartans. The concluding Chapter 9 re-examines the marketing strategies pursued by the heritage tourism industry as an aggregate and returns to some of the core themes presented in the first part of the book. Important contemporary sustainable marketing themes from general marketing literature are examined. It asks complex questions regarding feasibility and lessons to learn from a cross-over of marketing practices pursued by the non-tourism industry. The chapter concludes by furthering the proposed strategic sustainable heritage tourism marketing model based on important lessons derived from the illustrated case studies.

Acknowledgments

This book grew out of my years of teaching tourism marketing, where my interest was peaked about whether heritage can be successfully marketed in a sustainable manner. I have been struck by the results from my other body of work which shows stereotype notions of marketing are embraced by heritage institutions. It is considered a stigma by many traditional heritage institutions, which assume that marketing has a pronounced profitability slant. This book is therefore an attempt to highlight the benefits of marketing if planned in a sustainable and responsible manner.

What I initially conceived as being a quick and modest project turned into a lengthy and complex body of research work. I am enormously grateful to the scores of people and heritage institutions who provided assistance and support during the entire process. The bulk of the research and travel expenses were underwritten by awards and college funds. I thank my colleagues at the School of Community Resources and Development, especially Dallen Timothy for his initial encouragement to transform the sustainability discourse into a book. Also, I appreciate the help of Yuta Takeda, an undergraduate student of Arizona State University.

My field work was facilitated and enriched by a number of experts including Dr. Ann Marshall of Heard Museum (USA), Donna Abelli of Emily Dickenson Museum (USA), Catherine Terzaghi of Maison Tavel (Switzerland), Dr. Varsha Dass of Mahatma Gandhi Memorial Museum (India), Dr. Y.B. Singh of UP Tourism Office (India), Michael Davis of Culloden House Hotel (Scotland), and Mike Gibson of Southeast Heritage (UK).

Finally, I thank my family. This book is dedicated to my father, Dr. G.S. Chhabra and my late mother, Sharanjit Walia, who is no more with me but continues to inspire through the memories I will always have of her.

1 Marketing of Heritage Tourism

Heritage tourism has grown exponentially over the past several decades. It is a multifaceted term manifested with a wide range of meanings and, therefore, it is not uncommon to find sometimes polarized views of it in published literature. This chapter aims to develop conceptual material on heritage and heritage tourism based on the perusal of numerous discursive accounts. It is also known that marketing of heritage tourism is a complex phenomenon because akin to the heritage debate, a review of marketing literature points to a wide range of discussion on numerous marketing concepts. Marketing as a phenomenon has undergone many changes over the past several decades. The purpose of this chapter is also to identify recurrent themes in the terrain of marketing and conclude with a discussion of contemporary trends in heritage tourism marketing.

Heritage Tourism

Heritage has been a buzzword in tourism since the late nineteenth century. Much scholarly debate with regard to the nature of heritage tourism still persists, suggesting that heritage is an amorphous concept and a complex phenomenon. Myriad viewpoints shape its definition. This can be partially attributed to the positive and negative treatment accorded to heritage. The positive aspect of heritage aims to take care of culture and landscape for long-term use, whereas the negative aspect implies "manipulation and exploitation of the past for commercial ends" (Merriman 1991: 8).

Previous research has broadly classified heritage into two categories: tangible and intangible. Tangible heritage is inclusive of all assets that contain a degree of physical embodiment of cultural values (UNESCO 2000). Examples include cultural objects, movable items, historic towns, archaeological sites, and cultural landscapes. McKercher and du Cros define intangible heritage as "traditional culture, folklore, or popular culture that is performed or practiced with close ties to 'place' and with little complex technological accompaniment" (2002: 83). Heritage is also referred to as built heritage which can be classified into three categories (Prentice 1993):

- Historic and artistic: Examples include relics with physical/tangible characteristics.

- Scientific: This category refers to elements drawn from birds, animals, rocks etc.
- Cultural heritage: Examples include folk, fine arts, traditions, and languages.

In the context of tourism, the word 'heritage' has both cultural and natural connotations (Herbert 1989; Timothy and Boyd 2003; Zeppal and Hall 1992). For instance, Timothy and Boyd create a heritage spectrum that traverses multiple settings ranging from "natural and pristine to the built-urban and artificial" (2003: 9). The authors argue that heritage "represents some sort of inheritance to be passed down to current and future generations, both in terms of cultural traditions and physical artifacts" (2003: 2). Earlier, Richards (1996) defined heritage as a gamut inclusive of ancient monuments, the built urban settings, multiple features of the natural environment, and numerous facets of living culture and the arts. Howard describes heritage as "anything that someone wishes to conserve or collect and pass on to future generations" (2003: 6). Tourism thus stands to benefit from the heritage–tourism link in the range of heritage participation opportunities available across the globe. Convergence of tourism and heritage operations demonstrates the politics of power to control the past and its selected distribution to the tourist (McLean 1995). Heritage is a driving force of complexes which focuses on disseminating cultural capital. Thus, within the tourism context, heritage has become a commodity aimed to fulfill the needs of the contemporary tourist. According to Taylor (2001), heritage tourism is driven by monetary motivations and is being increasingly used today as a distinguishing base to surpass competition. Heritage tourism can exist at different levels: world, national, local, and personal (Graham, Ashworth and Tunbridge 2000).

While the above discussion highlights use of heritage from a tourism perspective, it is also worthy of mention that latent or non-use status of some kinds of heritage also exists. Timothy (2000) identifies several constraints to the latent demand of heritage such as inaccessibility (either physical or market such as work and family obligations and low income levels), lack of educational knowledge, disabilities (creating intrinsic, environmental, and communication barriers), and psychological barriers (such as a popular notion that historic sites are boring, lack of interest or desire). In such cases, deliberate marketing strategies are required to assist in addressing latent demand barriers.

What is heritage tourism? This is probably a simple question but nevertheless a difficult one to answer because so many definitions of heritage tourism adorn the academic radar. Heritage tourism studies have embraced a wide array of themes such as "the analysis of museums, landscapes, artifacts, and activities that concentrate on representing different aspects of the past" (Halewood and Hannam 2001: 566). Nevertheless, a monolithic approach to delineate boundaries is often followed in extant documented literature, thereby neglecting to acknowledge the broader underpinnings of heritage tourism (Apostolakis 2003).

The myriad viewpoints of heritage tourism can also be alluded to by its polarized definitional themes. The first theme is supply-centered and refers to both the tangible and the intangible nature of culture and heritage (Ashworth and Larkham 1994;

Garrod and Fyall 2001; Nuryunti 1996; Yale 1991). Examples include attractions, relics, artifacts, art objects in addition to traditions, languages, and folklore (Apostolakhis 2003: 799). This definitional group also recognizes that a heritage tourism activity comprises of two elements: primary (the main attraction) and secondary (which enhance or support the primary attraction).

The second theme has demand-side connotations and centers on perceptions, motivations, and experiences based on the consumption of heritage resources and, thus, it embodies an interpersonal element (Chhabra, Healy and Sills 2003; Moscardo 2001; Richards 1996; Silberberg 1995). Moscardo (2001) describe heritage tourism as an experience triggered by visitor–source interactions. The entire process is considered interactive. In common with the antecedent viewpoints, Richards (1996) refers to heritage tourism as either a product or a process guided by both demand and supply perspectives. Clearly, this view reinforces the multiple delineations of heritage tourism. The product-based approach refers to the tangible context of sites and museums while the experiential aspect has conceptual underpinnings associated with the motive and meaning attached to a heritage activity.

Poria, Butler and Airey (2001) define heritage tourism as a phenomenon created by visitor perceptions of a heritage site. As is evident, the fundamental tenet here pertains to cognitive perceptions, expectations, and motivations. Motivations for heritage tourism include nostalgia, social distinction, and desire for an 'authentic' experience (Poria *et al.* 2001). In fact, of paramount importance are nostalgia and authenticity as motivational factors facilitating demand for heritage tourism. As pointed out by Lowenthal, "if the past is a foreign country, nostalgia has made it the foreign country with the healthiest tourist trade of all" (1985: 4). This means that the past can be transformed into a 'palatable slice of nostalgia' in the capitalist economies. Also, popular demand for authenticity has existed since times immemorial and remains strong today (Jones 1993; Grayson and Martinec 2004). However, marketing researchers have only recently begun to take notice of this cult of authenticity.

Spearheading the list of aforesaid motivations across a range of heritage institutions is a pronounced message that "authenticity is a generic and uncontestable attribute of any primary heritage manifestation" (Chhabra, Healy *et al.* 2003). Authenticity has played a pivotal role in luring visitors to heritage sites (Chhabra, Healy *et al.* 2003; Halewood and Hannam 2001; Waitt 2000). It is a viable economic resource and can be used to tap and manage current and potential demand. This view resonates with Apostolakhis, who argues that "the concept of authenticity can be managed to generate a procedure through which product characteristics stemming from the supply side of the model can be adjusted accordingly to incorporate the multiplicity of market segments as these are presented through tourists' motivation patterns" (2003: 699).

Despite the potential significance of authenticity from conservation and consumption perspectives, it remains an elusive concept because of its multiple connotations. Halewood and Hannam (2001) provide an insightful discussion on the 'authenticity' perspectives of heritage tourism. The authors highlight three views: heritage is bogus and trash, heritage is staged authenticity, and heritage is commodified authenticity. In other words, heritage to them is one of the following (2001: 567):

- Landscapes of nostalgia – it implies that the contemporary growth of heritage tourism is fueled by nostalgia thereby offering a sense of security and stability against the contemporary era of uncertainty.
- Staged authenticity – it refers to contrived settings to satisfy tourists' quests for genuine experiences. This perspective echoes MacCannell's (1992) argument that staging develops a distinct tourism space apart from the real place and this distance ruins all chances of an authentic experience.
- Commodification – this suggests that heritage tourism may lead to the standardization of culture and transform it into a global commodity for consumption. In such cases then, authenticity becomes a marketing tool. Halewood and Hannam (2001) maintain this commoditization as a mixed blessing. It can prove to be lucrative for a host community although its mass consumption can make it inauthentic and disassociated from the original meaning. Bagnall (1996) locates two responses to this problematic term: the emotional realism response and the factual basis response. The first one refers to felt experience, feelings of consuming the past or obtaining a good view of what past life was like, whereas the second response is associated with the desire for experiences that are based on object genuineness and fact. A more detailed discursive view of authenticity is given in Chapter 2.

Regardless of the wide range of views related to heritage tourism, its economic significance helps build a common platform between the supply and demand perspectives. Heritage is of significance in tourism because it provides monetary benefits (Chhabra, Sills and Cubbage 2003; Chhabra, Healy *et al.* 2003; Leones, Colby and Crandall 1998; Davies and Mangan 1992; Garrod and Fyall 2001). It has been posited that the rapid growth of the heritage tourism industry mostly rests on its potential to generate economic benefits (Chhabra, Sills and Rea 2002; Fayissa, Nsiah and Tadasse 2007; Li, Wu and Cai 2008; Simpson 2008). Numerous studies have examined the economic impact of heritage tourism on host communities and its other stakeholders and have reported positive benefits (Chhabra, Healy *et al.* 2003; Crompton, Lee and Shuster 2001; Crompton 2006; Fayissa *et al.* 2007). It has been noted that residents and visitors make monetary contributions to the government in the form of taxes. The government uses some of these funds to subsidize tourism events, promotions, activities, or facilities that lure tourists to spend money within the local community (Crompton 2006). This new money generated by out-of-community visitors generates income and employment for local residents. Thus the host community benefits through the availability of new jobs and increase in household income.

In sum then, the core elements of heritage tourism center on economics, emotions/motivation, inheritance, past, common (shared), authenticity, and participation. Evidently, a precise definition of heritage tourism will be illusionary. But there is little doubt that a number of identifiable characteristics of heritage tourism exist. Having reviewed multiple themes and definitions of heritage tourism, it is now necessary to consider how concepts can be fused together to coin a holistic and fuller understanding of heritage tourism. To accomplish this task, this book coins a working definition of heritage tourism: a phenomenon that focuses on the management of past, inheritance, and authenticity to enhance participation and satisfy consumer motivations by evoking nostalgic emotions; its underlying purpose is to stimulate monetary benefits for its various constituencies such as the museums, historic houses, festivals, heritage hotels, and other stakeholders. To include a sustainable element to the definition of heritage tourism, one may add to the above while at the same time adhering to specific conservation principles.

Supply and Demand of Heritage Tourism

A fundamental assumption in heritage tourism is that it is an industry, consciously controlled and planned, with the purpose of producing a marketable product. This explains why heritage tourism has both supply and demand connotations. As a useful starting point, this section begins by defining the concepts of supply and demand. As described by Timothy and Boyd (2003: 61), "in traditional economic terms, demand refers to the quantities of products and services that are consumed at various prices." Supply, on the other hand, is taken to encompass a range of tourism resources and services in a given region. Supply factors often operate as pull factors and their strength helps determine the heritage destination appeal. Timothy and Boyd suggested a broad supply of heritage attractions:

> Museums such as arts, sports, music, industrial science, philatelic, and local history;
> War sites and atrocities such as battlefields, war graves, cemeteries, and memorials;
> Religious sites such as pilgrimages and sacred sites;
> Living culture of distinct groups such as traditions, ways of life, ceremonies, dances, agricultural practices, culinary habits, and arts and crafts;
> Festivals such as those focusing on culture and heritage;
> Industrial places such as mines, quarries, factories, harbors, ports, agricultural relics, railroads and railway museums;
> Literary sites, for example, fictional and real-life places of authors and playwrights. (2003: 59)

Attention in this paragraph shifts to demand. Literature reveals that demand for heritage sites has grown exponentially over the last few decades. This is evident from the increasing popularity of heritage sites in the United States. Within the heritage tourism context, different views of demand exist. For instance, four perspectives of demand are reported by Johnson and Thomas (1995):

1. Current or use demand – refers to the number of tourists to the heritage site.
2. Option demand – refers to the option of a future visit by potential visitors.

3. Existence demand –refers to the value placed on the heritage site regardless of any current or future use.
4. Bequeath demand – pertains to the desire to promote intergenerational equity; that is, the ability to be able to pass on to the future generations what is acquired from the ancestors.

Demand can also be examined from the source perspective. Significant demand sources include individuals and groups striving to promote heritage attractions, various government agencies, and heritage custodians (Timothy and Boyd 2003). Some authors such as Kerstetter, Confer and Bricker (1998) and Poria *et al.* (2001) relate to demand from the market perspective. Tourists and visitors and their preferences, activities, visitation, and spending potential constitute the market version of demand. Demand also refers to audience-related factors such as group and individual markets, consumer behavior, market segmentation, and target marketing. (Kotler, Bowen and Makens 2006)

Marketing

Attempts to define marketing have engaged the energies of many authors, both academics and those belonging to the managerial field. Given the ordeal of producing a precise and universally accepted definition, Schulz (2001) suggests that this term should cease to be used so that reflections can be geared toward its purpose and significance. In fact, the 2004 definition of marketing by the American Marketing Association was condemned by marketing academicians for its ignorance toward stakeholders, impact on society, and narrow organizational slant (Parsons and Maclaran 2009). Consequently, marketing is being redefined to include the overall society interests. Most recent meaning of marketing in non-tourism literature has thus centered on value co-creation, calling for intensive engagement with the consumers; the emphasis is on "creating systems that result in mutual value although actively supporting rather than directing, consumer creation of value" (Parsons and Maclaran 2009: 7). Arnould and Thompson also support the consumer culture framework and argue that contemporary marketing needs to represent all aspects of consumer phenomena such as "neglected experiential, social, and cultural dimensions of consumption" (2005: 869).

A perusal of marketing definitions in the tourism literature, on the other hand, reveals that tourism is still heavily slanted toward customer needs, satisfaction, and relationship building, although traces of society and stakeholder emphases are beginning to emerge. This book makes an attempt to define marketing as is understood and applied in the contemporary era. Dozens of acceptable definitions of marketing exist. Five well-considered definitions from the tourism terrain and two from the non-tourism field are identified:

•   Marketing is a tool to promote your product, a way to improve program attendance, advertising programs to the public, introduce programs to others, and sell what you offer. (Janes 2006: 5)

- Marketing is about anticipating demand, recognizing it, stimulating it, and finally satisfying it; in short, understanding customers' wants and needs, as to what can be sold, to whom, when, where and in what quantities. (Holloway 2004: 7)
- Creating and keeping customers are two inherent and inseparable words that define marketing. (Shoemaker, Lewis and Yesawich 2000: 20)
- Marketing is the effective management by an organization of its exchange relations with its various markets and publics. Marketing is the analysis, planning, implementation, and control of carefully formulated programs designed to bring about voluntary exchanges in values with target markets for the purpose of achieving organizational objectives. It relies heavily on designing the organization's offering in terms of the target markets' needs and desires, and on using effective pricing, communication, and distribution to inform, motivate, and service the markets. (Kotler 1982: xiii, 6)
- Marketing is a societal process by which individuals and groups obtain what they need and want through creating, offering, and exchanging products and value with others. (Kotler *et al.* 2006: 13)
- Marketing is the planning of activity for creating, communicating, delivering, and exchanging offerings that offer value for customers, clients, and society at large. (Lib 2007)
- Marketing is the activity, conducted by organizations and individuals that operates through a set of institutions and processes for creating, communicating, delivering, and exchanging market offerings that have value for customers, clients, marketer, and society at large. (revised definition by the American Marketing Association, AMA 2007)

This book draws on some of the core concepts presented by the aforesaid sources and defines marketing as:

A process sought to exchange ideas, relations, and products with the organization's various publics and stakeholders with objectives to enhance attendance, revenue, education, and interactive engagement with the consumers while

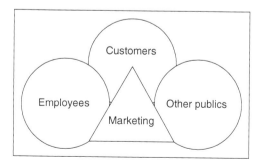

Figure 1.1 The Marketing Role

promoting sustainable environments and society interests at large for the enjoyment of both the current and future generations.

The role of marketing is to integrate different publics of a business or organization. Janes (2006) reports that marketing has become a core function in tourism organizations. Webster (1995) asserts that an integrated marketing culture can facilitate greater marketing effectiveness. As Figure 1.1 demonstrates, employees are an integral part of an organization who help to deliver products and promises in an efficient and timely manner. Lending a voice to this credence, Cony (2002) emphasizes on the significance of considering employees and volunteers as one category of target audience to promote internal marketing.

Philosophies of Marketing

All businesses or firms operate under a fundamental marketing philosophy or orientation and this philosophy is an integral part of the organizational culture. It serves to guide the marketing efforts. Six predominant philosophies can be identified from a perusal of literature: product and manufacturing, selling, marketing, relationship, tribal, and societal. In fact, the first five can be placed on a continuum ranging from transactional focus to 'communitas' relationship emphasis (as illustrated in Figure 1.2). A brief description of each is given below:

- *Product and Manufacturing Philosophy* – centers on the theme 'build it and they will come.' Organizations or businesses working under this philosophy "trumpet that their property has the best food, the finest chefs, designer-decorated lobbies, or even the best location" (Shoemaker, *et al*. 2000: 28). This philosophy was more popular in the 1960s and early 1970s (Janes 2006). Customer needs were not given priority. The focus was solely on operations. In the contemporary era also, it is not uncommon to come across this theme in some countries where demand is in excess of supply.
- *Selling Philosophy* – with the progress in technology, production became easy in the mid-1970s. However, competition became more intense and each business strived to excel in selling skills. The focus switched from production to selling. "Beating the competition by outselling them became the first priority" (Morrison 2002: 5). Efforts to find someone to walk through the hotel and restaurant doors became the central aim of marketing (Shoemaker *et al*. 2000). The aim of selling, thus, is to "get every possible sale, and not to worry about satisfaction after the sale or the revenue distribution of the sale" (Kotler *et al*. 2006: 25). Consequently, a long-term relationship with the customers is not given priority and efforts center on getting rid of the product.
- *Marketing Philosophy* – this became the locus of attention in the 1980s. This orientation is premised on the notion that 'Customer is King' and gives top priority to the needs and wants of the consumers. The key message is that

serving customers better is the "best way to earn profits" (Shoemaker *et al.* 2000: 29). Clearly, the willingness to be flexible and adapt to the changing customer needs constitutes the essential characteristic of this philosophy. Other principal characteristics include embrace of marketing research as an ongoing activity in the organization, understanding of customers' perceptions, frequently reviewing strengths and weaknesses relative to the competitors, planning long term, and valuing and encouraging interdepartmental cooperation (Shoemaker *et al.* 2000: 16). This philosophy continues to be highlighted by most of the travel and tourism businesses and organizations across the world.

• *Relationship Philosophy* – this orientation is the product of the 1990s and emphasizes integrating the customers into the organizational mission in a systematic manner. In Janes's words, it is about "connecting the organization to the consumer" (2006: 7). The theme centers around building valued relationships with customers. Here, organizations seek to "tie-in" customers and win customer retention (Gummesson 1999). Two integral elements of relationship marketing are the promise concept (Magrath 1992) and trust (Moorman, Deshpande and Zaltman 1993). Mutual giving and fulfillment of promises are important to achieve customer retention. In addition, customers' trust in the resource and the organization are equally important. Several leading businesses such as the Four Seasons Hotels and Resorts and Ritz Carlton follow this philosophy.

• *Tribal Marketing Philosophy* – Cova (1997) argues that the conventional relationship focus is shortsighted because it aims at creating and developing a relation between an organization/firm and the consumer. The author offers a communal perspective to relationship marketing that accords priority to restructuring and supporting the relationship among consumers or different members of the audience. Products, physical products, and employees are used to support the communal structure instead of offering a substitute product for it (Cova 1997). Tribal marketing thus emphasizes shared experience and advocates against exploitation of consumers in their "contemporary individualization" (Cova and Cova 2002: 595). This school of thought focuses on the reverse movement to address the postmodernity concerns of "severe dissolution and extreme individualism" (Cova 1997: 300) as a result of fragmented clutter of consumption made possible by the contemporary experience economy. Marketing, in this case, becomes a system to fill the void created by individualized fragmentations and lack of community.

• *Societal Marketing Philosophy* – this concept holds that products should be marketed to customers in a responsible manner. In other words, "the organization should determine the needs, wants, and interests of target markets and deliver the desired satisfactions more effectively and efficiently than competitors in a way that maintains or improves the consumer's and society's well being" (Kotler *et al.* 2006: 27). Supporters of this philosophy seek active coordination between public interest groups and the travel and tourism industry. The aim is to guide the industry so that long term benefits can be sought for the society as a whole.

The first three philosophies can be paraphrased as a 'marketing myopia.' This implies that, businesses are "unable or unwilling to think, see, and plan beyond the short term. Managers are short-sighted and often fail to realize that there's no such thing as a perpetual growth industry" (Morrison 2002: 24). Events such as energy crisis in the mid. 1970s and invasion of Kuwait by Saddam Hussein in the 1980s, and World Trade Center attacks have shown that it is a strategic error to confidently predict a consistent upward growth of the tourism industry. Proper planning and awareness of unpredictable changes are important to ensure continued success of tourism businesses. Additionally, as stated by Morrison (2002), organizations with production orientation define their businesses in a narrow manner and fail to tap lucrative marketing opportunities. Furthermore, these philosophies do not taken customer needs into consideration and take an inside-out perspective. This can be detrimental for organizations existing in competitive environments.

The marketing philosophy, on the other hand, embraces an outside perspective and strives to "meet the organizational goals by creating long-term customer relationships based on customer value and satisfaction" (Kotler *et al.* 2006: 26). The relationship concept furthers the marketing perspective and is centered on the "development and maintenance of mutually satisfying long-term relationships with customers" (Gilbert 1996: 576). The tribal perspective takes the relationship approach to a next level by advocating active engagement not only between the organization/firm and the customers but also between the customers to enhance shared values and engaged experiences.

Parallel to this progressing continuum is the emergence and progress of the societal marketing philosophy in tourism. This concept seeks awareness of negative impacts on the society. In the words of Kotler *et al.*, "the hospitality and travel industries cannot insulate themselves from the continuing need for societal approval" (2006: 28). A strong link of this orientation can be found in social marketing which aims to seek cognitive, action, behavioral or value changes in a society. Social marketing can be described as "the design, implementation, and control of programs seeking to increase the acceptability of a social idea or cause in a target group (s). It utilizes the concept of market segmentation, consumer research,

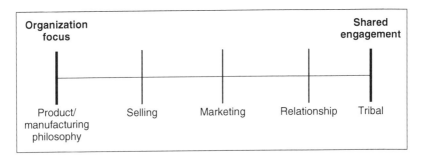

Figure 1.2 Marketing Philosophies

concept development, communication, facilitation, incentives, and exchange theory to maximize target group response" (Kotler 1982: 490).

Marketing for For-Profit and Non-Profit

In today's tourism environment, marketing is crucial not only for for-profit organizations but also for non-profit and public agencies. Not withstanding any reluctance among non-profit, for-profit, and public agencies to work together, developing a coordinated framework is no simple task. It might be expected that each of these organizations will follow different objectives, but "the distinctions historically created between public and private, nonprofit and for-profit tourism organizations, are slowly blending. Every organization, regardless of profit status has specific objectives from which to guide the decisions of the organization" (Janes 2006: 20). The most pronounced issue dominating the goals of non-profit and public agencies is decrease in funding. Traditional sources such as taxation, grants, and donations for securing operating and financial budgets are becoming redundant today. Increasing reliance on user fees and revenue earned from ancillary services such as souvenir shops and onsite restaurants have blurred the demarcating line between for-profit and non-profit/public marketing strategies. Therefore, it will not be unrealistic to say in this era that one single marketing strategy can be designed to cross different frontiers.

Marketing of Heritage Tourism

Much of the recent research focus of heritage tourism marketing is centered on the following recurrent themes: market segmentation, consumer behavior, communication and promotion (mostly advertising), and partnerships. In fact, there has been a growing body of work in heritage tourism literature that seeks to identify different market segments so that tailor-made products can be designed for profitable target markets. A distinct basis for segmentation has been identified to be demographics (Chen and Hsu 2000; Misiura 2006), perceptions (Chhabra, Healy *et al.* 2003; Waitt 2000), motivation (Kerstetter, Confer and Graefe 2001), activities (Sung 2004), attitude (Poria, Butler and Airey 2003), benefits (Frochot 2005), and spending propensity (Chhabra *et al.* 2002; Caserta and Russo 2002). Several of these aforementioned authors conclude that market segmentation research is crucial to decision-precise promotional strategies (Cooper and Inoue 1996). As noted by Chhabra (2009), the main goal has been to stay competitive, satisfy consumer needs, increase marketing effectiveness, and provide a base for target markets and help identify opportunities and threats.

Documented literature classifies communication channels into two categories: interpersonal (occurring on a personal level) and impersonal (mass and promotion based) (Schiffman and Kanuk 1991). Mixed use of these channels has been reported in heritage tourism literature. Several studies have reported reliance on interpersonal communication channels (Stynes and Mahoney 1986; Chhabra *et al.* 2002). External marketing communications often take the shape of intended messages directed at target markets. Different strategies are known to apply to first time and repeat visitors. External communications or promotions have mainly focused on informative messages for prospects and relevance-, memory-, or connection-based messages for repeat markets (Reid and Reid 1993; Walters, Sparks and Herington *et al.* 2007). Furthermore, print ads are extensively used to promote heritage tourism (Smith and McKay 2001; Manfredo, Bright and Haas 1992). Main focus is on advertising and the measurement of its effectiveness among selected target markets in heritage tourism literature (Xiao and Mair 2006). Advertising-related research in heritage tourism has centered on brochures, newspapers, radio, television etc., to examine word meanings and imagery perspectives to gauge the impact of messages (MacInnis and Price 1987; Gartner 1993). For instance, Walters *et al.* (2007) examine the effectiveness of external stimuli in evoking consumers' visionary responses to advertising material.

In sum, the aforesaid discussion reveals that regardless of the communication strategy used, the core focus of heritage tourism marketing has been on designing promotional strategies and message content appropriate for selected or suggested target markets. The messages are designed to appeal to target markets so that more profits can be generated. Therefore, it is evident that exploration of a unified and harmonious blend of marketing, authenticity, culture, commodification, and conservation is remiss. Nevertheless, works of Misiura (2006), Rowan and Baram (2004), and McLean (2002) need to be commended and are worthy of discussion:

- Misiura (2006) centralizes the customer while explaining the dynamics of heritage marketing. She summarizes her understanding of marketing derived from the work of Dibb and Simkin who maintain that "the aim of marketing is to know and understand the customer so well that the product or service fits him/her but allows the organization to achieve its goals" (2006: 2). Misiura's heritage marketing model refers to the influence of environmental factors on the heritage suppliers, market segmentation, and the marketing mix. The underlying connotation behind the model is relationship building through focus on quality, customer service, and service issues. Misiura's suggests that the marketer should act as an ethnographer and try to understand the consumers. On heritage and identity, she talks about the organizational need to establish corporate identity and make heritage symbolic. According to her, heritage links people to consumer brands and emotional and spiritual assets of communities are offered for experience. She suggests further research to explore the relationship between heritage and identity to enable the marketers to target niche markets effectively. She raises the issue of heritage inclusivity. Additionally, she expresses concerns about the limited information available from the minority groups. Nostophobia is what she focuses on when discussing the past. According to her, because there is a past to be told, it should be marketed and sold wherever possible.
- In their seminal work on marketing archaeology, Rowan and Baram (2004) focus on archeology and consumption of the past. The authors refer to market-

ing from a material, corporate, and consumerism perspective and demonstrate concern over the increasing commodification of archaeology and the past. They are skeptical of the term 'heritage.' They also state that the proliferation of commodity production, distribution, and consumption can be understood in the context of power dynamics. According to Rowan and Baram, "the commodification of the past is part of a trajectory on which more and more aspects of social life and localized resources become objects for consumption" (2004: 6). The authors imply that marketing uses the past for a specific purpose and parallel this with heritage explained as a "complex notion, involving the past, contemporary social understandings of places and the active construction of the past" (Rowan and Baram 2004: 5). To conclude, the authors explore the association between the material remains of the past and their access, using a global perspective. Their central theme focuses on the "contemporary consequences and long-term scholarly implications of globally generated and situated presentations of the past" (Rowan and Baram 2004: 3). Heritage tourism is referred to as a consumerist phenomenon. By adding an economic element to this dynamism, the entire phenomenon of tourism use of the past and archeology distracts from the core purpose resulting in a discourse between scholarly and corporate implications.

- McLean (2002) focuses on museums and discusses marketing strategies and concepts within the museum environments. According to the author, "marketing in museums is misunderstood. What is required is an understanding of marketing developed specifically for the museum context, one which reflects the purpose of the museum" (McLean 2002: 21). The author is of the opinion that marketing should be considered as one of the many tools used to accomplish the museum's collection and preservation objectives. She argues that "marketing at its lowest denominator is about building a relationship between the museum and the public" (McLean 2002:2).

The author displays concern over the misuse and misunderstanding of marketing in the museum world. She questions the credentials of marketing with its multiple connotations, commonly understood as focusing on the needs of the consumer and supplier strategies to meet those needs. According to the author "without people, there would be no need for marketing" (2002: 1). The author contends that the expectation of designing museum marketing to reflect social goals (based on the notion that museums exist for the public benefit) can be detrimental to the overall preservation and collection ethos.

Museology, she points out is not a straightforward concept and the new museum ethos requires society values to be inherent in the interpretation content of museums (McLean 2002). Within this principle, marketing is a tool for survival, and "the public only needs to be persuaded and cajoled to visit and marketing needs should be specifically developed for the museum context, one which reflects the purpose of the museum" (McLean 2002: 2). Marketing can be corrupt and unethical and often lead to manipulations and distortions albeit it can serve a useful function if embraced by museums as a last resort (out of desperation).

Trends in Heritage Tourism

More recently, it has been pointed out that heritage tourism marketing fails to take into consideration significant trends that are likely to affect the heritage industries and also neglects the agendas of heritage managers (Ashworth and Tunbridge 2000). Therefore, it is necessary to outline trends suggested by existing literature as they have the potential to influence the planning and success thereof the marketing strategies within the realm of heritage tourism. These include:

- *Demand trends* – heritage tourism continues to grow as more and more people are interested in peeking into the past and cultures of the 'other.' This growing demand will continue to impose a drain on heritage resources and living cultures.
- *Increasing competition* – Timothy and Boyd (2003) claim that there is an over-supply of heritage today accompanied by the race to divorce heritage attractions from their original settings. This can be partly attributed to the "current level of interest which is creating a situation where destinations seeking to capitalize on this market are continuously expanding their attraction bases, often placing the ever more popular heritage label on existing features to create new demand, for example, heritage rivers, heritage railways etc." (Timothy and Boyd 2003: 282).
- *Gazinta philosophy* – the term 'gazinta' implies optimal effective use of time (Burns 1993). Time has become a precious commodity and consumers today desire to participate in a wide range of activities rather than devote their time on a few. Consequently, tourism suppliers are offering a wider spectrum of activities and experiences under one roof. Yeoman, Brass and McMahon-Beattie suggest that in the foreseen future, "people's leisure portfolios will incorporate a wide range of 'shortburst,' simultaneous or integrated activities taking place alongside spells of longer, less hectic activity which can described as 'time oasis leisure' today" (2007: 1132).
- *Growing demand for authenticity* – Yeoman *et al.* (2007) also identifies a growing trend among visitors to Scotland to obtain original and real experiences and products instead of fake ones. This view is also maintained by Wang (1999) and Wilmott and Nelson (2003). Consumer decisions today are "based on how real they perceive the product/service offering to be" (Yeoman *et al.* 2007: 1128). As concluded by Taylor (1991), today's consumer feels more secure in the past as the future becomes more uncertain with ongoing environmental, political, and economic issues. Feelings of nostalgia and need for a secure environment lure them to seek their legacy and inheritance.
- *Ethical consumption and volunteering* – Wilmott (2003) reports that ethical consumption is emerging as a significant tourism trend. The affluence tourist

market is interested in contributing to the society. This view is evident in the growing demand for volunteer tourism (Gray and Campbell 2007; McGehee and Santos 2005; Mustonen 2006). In fact, volunteering is considered trendy today. Also, it is purported that awareness of heritage will continue to grow significantly for the overall wellbeing, education, and health of the society (Brown 2005; Cossons 1989).

- *Continued relationship with politics and the accountability thereof* – as maintained by Timothy and Boyd (2006), heritage is a highly contested and a highly political phenomenon. For instance, selective memory (referred to as social/collective amnesia) is often used to highlight certain events and history. The ethnic groups in power suppress some other pasts of non-desirable people or write them out of documented history or ignore indigenous heritage as is the case in South Africa and with the Native Americans in the United States. In fact, "dissonant views of history and the perceived superiority of various heritages have been at the root of many conflicts" (Timothy and Boyd 2006: 3). Also, heritage places and events are commonly used to instill selected nationalist images and patriotism (Chronis and Hampton 2008; Pretes 2003). Trends today are pointing to a consumer desire to seek more balanced and accurate views of history and this will help unveil forgotten or discarded pasts (Goodwin and Francis 2003; Weeden 2005).

- *Experience-based economy* – today, consumers prefer products that provide meaningful experiences and can enrich their lives, and more and more organizations/businesses are promoting this trend. In fact, they are seeking a real sense of place and attachment with places they visit (Stamboulis and Skayannis 2003). Such experiences forge a personal connection between the supplier and the consumer, commanding dedicated engagement and loyalty, thereby providing a distinct marketing advantage (Pine and Gilmore 1999). This has generated greater demand for interactive events and exhibits in museums, festivals and other heritage institutions (Chhabra 2008; Henderson 2005). Pine and Gilmore identify four distinct categories of experiences: entertainment, education, esthetic, and escapist (see Figure 1.3). According to the authors, the escapist experience fully immerses the participant and involves active participation (for example white water rafting), whereas the esthetic realm offers a fully immersive but passive kind of experience (for example visiting a museum). The educational offers active engagement to the participant (for example, attending a seminar). And the entertainment category of experiences is absorbing but passive. Examples in the later category include watching a movie or television. The authors believe that the most compelling experiences are the ones that congregate in the center of the experience model (see Figure 1.3). It is suggested that heritage organizations should aim to provide compelling experiences to capture audience interest and loyalty.

- *Resistance to marketing by both consumers and conventional suppliers of heritage* – trends point to a future world of 'No Logos' (Klein 2001). Yeoman *et al.* (2007) report that a hospital in Norfolk had banned McDonalds from

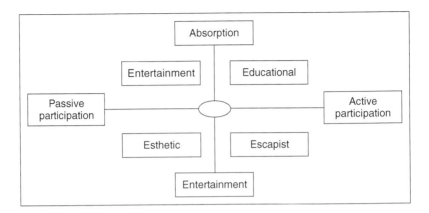

Figure 1.3 The Four Realms of Experience
Source: Pine and Gilmore (1998: 7)

distributing meal vouchers to the families of ailing young patients. Consumers are becoming increasingly wary and distrustful of con marketing strategies employed by big companies and popular brands. Skepticism toward advertising was also evident in 2005, when despite the fact that consumers were bombarded with 5000 messages everyday, the conversion rates were not impressive (Yeoman *et al.* 2007).

- *Multiculturalism* – this is a growing trend. Yeoman *et al.* state that "the internet boom, the expansion in specialist and minority television channels, and the relentless growth in international tourism etc., combine to stretch perceptions" (2007: 1132). In fact, consumers live in multicultural environments and demand the same when they travel.
- *Heritage economics* – the economic prospect of heritage tourism is enormous and yet untapped to its full potential. Benefits to ancillary sectors such as restaurants, souvenir shops, lodging establishments, gasoline stations, etc. and ripple effects of resulting multipliers will continue to garner future support for heritage tourism from both public and private sectors. Also, as public funds continue to dwindle, creative and innovative strategies are likely to be the priority of heritage site managers (Ames 1988; Gorgas 2001). These will include efforts to secure grants, fund raising activities, and actively seeking donations and sponsorships (AAM 2009; Burgers 2000; Chhabra 2008).

While the above trends may seem to evoke a sense of obstacles in the path of sustained success of heritage tourism, they also unveil a string of opportunities waiting to unfold in the heritage tourism arena for the present and future suppliers and consumers of heritage tourism.

Summary

This chapter has presented different notions of heritage, heritage tourism, and marketing. As can be seen from the multitude perspectives of heritage, it is a complex phenomenon and has both supply and demand side connotations. The discussion in this chapter clearly suggests recurrent characteristics of heritage tourism to be economics, emotions/motivation, inheritance, past, common (shared), authenticity, and participation. A working definition of heritage tourism is presented for the purpose of this book:

> A phenomenon that focuses on the management of past, inheritance, and authenticity to enhance participation and satisfy consumer motivations by evoking nostalgic emotions; its underlying purpose is to stimulate monetary benefits for its various constituencies and custodian of heritage such as the museums, historic houses, festivals, heritage hotels and other stakeholders.

Drawing some of the core concepts of marketing from published literature, this chapter presents a definition of marketing that facilitates exchange of ideas, relations, and products with the organization's various publics with the core purpose of enhancing attendance, revenue, and education. At the same time, the definition suggests promotion of sustainable environments for the enjoyment of the current and future generations. Also, because heritage tourism spans multiple environments managed by for-profit, public, and non-profit agencies, it is stressed that marketing strategies develop a coordinated crossroad of frameworks applicable to different settings.

Any heritage tourism marketing strategy needs to be guided by a philosophy. This point has been stressed in this chapter. It is important that heritage tourism follows a mixed approach by embracing elements of manufacturing, marketing, relationship-building, tribal, and societal philosophies. Manufacturing orientation can assist in keeping the heritage product intact in its current state without many modifications as are expected in a pure marketing-driven world perspective. Marketing and relationship building are becoming important as non-profit and public agencies compete for consumer dollars with each other and with for-profit businesses. Tribal advocacy can facilitate interactive engagements and personal selling tools such as 'word of mouth' and make visible shared emotional values between groups of like-minded consumers. This view also resonates with the contemporary direction advocated by non-tourism marketing professionals. While making the best use of the aforesaid orientations, a heritage agency should not discount benefits to the society. A strong focus on societal philosophy is equally important. Of paramount importance is the consideration of prevailing trends in heritage tourism that are likely to impact planning and management of marketing policies. Having discussed the basic tenets of heritage tourism marketing, the next chapter turns to sustainability and sustainable marketing of heritage tourism.

Questions

1. Why is heritage considered a complex phenomenon?
2. What are the different perspectives of heritage tourism?
3. What are the common characteristics of heritage tourism?
4. Discuss different philosophies of marketing within the context of heritage tourism.
5. What are some of the contemporary trends that may impact marketing of heritage tourism?

2   Setting a Sustainability Stage for Heritage Tourism

In the preface to this text, extant review of existing literature informed a preliminary discussion with some graduate students and academicians at a southwestern university in the United States on the use of the term 'sustainable development of tourism.' This provided some guidance as to the focus of this chapter. Extant literature demonstrates that defining sustainability and sustainable development is not an easy task. A complete understanding of the discourse can only be possible if one examines these concepts from their early stages.

The concept of sustainable development, in fact, gained prominence in the 1970s. But it was in the 1980s that the role and value of unchecked tourism in destinations was questioned and reassessment of the entire situation called. This partly resulted from the rising environmental consciousness and partly from the revelation that tourism creates negative impacts. It was considered crucial to address the major impacts of tourism and these views formed the underpinnings of the sustainable development concept as presented by the Brundtland Report titled 'Our Common Future.' The report defines sustainability as "meeting the needs of the present without compromising the ability of future generations to meet their own needs" (World Commission for Environment and Development 1987). Within this context, emphasis is thus placed on the long-term preservation of the environment.

I would like to point out that sustainability, sustainable tourism, and sustainable development are broad terms which are often used interchangeably in tourism literature (Liu 2003). It is, however, important to understand what each term signifies. Although the notion of sustainability can be mapped back to the thirteenth century, it was in the 1970s that it gained attention in the environmental literature (Kamara, Coff and Wynne 2006). Sustainability is a focused state which takes into consideration future generations (Harris and Leiper 1995; Liu 2003). Bramwell and Lane describe sustainability as "a positive approach intended to reduce the tensions and friction created by the complex interactions between the tourism industry, visitors, the environment and the communities which are host to holiday makers" (1993: 2). Callicot and Mumford define it as "meeting human needs without compromising the health of ecosystems" (1997: 33). More recent definitions adopt a collectivist perspective and strive to promote equity among all people (Jones, Clarke-Hill and Comfort 2008).

Sustainability has earned widespread support of both the private and the public sectors and has been applied not only to sustainable development of tourism but also to create sustainable communities, sustainable railways, and sustainable daily utility products. Sustainable development has a processual focus. Prosser (1994) postulates that the need for sustainable development stems from four mechanisms of social change:

- Lack of satisfaction with existing products;
- Growing need to be environmentally and culturally sensitive, increasing awareness of limited resources by the destinations and the need to preserve them;
- Attitudes of tourism suppliers such as the developers, the tour operators and lodging establishments;
- Tax incentives.

Manning and Dougherty describe sustainable development as "the use of natural resources to support economic activity without compromising the environment's carrying capacity, which is its ability to continue producing those economic goods and services" (1995: 30). Therefore, sustainable development pertains to the management of changes that strive to bring improvement to the environment (Dinan and Sargeant 2000; Fyall and Garrod 1998; Miller 2001). As noted by Sampson, UN-WTO defines sustainable development as a process that can assist in "securing a growth path where providing for the needs of the present generation does not mean compromising the ability of future generations to meet their own needs" (2001: 6).

The concept of sustainable development helps to set an agenda for sustainable tourism. The notion of sustainable tourism has acquired attention in part due to concerns associated with tourism impacts and in part due to the advocacy of organizations campaigning for a better environment (Dinan 2000). Sustainable tourism refers to all types of alternative tourism that have compatibility with sustainable development (Hughes 1995; Miller 2001). In line with this view, Kaul and Gupta maintain that "sustainable tourism is responsible tourism intended to generate employment and income, thereby reducing any deeper impact on the environment and local culture" (2009: 13). Liu asserts that "sustainable tourism requires both the sustainable growth of tourism's contribution to the economy and society and the sustained use of resources and environment and successful development in the long term necessitates a balance of supply and demand in terms of range, quality, quantity, and price" (2003: 462). This chapter discusses a blueprint for sustainable tourism development. Issues, associated with the sustainable development of heritage tourism, are also unfolded. The chapter closes with a description of sustainable heritage tourism marketing models derived from documented literature.

Blueprint for Sustainable Tourism Development

As the visibility of environmental and sustainable problems continued to grow, the historical 1992 United Nations Conference on Environment and Development was called and Agenda 21 was born. Agenda 21 was a 'detailed blueprint for implementing sustainable development, whilst not binding, agreements reached at the Earth Summit laid down principles for global sustainable development' (Berry and Ladkin 1997: 434).

The Agenda set forth a range of principles and guidelines to achieve sustainable development. It contained twelve principles for sustainable development, nine principles for governments across the globe, and ten set for the private sector. Agenda 21 identified travel and tourism as one industry that could help create a healthy planet. As a follow up on Agenda 21, Carter (1993) presented tripartite objectives of sustainability: adhere to the short-term and long-term needs of the local population, satisfy tourist needs, and protect the environment while fulfilling the first two objectives.

Consequently, several guidelines for acceptable development were issued by the public sector at the national and local levels. For instance, the English Tourist Board in the United Kingdom created an agenda for national parks and produced guidelines for balancing tourism development and issues associated with its environment. The principles set forth by the United Kingdom's Department of Environment were based on mutual respect, harmony, better management of resources, coordination, and inter-generational equity (Hassan 2000). Similar guidelines were issued by New Zealand, Canada, and Australia. Taken in aggregate, most studies suggest similar key words or emphases areas of sustainable development:

- Longer viability and quality of natural and human resources;
- Reducing friction in the complex interactions between stakeholders of diverse interests;
- Adhering to host population needs and quality of life;
- Benefiting the future generations;
- Balancing visitor numbers based on preservation guidelines to maintain of long-term biological and cultural diversity;
- Reassessing role of tourism in host society;
- Maintaining cultural integrity.

A broad spectrum of views thus exist on sustainable development. However, regardless of this heterogeneity, most strive to achieve a balance between conservation of cultural/natural environments of host communities and commercialization. For instance, Turner, Pearce and Bateman (1994) place different levels of sustainable development on a continuum with 'very weak' and 'very strong' at the polarized ends. Hunter (1997) argues that the center point of the sustainability scale requires balancing sustainable development with continued economic progress. That is, the focus should be on achieving compatible goals. Turner *et al.* (1994) note that the extreme positions should be discarded to reach a consensus on sustainable tourism development guidelines. Therefore, the middle approach has been the most common approach advocated by the supporters of sustainable development (Miller 2001).

Within the context of heritage tourism, adherence to sustainability and sustainable development suggests a need to develop an effective management of heritage resources for the benefit of future generations. In line with this view, Fyall and Garrod posit that "each generation passes on to the next a heritage asset based on at least equivalent size and quality as they themselves inherited from their forebears" (1998: 214). Boyd (2002) also indicates the necessity to ensure long-term viability of heritage using sustainable promotion techniques. Coccossis (2008) stresses the need for controlled development, management of land use conflicts, appropriate access to local heritage resources and services, and sustained use of infrastructure and support systems such as water, sewage etc. Coccossis (2008) states that the management of the aforesaid issues is crucial to balance conservation needs with the socio-economic development of the art and heritage cities.

A wide range of sustainable measures are suggested by scholars of heritage tourism. For instance, carrying capacity control is highlighted by Saarinen (2006) to achieve sustainable development of heritage tourism. According to the authors, heritage sustainability can be achieved through "a negotiation process, which indicates that the limits of growth are socially constructed" (Saarinen 2006: 1130). Kaul and Gupta (2009) emphasize training and educational programs and active involvement of the local community. Jamieson (2000) points out that preservation of culture and heritage is a process that should be focused on monitoring and managing change. The following objectives are proposed by the author: conservation of cultural resources, accurate interpretation of heritage resources, provision of authentic experiences, and stimulation of economic earnings from culture and heritage resources. Boyd identifies five themes for the sustainable development of the heritage industry in Canada:

- Mutually beneficial partnership
- A national strategy with local linkage
- Integration of public and private sectors
- Knowledge-based local communities
- Greater attention to culture and heritage within the context of a wider view of tourism in general. (2002: 228)

Sustainable planning has also been postulated as an injunction for change in heritage tourism (du Cros 2001) for the conservation and economic health of heritage sites. According to du Cros (2001), two areas of crucial focus should be: 1) the most appropriate heritage sites and locations to develop tourism; and 2) effective management of these places to achieve sustainability. Hughes (1995) points out that the regulation of consumption and development patterns of tourism commands mediation at both global and personal levels of an organization. The author further notes that the drive for sustainability in heritage tourism stems from moral or ethical imperatives, symptoms of which are manifested in terms such as 'care' and 'concern' to retain the sanctity of the earth and its variant cultures. Caserta and Russo (2002) also refer to sustainable development in heritage tourism as a balancing process aimed to address the on-going banalization of heritage products.

Evidently, sustainable heritage tourism aims to promote responsible use of heritage products and its surrounding environment, while aiming for economic numerations. But ambiguity issues often shadow efforts to obtain a clear and precise paradigm of sustainable development. To avoid the ambiguities implicit in the multiple perspectives of sustainable development of heritage tourism, this book adopts a 'working definition' of sustainable heritage tourism:

> Having the potential to consistently advocate long-term economic, social, cultural/heritage viability, and local welfare and education while striving to become a locally inclusive, collaborative, and ecologically balanced industry.

Sustainable Development Issues in Heritage Tourism

Before embarking on sustainable development issues specific to heritage tourism, it is important to highlight general problems associated with sustainable tourism because of their far-reaching implications on heritage tourism. The first one is associated with lack of clarity. Despite global acknowledgment that sustainable principles have provided a stage to set a "useful way forward for sustainable development" (Berry and Ladkin 1997), they are vague. It has been argued that they are general and not specific to be effective in achieving meaningful and measurable improvements in the environment (Fyall and Garrod 1998; Miller 2001). Another issue refers to application. According to Pigram (1990), a large gap exists between sustainable development policy endorsement by international charters and national and local governments and their implementation at the global, national, and local levels. Failure in implementation has been attributed to the conflict between various stakeholders such as the management agencies, the local communities, and the tourism developers and planners. Thus, there is missing a common platform between the various stakeholders of tourism development (Timur and Getz 2009).

On the topic of converting sustainable concepts to workable practices, highlighted issues are also associated with accessibility in regard to infrastructure, road improvements and congestion, need for good marketing to spread people to places which have better ability to accommodate numbers, and lack of education for visitors and the local community alike. One issue is raised by Berry and Ladkin (1997), who bring to light local community perceptions that sustainability is not well defined and often misused as a marketing ploy. 'Eco,' 'green,' and responsible tourism are all considered jargon without any rationale. Another recurrent issue is associated with the need to educate local communities and the private sector about ways to achieve energy conservation (Kaul and Gupta 2009). In summary, several areas requiring consideration are brought forward by aforesaid scholars, which include: the need for tourism to encompass community activity; increasing role of the public sector as a coordinator of stakeholder activities; defining roles for people in charge of infrastructure management, development, and regulation; simple, clear, and concise ideas on how to promote 'green' activities; and understanding local issues and their impact on the environment.

The problem of a clear understanding of sustainable development and what it requires is also pointed out by Hunter (1997). Hunter provides a comprehensive list of multifaceted roles required of sustainable development tools (1997: 852):

- The role of economic growth in promoting human well being;
- The impact and importance of human population growth;
- The effective existence of environmental limits to growth;
- The substitutability of natural resources with human-made capital created through economic growth and technical innovation;
- The differential interpretation of the criticality of various components of the natural resource base, and therefore the potential for substitution;
- The ability of technologies to decouple economic growth and unwanted environmental side efforts, the meaning of the value attributed to the natural world and the rights of human species;
- The degree to which a systems (ecosystems) perspective should be adopted and the importance of maintaining the functional integrity of ecosystems.

Hunter (1997) also brings forth the issue of distributional equity. He illustrates how the equity of access to natural resources can be ensured so that human well-being receives top priority and benefits and costs are dispersed in an equitable manner. According to Hunter, "equity implies attempting to meet all basic human needs and perhaps, the satisfaction of human wants, both now and in the future" (1997: 851). Liu (2003) is concerned with the lack of attention toward tourism demand, poor understanding of the dynamic nature of existing resources (because they evolve and change with changing needs and development of the society), and minimal focus on intra-generational equity (that is, fairness to all existing stakeholders of sustainable tourism). Other issues are linked with:

- Fair dispersement of economic benefits among the host community;
- Over emphasis on economic benefits, thereby compromising other priorities such as the examination of social cultural impacts on host societies;
- Need for conceptual clarity of limits or thresholds of development pace;
- Last, need for more sophisticated and clear implementation policies to devise measures (to promote and apply sustainable development strategies).

Where socio-cultural impacts are concerned, extant literature has focused on resident perceptions of impacts of tourism development. Three broad dimensions are confirmed: social, economic, and environmental (Liu, Sheldon and Var 1987; Besculides, Lee and McCormick 2002). Economic benefits are related to increased employment investments, profitable local businesses, improved tax revenue, increase in personal income, higher standard of living, and increase in prices of good and services. Negative economic impacts include low multiplier effects, increase in prices of goods and services, and negative effect on other area businesses. Socio-cultural benefits have included opportunity to socialize, opportunity for learning, revival of old traditions, and pride in local culture, while associated costs refer to loss of resident identity and local culture, increase in crime rates, social conflicts, demonstration effect, and materialism. Finally, environmental benefits are associated with better infrastructure while costs include crowding, noise and traffic pollution, and graffiti. As the nature of the effects illustrate, these dimensions have resulted in benefit-cost dichotomies (Gursoy, Jurowski and Uysal 2002) thereby providing justification of or criticism for tourism development on the basis of discerned benefits and costs. However, despite a comprehensive dissection of the aforesaid impacts, their relevance within the context of sustainable development of heritage tourism remains lacking.

While many of the issues associated with sustainable development of heritage tourism are nested within the general tourism praxis, there are some that are specific and unique within the heritage realm. Documented literature suggests nine prominent issues in the contemporary heritage tourism terrain:

1. *Marrying cultural heritage management with tourism* – cultural heritage management (CHM) has global implications. It has been defined as "the systematic care taken to maintain the cultural values of cultural heritage assets for the enjoyment of present and future generations" (McKercher and du Cros 2002: 43). CHM is concerned about the overuse and misuse of heritage sites and unlawful trade of artifacts (McKercher and du Cros 2002). As CHM is becoming more and more cash starved, it is associating itself with tourism to explore economic opportunities. This has brought to the fore a conflict between the ideologies pursued by CHM and the commercial goals of tourism. The biggest challenge lies in establishing a cordial and mutually beneficial relationship between CHM and tourism. For instance, CHM deliberations have often been concerned with the negative impacts of tourism such as tourist behavior, unplanned tourism infrastructure development, loss of control over cultural property and physical deterioration of heritage assets (Mercer 1996; Pearce 1995; Hollinshead 1999; McKercher and du Cros 2002). Because of frequent conflicts between tourism needs and conservation requirements, the management is frequently faced with an arduous task of achieving a balance between the two. The enormity of this issue can be specifically viewed using the example of World Heritage sites. In her study of three World Heritage Sites in the United Kingdom, Lyon (2007) notes that achieving an appropriate nexus between heritage and tourism is a complex task as it requires apposite interpretation techniques, at both the content and the medium levels.

2. *Revenue sources and the user fee debate* – it is known that economic fluctuations in the macro environment have triggered budgetary constraints in the heritage tourism sector. In the contemporary fiscal deficit times, heritage institutions have taken upon themselves to design cost-effective management and operation strategies (Silberg 1995; Smith, 1989; Garrod and Fyall 2001). Simultaneously, they have strived to gain revenue from a variety of sources such as special events, user fees, retailing, lodging and catering, interpretation, grants, sponsorship, and donations (Timothy and Boyd 2003).

Several studies have highlighted the conflict between pricing and sustainability. With budgetary restraints, free admission policies have received a setback in many heritage institutions across the globe. Token admission prices (used to cover the cost of keeping the heritage site open to the public and as a visitor tracking mechanism) are adopted by many in the heritage sector. Additionally, admission prices offer a way to curtail growing visitor numbers to heritage attractions. This has dovetailed into more intractable problems such as accommodating the needs of a wide array of visitors and managing their impacts while at the same time maintaining the authentic experience of the site. By diluting and distorting pasts to meet visitor demand, there is a fear that contemporary heritage tourism will be "gradually disinheriting future generations from their own past" (Fyall and Garrod 1998: 217).

The pricing for sustainability approach has been examined by several authors. The 'user pays' principle implies that visitors shoulder the responsibility of promoting/producing and market prices should be amended so that "users, i.e. visitors are confronted with the full costs and benefits associated with the heritage assets that are being employed" (Fyall and Garrod 1998: 220). This view is supported by Laarman and Gregersen, who assert that pricing provides prospects for "greater efficiency, fairness, and environmentally sustainable management" (1996: 220). Similar arguments are echoed by Prentice (1989) and Smith (1989). That said, this approach is not without limitations. Rogers (1995) describes several reasons for heritage attraction managers' reluctance to address revenue deficit by levying increased admission fees. Also evident is the ineffective use of pricing as a management tool which is often attributed to inadequate experience in pricing techniques, lack of understanding and training in using price as a competitive mechanism, and concern over being marked with an 'expensive' label.

3. *Interpretation issues* – heritage tourism relies in enormity on interpretive material to engage its audience in terms of involvement and deliver its key messages. The development of interpretive material requires a substantial amount of time and extensive use of resources. Additionally, the narration content and format is an arduous task. For instance, decisions have to be made with regard to "what story should be told?" and "how it should be told" (Hede 2007: 139). Interpretation can interfere with visitor's own experience at a heritage site (Moscardo 2001; Timothy and Boyd 2003). In some cases, the spectacle and show takes priority over the need to communicate authentic messages of the site itself. Bramwell and Lane (1993) note that interpretation driven by economic numerations is profit-centered and modification of the core essence of a heritage setting or content to meet visitor needs comprises the sanctity of the site. An important issue described by Urry (1990) is the danger associated with over-interpretation leading to the trivialization of the significance and a diminished engaging experience between the site and the visitor.

An additional challenging aspect of interpretation seeks to strike a balance of education with entertainment. Earlier, pleasure and enjoyment were considered separate and incompatible with education by heritage sites (Light 1996). Today, these are not regarded as polarized. 'Edutainment' is the new trend pursued by most of the heritage site managers who desire to capture visitor interest. According to Timothy and Wall (1997), this approach can help draw leisure visitors, enhance appeal of the heritage site, and maximize economic numerations. That said, this approach is not without problems. Timothy and Boyd find that "there has always been a fundamental problem in knowing when the entertainment stops and the education starts" (2003: 202). Hence careful management strategies are required to address the aforementioned interpretation issues.

4. *Congestion management* – previously, congestion referred to individual issues such as traffic, crowding, and queue management (du Cros 2007). In line with this view, UN-WTO (previously known as WTO) states that congestion happens "when physical obstructions block the natural flow or narrow passages cause the flow to slow down (2004). Today, a holistic and integrated framework is needed to embrace the demand, destination, and site level perspectives. Congestion occurrence needs to be addressed at both the consistent and the fluctuating levels so that appropriate management strategies can be designed. Consistency that implies recurrent overcrowding and fluctuating congestion is associated with peak periods only such as public holidays and vacations (du Cros 2007). Congestion can also be associated with the overuse or overdevelopment of ancillary supply such as too many lodging facilities or traffic issues associated with connecting corridors. Three factors are identified by Goulding (2000) to tackle crowding issues so that visitor experiences may be optimized: scene setting, routing and mapping, and crowding density levels.

Congestion in heritage tourism is not solely a physical phenomenon. Perceptual crowding can also prove to be detrimental to visitor experience and engagement. From a psychological perspective, it is important to gauge levels at which visitors feel distracted. Literature suggests several measures to deal with congestion problems such as allowing groups by appointment, dispersement of foot and vehicular traffic, quota systems, zoning and effective land use planning, and directing tourist attention from vulnerable locations (Timothy and Boyd, 2003). Additionally, Page (1992) suggests reducing traffic in the local areas by taking measures such as routing patterns and setting lower speed limits, establishing park-and-ride facilities, etc.

5. *Heritage politics* – this line of inquiry mainly suggests dominance of selective heritage representations. Certain pasts are ignored and certain cultures are marginalized. As asserted by Timothy and Boyd, "throughout history, special interest groups and proponents of heritage commemoration are forcing legislators and other public officials and organizations to acknowledge the atrocities of the past and commemorate them" (2007: 3). Heritage and history are often contested by the host communities, the stakeholders, and the policymakers, thereby causing dissonance. Tunbridge and Ashworth define dissonant heritage as "a discordance or a lack of agreement and consistency in understanding and portraying what is or is not heritage" (1996: 20). Three types of contested (dissonant) heritage are identified by Olsen (2000):

1. Overlapping heritage – this category comprises two or more groups establishing a claim for the same or overlapping heritage. Contestations can be the result of diverse or conflicting views and interpretations.

2. Divided heritage – this suggests divisions within the same group over what elements of heritage to display and share with the audience.
3. Indigenous versus colonial heritage – this category refers to two different kinds of groups who have parallel heritages. Debates within this category center on whose and which heritage to preserve.

6. *Globalization effects: the fragmented heritage issue* – Boniface and Fowler (1993) provide noteworthy deliberations on the concept of globalization and assert that technology has created global citizens. The authors argue that disparity among citizens across the world will always exist because of the grass root level cultures local to different regions. The ordeal of presenting moving or static heritage to a global audience is complex because much of the endeavors are dictated by power groups. That is, official agencies control and legitimize the moving object movement (Boniface and Fowler 1993: 136). For instance, The Canadian Cultural Property Import and Export Act of 1974 offers tax incentives to encourage local people to donate their antiques to public agencies. It also includes procedures to seek recovery of illegally exported objects from the country in question. Thus, it aims to regulate both the export and the import of heritage objects.

Many countries across the globe today consider it important to conserve the objects in their place of origin. An interesting argument is given by Boniface and Fowler to support this statement:

> Because culture is seen as integral to identity, especially of statehood at official level, and because of its economic significance in terms of tourism around 'the global village.' To put it crudely, if you have not got heritage, can you exist in a meaningful, particularly political sense? And if you have not kept your 'cultural loot,' how can you capture a segment of international cultural tourism. (1993: 142)

That is, keeping another country's loot and retaining preferred heritage originating from one's own country of origin are both desired prerogatives. It will not be wrong to say then that both strategies promote global heritage and movements of international visitors. Moving objects are thus caught in the web of intergovernmental politics. Boniface and Fowler (1993) present culture clash in the global village and point out that lack of understanding exists at the heritage tourism level to cope with this global issue. Heritage continues to be re-evaluated and selected and the world citizens of today possess dual heritage: global and local. As stated by Naisbitt and Aburdene (1990), people will strive to preserve their national and local identities in the face of the threat posed by global homogenization. In other words, the more humanity sees itself standardized and losing its identity, the greater will be the need for each culture to possess a unique slice of heritage. The heritage tourism industry needs to acknowledge all frontiers (in all their intricacies and complexities) and give due recognition to multiple and diverse themes (Boniface and Fowler 1993).

7. *Use of technology* – over the last three decades, technology has played an increasingly important role in shaping the heritage tourism resources. It has helped

enhance visitor experience while at the same time offered alternative prospects for a better use of heritage resources. Disparate sources of information and common threads can be examined quickly. For instance, technology has unveiled new possibilities for cultural heritage venues, provided paths to create unique and new experiences and helped explore new revenue-seeking opportunities (Arnold 2005).

It is also important to point out that new technology is making an overwhelming impact on marketing research outside the heritage tourism turf. There has been an increasing use of ethnographic methods, using visual and the textual/linguistic to understand consumers. These offer important inferences for the marketing managers of heritage tourism. Most advances can be noted in the use of consumer data technologies. These include videography, netnography, blogging, and virtual life worlds (Parsons and Maclaran 2009):

- Videography – this method makes use of video cameras. Belk and Kozinet report three main ways in which this technique has been applied. First, individual or group interviews are videoed which makes possible a study of facial expressions and gestures of interviewees in addition to group dynamics. Naturalistic observation is the second applied example where effort is made to get on the consumer level and understand the words as they see it. Third, autovideography makes use of videos directed by the informant. In other words, the informants video themselves and their experiences. Therefore, they contain material relevant to the participant. Webcam footage is also an important tool. Video footage in public areas such as parks and shopping malls can provide a glimpse of the consumption behavior and rituals of consumers.

- Netnography and online communities – Netnography, a relatively new research method, makes use of "ethnographic research techniques to study cultures and communities that are emerging through computer-mediated communications. These offer a window into naturally occurring behaviors" (Kozinets 2002: 62). Online community discussions are mostly directed by the consumers and relevant excerpts of conversations can be downloaded by researchers. Sensitive research topics are easy to explore because this method is unobtrusive. However, there is an issue of representativeness of the sample size because it is limited to only online users. Other issues are related to ethics. For instance, some communities have their own internal norms, hierarchies, and vernacular which need to be observed before participating in discussions. Also, "privacy of publicly private nature of online communications" should be observed (Maclaran and Cattarall 2002: 324). It is also important to note that online communities develop relationships in online environments which may be transient. Four types of online users are identified by Kozinets (1999): tourists (only casually related to the community), minglers (interested in the social function rather than the topic of discussion), devotees (have keen interest but are not attached to the group), and insiders (the most dedicated in terms of socialization and interest and are founding members of the community). Further, it is important to know different types of virtual communities. Five categories were identified by Kozinet (2002):

    i. Boards – these perform the role of electronic bulletin boards such as news-groups.

    ii. Web rings – web pages linked based on a theme.

    iii. Lists – in this category, users have access to email lists of those who share their interests.

    iv. Multi-user dungeons – themed virtual spaces using role-playing techniques to facilitate interactions.

    v. Chat rooms – non-themed locations based on shared interests.

- Blogs and blogging – blogs are mainly about individual expressions and often involve a high degree of personal creativity. This method offers many opportunities which still remain untapped for marketing researchers. Blogs can perform important functions. They can help facilitate interactions between the company and the consumer. This way feedback on the product usage and experience can be obtained.
- Virtual Life Worlds – examples include Second Life, Entropia Universe, and There.com. These are underused and offer many opportunities to both tourism and non-tourism agencies and industries. These further the function of blogs and take self-presentation to the next level. They offer an interactive commercial environment to facilitate online purchases. Novak and Anderson, based on another research study, noted two key motivations for using Second Life: a creative opening and to escape daily mundane life.
- Data Capture Data Mining – here, companies collect vast amounts of data on consumer spending histories and follow the consumer trail of transactions (Parsons and Maclaran 2009). Thus data of online point of purchase transactions and other online transactions is assembled into big databases called warehouses. Data models are later built to identify trends. The collected data is data mined to gain insights into consumer buying and expenditure patterns. Data mining offers a wide range of functions such as assistance with customer acquisition (identifying traits that help predict responses to different promotional techniques), customer retention (identifying lucrative consumers who are likely to switch loyalty), customer abandonment (consumer histories are purchased to identify market segments that are costing more than their contributions), and market-based analysis (here purchase histories are used to identify product and brand preferences) (Peacock 1998). Parsons and Maclaran also point out that data mining can be useful in "developing new products, discovering new cross-selling opportunities, managing customer churn, discovering patterns in customers' satisfaction, and tracking studies." (2009: 189)

However, barriers to the proper use of technology and resources still remain enormous and appropriate education and training is required. Also, a strategic framework is needed to integrate technology within the broader context of cultural heritage experiences. It is suggested that despite the augmented role "of the global nature of Internet and other new technological devices (such as mobile devices, mobile phones, and interactive television) in fostering the creation of global heritage space" (Sigala 2005: 172), virtual community tools need to support community and sustainable tourism development by enhancing or integrating with destination management systems. Moreover, although virtual reality keeps making progress by leaps and bounds and is keenly pursued by the heritage industry, its fast rate of development has raised attention to issues such as "morality, privacy, personal identity and the prospect of fundamental change in human nature" (Rheingold 1991). The tourist experience today has become a journey through different dreamlands.

8. *Tension between commodification and conservation* – extant literature decrees commodification as a serious threat to a large variety of heritage assets. McKercher and du Cros (2002) note that commodification in the form of site hardening has led to the physical deterioration of assets. Supporters of conservation, on the other hand, contend that conservation of heritage produces social good. Conservation is mainly concerned with the protection of the past and it is one of the fundamental tenets of sustainable development of heritage. Its guiding philosophy centers on responsible and wise use of resources.

An important issue arising from the efforts to conserve past for heritage tourism is centered on the past itself. McKercher and du Cros (2002) raise an interesting question: Why conserve the past? Lowenthal is of the view that the past is a foreign country, nostalgia has made it "the foreign country with healthiest tourist trade of all" (2000: 7). In fact, nostalgia has both produced and promoted time-travelers (people who like delving into the past to remember old times). America's Nostalgia Book Club takes people years behind the times – by choice, of course. In the words of Lowenthal:

> Nostalgia's profitability has lured real estate agents 'to drum up interest by digging out every shred of history' where the connection is made with a king or a pop star; no echo is too bizarre to appeal. Once a menace, nostalgia now is the new buzzword. It attracts or afflicts most levels of society. Ancestor hunters search archives for their roots; millions throng to historic houses; antiques engross middle class; souvenirs flood consumer markets. (2000: 56)

For the first time in man's history, man is desperate to escape the present and nostalgia is a panacea to escape the present dilemma. That said, the past and its nostalgia can bring forth problems such as disappointment, coping inabilities, problem of returning to the present, and putting the temporal fabric at risk (Lowenthal 2000). The past can be examined within the context of the following questions: Is it healthy for heritage tourism to use the past as a bait to draw tourist attention? Can heritage tourism exist without the past?

Lowenthal reviews nostalgia from both malaise and blessing perspectives. According to him, nostalgia is often blamed for alienating people from the present. At the same time, nostalgia brings compensating virtues with it. That is, attachment to familiar places may buffer social upheaval and attachment to familiar faces may be necessary for enduring association. Nostalgia reaffirms identities bruised by recent turmoil. However, the norm of over-selling the past can be detrimental and its repercussions are likely to have far-reaching effects on the human mind in terms of progress into the future. Careful handling of the past and nostalgic emotions is needed today.

9. *Partnerships and stakeholder management* – most of the existing collaborations and partnerships in heritage tourism are driven by revenue-seeking goals. More than often, the purpose has been increase in net income and desire to promote a strong customer base (Markwell, Bennett and Ravenscroft, 1997), and the need to formulate strategies compatible with the market needs and economic viability (Hassan 2000). Research on partnerships with stakeholders is also premised on economic goals. For instance, Silberberg (1995) examines partnerships to increase attendance so that operating expenses can be managed. Additionally, stakeholders such as the local community are often neglected or ignored. As pointed out by Chang, "the tourist-local balance is tipped in favor of visitors while the needs of residents are marginalized or totally neglected. Not only does this view fail to appreciate the non-tourist as a heritage consumer, it also underestimates the flexibility of those in charge of heritage development and the malleability of the heritage product" (1997: 48).

Conceptual frameworks exist in literature which measure the effectiveness of continuing partnerships. For instance, four aspects of collaboration are examined by Aas, Ladkin and Fletcher (2005) in their study of a UNESCO-sponsored Norwegian project. These are: "channels of communication between the heritage and tourism groups, generating income for heritage conservation and management, involving local community in decision making and tourism activities, and assessment of the extent and success of stakeholder collaboration" (2005: 31–35). However, several barriers to collaboration are reported by the authors which include lack of leadership, initiative, direction, and effective communication techniques between stakeholders. Likewise, McKercher, Ho and du Cros (2004) identify seven different relationships between stakeholders ranging from full cooperation to full conflict and report that partnerships are rare and usually conflicting in heritage institutions. Li and Bong (2004) attribute lack of success in partnerships to poor leadership and strategic planning. Chhabra (2009) notes that a sustained applied approach to formulate partnerships and collaboration is not an easy task and has a lot to accomplish.

Authenticity Deliberations

Given the significance of authenticity for both the users and the suppliers, this subject warrants special attention in this chapter. Use of authenticity in heritage tourism is complex and laden with polarized perspectives. Nevertheless, a discursive path can be mapped to reflect its academic progress over the past few decades. As noted earlier, the concept of authenticity is of pivotal significance in heritage tourism settings. It is one of the most significant elements for cultural heritage and tourism management. However, the authenticity notion has been conceptualized and reconceptualized over the past three decades. In the words of Olsen

(2002: 163), it is a "heteroglot," with multiple connotations. In fact, the vigorous and spirited debate around this topic, mostly sparked in rejoinder to MacCannell's (1973) concept of staged authenticity, has centered on not only what authenticity is but also extends to a discursive approach on the ways visitors have sought and perceived authenticity over the past few decades. This section inquires into the paths of alteration that the authenticity concept has undergone since MacCannell's introduction of it to the tourism field.

MacCannell's (1973) notion of staged authenticity implies that real culture is increasingly concealed from the tourists' sight. Instead, staged artificial story and experiences are offered for consumption. MacCannell (1992) describes modern tourists in search of genuine experiences which are assumed to lie outside the realm of tourists' day-to-day life environments. It is this quest that leads to victimization and contrived experiences. MaCannell thus proposes that real authenticity is in existence but hidden. This view is in contrast with Boorstin's (1964) notion that tourists actively desire pseudo events which he defines as fake. These views have taken a front seat in many sociological paradigms which aim to understand the social dynamics of heritage tourism. Four schools of thought capture the authenticity discourse from the past few decades: conventional/essentialist, negotiated, constructed/constructivist, and subjective/existentialist.

Objective or Essentialist Authenticity

The conventional framework of authenticity often described as objective authenticity invokes overlapping terms such as: 'origins' (Bruner 1994; Trilling 1972) judged on traditional and antiquity criteria; genuineness (Theobald 1998), pristinity (Cohen 1988), sincerity (Taylor 2001), and creativity (Daniel 1996); "flow of life, not interfered with by the 'framing' of sights, sites, objects, and events for touristic purposes, by various overt markers" (Cohen 2007: 76); and 'cool' (Selwyn 1996). Chhabra (2005) provides a brief overview of this paradigm using an 'essentialist' label and argues that cultural signifiers endorsed by heritage authorities or custodians are needed to stamp a heritage object as 'objectively' authentic.

This school of thought embraces the museology concept and advocates non-intervention within the natural phenomena. Many heritage attractions, cultural heritage managers, and museums continue to treat authenticity in the spirit of frozen or 'museumfied' heritage. This view has been strengthened in the light of issues posed both by ongoing culture changes (such as commodification) and by demand for heritage tourism happening across the globe today.

Constructed or Constructivist Authenticity

The constructed paradigm of authenticity is premised on the notion that all judgments are influenced by the existing market forces and environments. This school of thought supports the demand perspective; that is, the tourists' perceptions of authenticity rather than restricting the right to judge to the heritage custodians (Chhabra, Healy *et al.* 2003; McIntosh and Prentice 1999).

The constructivist paradigm supports the commodified forms of authenticity, such as nostalgia and heritage in hyperreal settings and deliberately constructed pseudo-backstages (MacCannell 1992). As Medina points out, in fake settings, cultures "are continually produced and consumed through the actions of archaeologists, tourism promoters, tourists, tours guides, curators, and vendors of artisanal production." (2003: 357) Authenticity is thus modified to suit the needs of the audience. Hence a capitalist approach is pursued which facilitates commercialized use of heritage, leading to its commodification. Commodification concerns mostly stem from the constructivist use of authenticity.

Negotiated Authenticity

This ideology is regarded as a jointly constructed process between the suppliers and the consumers (Adams 1996). Justified under the umbrella of emergent authenticity, Cohen argues about its useful function: "commodification often hits a culture not when it is flourishing but when it is in the decline owing to the outside forces preceding tourism. Under such circumstances, the emergence of a cultural tourist market frequently facilitates the preservation of a cultural tradition which would otherwise perish" (1988: 382). This discourse suggests that authenticity can be sustained in the re-creation process while focusing on the requirements of the market. And if commodified carefully, it can "preserve traditions by generating demand or attributing value to them" (Medina 2003:354). Commodification can thus serve a useful purpose if the intent is to establish a middle path between demand and supply. This stance follows a middle path while retaining significant features of both essentialist and constructivist ideologies. In a way, it strives to strike a compromise between the two.

Subjective or Existentialist Authenticity

At the end of the twentieth century, the notion of authenticity shifted the constructivist focus to a purely 'subjective' perspective. This school of thought argues that subjective negotiation of meanings defines an authentic experience (Uriely 2005). This view is echoed by post-structuralists such as Goss (1993) and Selwyn (1996) who argue that authenticity is not an absolute concept and continues to stay in a state of flux. Terms such as 'self discovery,' 'being true to oneself' (Steiner and Reisinger 2006: 299), exalted living within tourist moments, taking into account one's own genuine experience; in other words, existentialists (Wang 1999) define this view. Similar experiences have been echoed by Maslow's (1970) self-actualization stage and Csikszentmihalyi's (1996) optimal experience. In retrospect to extant literature perspectives, Reisinger and Steiner came to a pessimistic conclusion that "authenticity should be abandoned because it was too unstable to claim the paradigmatic status of a basic theoretical concept" (2006: 66). However, the authors retreat from their claims later and argue that the objective and essentialist concepts are not polarized; but they have completely different meanings and need to be separated. In other words, Steiner and Resinger postulate that the authenticity term can be used from two different angles "as genuineness or realness of artifacts or events and also as a human attribute signifying being one's true self or being true to one's essential nature" (2006: 299). This conclusion echoes and confirms two conceptual rifts in the authenticity debate. As noted by Cohen the "two splits represent two distinct levels of reality: as a quality of the lived-in world or of an experience" (Cohen 2007: 75).

In sum, most of the above discussions have centered on conceptual explorations. Some have taken supply and demand perspectives. The supply perspectives pertaining to conventional heritage attractions center on the objective notion of authenticity. Several studies have confirmed this argument (Chhabra 2005; Chhabra 2007; Boyd 2002; Littrell, Anderson and Brown 1993; Reisinger and Steiner 2006). A more liberal supply stance has been constructivist where messages and objects are commodified to match the market need. The demand perspectives have struggled with subjectivity and have been criticized by the traditional supporters for ruining the objective versions of authenticity. The underpinnings to this condemnation stems from the conclusion that most visitors do not desire objective authenticity and hence it should cease to exist. If they desire instant gratification and exalted tourist moments to be in touch with themselves, then there is no need to support heritage institutions because they are no longer in demand. Most studies that provide an empirical explanation to these arguments are based on explorations of the general market or mainly the baby boomer segment. A recent study of Generation X by the author reports a different view: future adults desire objectivist authenticity instead of the existentialist kind of experiences at heritage attractions.

Sustainable Development Indicators

There has been much debate within tourism literature on what constitutes the most appropriate approach to promote sustainable development of tourism. A detailed discussion of these approaches is important so that suitable inferences can be drawn for heritage tourism. Clarke (1997) identifies three frameworks for sustainable tourism from documented literature:

- *Polar opposites and the continuum* – this position takes a dichotomous stance and regards mass tourism and sustainable tourism as two opposites (Pearce 1992). Continuum is an extension of the polarized opposites. It suggests variations along the sustainable spectrum. However, these approaches have been condemned for being too simplistic and impractical. According to Butler (1980), the concept of labeling two polar extremes as right and wrong is misleading because the extreme positions do not capture the dynamics of tourism. It is argued that tourism is fluid not static. Wheeller (1993) supports Butler's argument by stating that the 'continuum' position aims to provide a micro solution to a macro problem. Clarke echoes this view by stating that the continuum approach is "inward-looking, failing to recognize other industry sectors and the wider perspective of sustainable development, elitism, problems of ensuring local ownership and control and imbalances of power" (Clarke 1997: 226).

- *Movement* – this paradigm suggests fragmentation of mass tourism into sustainable forms (Krippendorf 1987). The underlying objective is to promote large-scale tourism and discourage mass tourism because of consideration and significance associated with environmental quality, involvement of large-scale operators to foster interest in sustainable tourism in the consumer market, and the advantage of large size in terms of support for the suppliers and distributors. It is hoped that the advantage will act as a persuasive force. Additionally, the position contends that less altruistic reasons, in the form of regulatory control, can serve to fuel support for sustainable tourism. This position signals that the conceptual premise of "profit with principle" has moved from the fringe to the mainstream (Clarke 1997: 229). A proactive rather than a reactive approach is suggested by this school of thought. Many examples can be drawn from the industry of proactive involvement to achieve the sustainable tourism goal.
- *Convergence* – this position is an extension of the third position and aims to present a contemporary take on sustainable tourism and reiterate the evolving nature of sustainable tourism. It postulates that all tourism should practice sustainability. Two interpretations of sustainable tourism underpin this position: "a dominant physical/ecological perspective expressed as a business orientation and a small scale interpretation perspective of sustainable tourism which offers a social slant using a local or destination platform" (Clarke 1997: 229). In other words, environmentally friendly tourist behavior inducement by the tourism industry is the focus.

Gunn (1994: 87) suggests several guidelines for a well-designed approach to plan sustainable tourism which include:

- Developing tourism goals and objectives linked to the broader comprehensive plan for a region and/or community;
- Formulating a set of indicators reflecting the objectives of tourism development;
- Implementing management strategies designed to direct tourism toward the achievement of the stated objectives;
- Monitoring the performance of tourism based on the indicators; evaluating the effectiveness of selected management strategies in influencing the performance of tourism with respect to the indicators;
- Developing strategic policies for tourism management based upon the monitored effectiveness of these techniques.

Another alternate framework is suggested by the World Resources Institute to address two key environmental issues (Jamieson, 1997): 1) visitor impacts associated with natural site degradation; and 2) visitor impacts pertaining to culture loss and tension. The first issue creates overcrowding at natural heritage sites resulting in vegetation destruction, physical infrastructure, degradation, and habitat loss.

The desirable response to this issue is suggested to be zoning, which can help protect fragile areas, limit access, and obtain expenditures to manage conservation. The second issue is concerned with high-demand effects on visited local religious/cultural events and ceremonies. The outcome of high demand is that local residents are reluctant to attend their own festivals. Consequently, the cultural and religious events lose their authenticity and residents are likely to exhibit anger and antagonism toward visitors for intrusion. Suggested response to improve the existing state includes allowing visitors access to a limited number of events and involving local residents to help determine carrying capacity. Also included in the portfolio is consideration of residents' perspectives to craft strategies for improving local benefits and developing code of ethics for visitor behavior.

Ehrlich and Ehrlich's (1990) approach is also worthy of attention. The authors develop a master equation to visualize and isolate the key forces imposing a burden on ecosystems. Their equation ($I = PAT$) defines environmental impact (I) as a function of population (P), affluence (A), and technology (T). According to the equation, population is the key factor that generates impacts because it represents the number of consumers whose needs have to be fulfilled. Per capital gross domestic product defines affluence (A) and it is considered a proxy for aspirations of the less developed world population to pursue resource-rich Western lifestyles. Current level of efficiency defines the technology coefficient. This efficiency plays a key role in transforming resources into products desired by the markets. The authors argue that both population and affluence cannot be controlled by marketing managers. Therefore, it is argued that to achieve sustainability through marketing, marketing strategy decisions should be incorporated into the technology coefficient. For instance, "technology applications, which reflect a propensity to consume resources and generate waste, influence the product forms offered; the amounts and types of materials and energy used to make products; and the relative efficiency at which production, marketing, and consumption activities are carried out" (Ehrlich and Ehrlich 1990: 8).

Several measures worthy of note also exist in literature (Butler 1999a; Cracolici, Cuffaro and Nijkamp 2008; Garrod and Fyall 1998; Kaul and Gupta 2009; Hassan 2000; Notarstefano 2008). For instance, Miller (1999) summarizes sustainable measures based on previous studies. Most recurrent indicators are reported to be regulatory, maximize economic benefit, are self-regulatory, observe carrying capacity, promote intergenerational equality, make efficient use of resources, utilize the technology-based approach, take a long-term view, enable local involvement, encourage local revitalization, improve level of natural capital stock, ensure resident satisfaction, ensure customer satisfaction, maintain levels of natural capital stock, contain well-developed tourism plans, and minimize non-economic impact. Using a Delphi technique, Miller (1999) later elicits top five preferences from the aforementioned list. These are:

- Take a long view;
- Contain well-developed tourism plans;
- Make efficient use of resources;

- Enable local involvement;
- Maintain levels of natural capital stock.

Butler (1999a) emphasizes measuring and controlling carrying capacity and planning and control of development and operation of tourism to achieve sustainability. Hassan (2000) also utilizes a model centered on cooperation and partnership between the public and private sectors so that relationships can be built and alliances made to strengthen the economic network of local communities. Sirkaya, Jamal and Choi (2002) point out the need to encompass multiple dimensions of sustainable development when designing indicators such as ecological, social, economic, institutional, cultural, and psychological at international, national, regional, and community levels.

Garrod and Fyall (1998) take an economic perspective by using monetary valuation to appropriately account for measures. The main idea is that through the monetary valuation a proper account can be made for the environmental impacts and concerns using techniques such as the contingent valuation method, the hedonic pricing, and the travel cost methods. Notarstefano (2008) suggests an integrated approach to help Europe achieve competitive and sustainable progress in tourism. He proposes the integration of the following measures: economic viability, local prosperity, employment quality, social equity, visitor fulfillment, local control, community well-being, cultural richness, physical integrity, biological diversity, resource efficiency, and environmental purity. His proposed agenda is centered on two elements (Notarstefano 2008: 47):

1. The ability of tourism to continue as an activity in the future, ensuring that the conditions are right for this.
2. The ability of society and the environment to absorb and benefit from the impacts of tourism in a sustainable way.

Cracolici *et al.* (2008) propose a technique to gauge tourism sustainability using appropriate measures of efficiency. The authors introduce the terms 'eco-efficiency' and 'economic efficiency' to represent the 'Sustainable Tourism Efficiency' indicators. They employ an Activity Analysis method to obtain eco-efficiencies and economic efficiencies for select provinces in Italy. According to Cracolici *et al.* (2008), destination performance in terms of efficiency can be evaluated using a guest-production function where physical and human resources make up the production process and output is represented by measures such as arrivals, bednights, value added, employment, or customer satisfaction. Here two kind of outputs can be used: good (desirable) and bad (undesirable) premised on the notion that production of tourist output can cause serious inconvenience to the tourist area and no good output can be produced without the production of bad output (2008: 41):

Tourist output: f(material capital, cultural heritage, human capital, labor)

The left side of the equation consists of some measures of both bad and good outputs. Multiple inputs and outputs can be employed. The authors use bed nights per capita and average length of stay as proxies for bad outputs. The proxies for material capital, cultural heritage, human capital, and labor include number of beds in the hotels over population, provincial state-owned artistic patrimony (number of museums, monuments, and archaeological areas) divided by the population; tourist school graduates divided by the population; and labor units of the tourism sector is divided by the total labor units for the region. This way, they were able to calculate Sustainable Tourism Efficiency. Places with high STE and EE scores are reported as an expression of good tourism quality.

Use of indicators steadily increased since the 'Social Indicators Movement' in the late 1960s and these are commonly employed to monitor social and biophysical changes (Wallace 1993). As Table 2.1 illustrates, most traditional studies have focused on four types of indicators: social, cultural, environmental/ ecological, and economic.

Table 2.1 Commonly Cited Indicators of Sustainability

Theme	*Key Issues*	*Indicator*
Sirakaya *et al.*	Cultural	Degree to which initiative builds on cultural heritage of community and is culturally appropriate, and not conflicting with community vision or plan
Sirakaya *et al.*	Ecological	Changes in biodiversity, naturalness at all levels
Marsh	Ecological	Species demographics
		Water quality, quality and use
		Air quality
		Recycling practices
		Efficiency of resource use
		Scenery degradation
Sirkaya *et al.*	Social	Changes in social relations and organization – qualitative changes in attributes of social sustainability including variables of the nature subsistence activities, family and/or kinship structures and decision-making structures for allocating resources
Marsh	Social	Community
		Jobs
		Migration in and out of community
		Complaints about tourism
		Quality of life
		Impact on lifestyle
		Tourists
		Number of visitors, and trends
		Proportion of repeat visitors
		Length of stay
		Tourist satisfaction and complaints
		Institutional
		Laws and regulations regarding tourism
		Infractions and court cases

		Recognition of tourism in official plans
		Existence of tourism plans
		Tourist and interpretive information
		Government and private tourism organizations
		Non-Government Organization response to tourism
		Existence of code of ethics for tourists and the tourism industry
Sirakaya *et al.*	Economic	Changes in the structure of employment opportunities
		Income distribution at national, provincial, and regional levels
		Regional and community balance of trade impacts of tourism initiatives, strategies or plans
		Backward and forward linkage between tourism activity and other formal and informal activity in the community
Timur and Getz	Collaborations	Diverse group of stakeholders
Aas *et al.*		Effective partnership between stakeholders
		Effective leadership
McKercher and Du Cros Du Cros	Conservation Robusticity	Retaining Authenticity

After Sirakaya, Jamal and Choi (2002)

Sustainable Heritage Tourism Marketing Models

Sustainable heritage tourism frameworks are mostly remiss in academic literature. Of the few that have been presented, the ones by du Cros (2001) and Chhabra (2009) are worthy of attention. Du Cros suggests a scale which has conservation and commodification at its opposite ends. The author develops a matrix indicating dynamic relationships across the spectrum between robusticity and market appeal (see Figure 2.1). According to the author, "within the matrix, heritage places can be plotted based on their appeal to tourists and their robusticity or ability to withstand high levels of visitation" (du Cros 2001: 168). One aspect of the figure reflects positioning of a heritage attraction based on the status of conservation or robusticity and this scale is of utmost significance for managers who prioritize long-term conservation of cultural values. The other end of the continuum is of interest to the tourism sector assumed to be keen on assessing worth of a heritage attraction based on market appeal. The author further suggests inclusion of indicators specific to each heritage attraction to measure the place's position along the robusticity and market appeal continuums. This can, in turn, guide tourism development and conservation management policies. Additionally, du Cros suggests the inclusion of political considerations and local community concerns to address the diverse perspectives of heritage management and tourism.

Chhabra (2009) proposes a Sustainable Heritage Tourism Marketing model (SHTM) based on a nationwide study of heritage museums. As Figure 2.2 shows the SHTM model comprises of the following core elements:

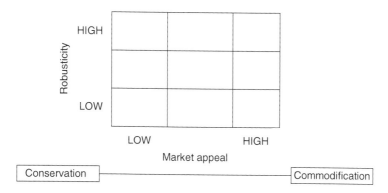

Figure 2.1 Robusticity and Market Appeal Matrix
Source: Du Cros (2001: 166)

1. Mission statement and communication mix (interpersonal and impersonal). Interpersonal focuses on methods such as personal selling and word of mouth) and impersonal employs techniques such as advertising and sales promotion.
2. Additionally, the model suggests important influences on the communication mix by market segmentation, external and internal environment factors, level of types of partnerships, and research function.

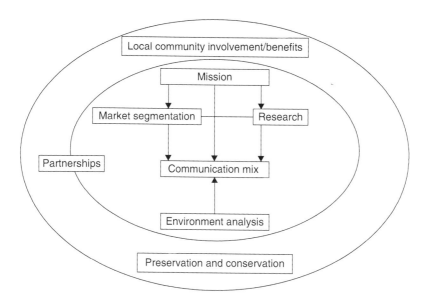

Figure 2.2 Proposed Sustainable Heritage Tourism Marketing Model
Source: Chhabra (2009: 313)

Chhabra (2009) speculates that these influences aid information and formulation of communication strategy for museums. The key message of the model is "to suggest that marketing decisions need to be guided by conservation and preservation principles that underpin the traditional role of museums in addition to local community involvement and benefits" (Chhabra, 2009: 313).

Chhabra's model suggests advocacy of 'green' heritage tourism. In sum, the author comes up with the following suggestions for contemporary museums:

> focus on long term strategic planning; follow a product driven philosophy; educate the target markets so that they feel responsive towards your sustainable strategies; design promotional strategies that explain why you choose to revert back to the traditional stance of preservation and conservation; increasingly involve the local community in your marketing endeavors; keep traditional research at the forefront; and make conservation and preservation your primary objective. (2009: 317)

Summary

Upon completion of this chapter, the reader should become familiar with the meaning of sustainability, sustainable development, and sustainable tourism.

A broad spectrum of views on what guidelines and principles define sustainable development adorn the academic radar. Nevertheless, all advocate a balance between conservation of cultural/natural environments of host communities and commodification. While it is difficult to define sustainable heritage tourism, based on recurrent themes, this book coins a working definition which emphasizes long-term economic and cultural viability, local welfare, collaborative, and ecological harmony.

It is crucial to outline barriers which have the potential to impede the progress of sustainable development. In this chapter, nine issues within the heritage tourism realm are highlighted. These refer to the marriage of cultural heritage management with tourism, budget deficit and user fee debate, interpretation constraints, congestion management, politics of heritage, mixed benefits of technology on heritage, commodification versus conservation, and creating effective partnerships and stakeholder management. Awareness of these issues can guide relevant and effective marketing strategies.

The chapter also provides a detailed review of the authenticity debate as applicable to heritage tourism. The crucial and central role of authenticity in heritage tourism is highlighted. It is hoped that the discourse enhances the in-depth understanding and descriptive power of the term and helps the reader to rethink its meaning using a fresh perspective. Traditional heritage institutions continue to employ and promote the objective version of authenticity.

Numerous indicators to gauge sustainability levels are identified. These can be broadly grouped into cultural, economic, ecological, social, partnership, and conservation indicators. It is purported that heritage providers promote sustainable development by taking a strategic marketing perspective. What is also beginning to emerge is the need for a holistic approach that promotes both intergenerational and intra-generational equity. It is of surprise then that scant attention has been given to sustainable marketing paradigms in heritage tourism. The next chapter aims to fill this vacuum by extending Chhabra's (2009) sustainable framework.

Questions

1. Define the following terms: sustainability, sustainable tourism, and sustainable development of tourism.
2. Describe some of the prominent issues associated with heritage tourism.
3. Briefly describe the authenticity debate. Which stance is most applicable to the sustainable development of heritage tourism?
4. Critique du Cros's model within the context of the sustainable development indicators presented in this chapter.

3   Strategic Sustainable Heritage Tourism Marketing Model

This chapter is structured around the sustainable heritage tourism marketing model. The central question guiding this chapter relates to how each element of the model can contribute to sustainability. Each theme in the portfolio is identified based on an extensive review of literature and consultations with colleagues and various members of the heritage tourism industry. The chapter begins with a detailed explanation of the marketing mix. Attention is then turned to the factors that exert significant influence on the marketing mix. In closing, the crucial features of sustainability are discussed. These are then embedded into the proposed strategic sustainable heritage tourism marketing model.

Marketing Mix

'Marketing mix' is a multifaceted term. Many succinct and convenient classifications of marketing mix activities are suggested in documented literature (Frey 1961; Lazer and Kelly, 1962; McCarthy 1960), of which McCarthy's '4P' classification has been the dominant paradigm since the 1960s. It consists of four components; product, price, place (distribution), and promotion. The underlying premise of this classification is that promotion strategies for a product need to take into consideration other features such as the product, price, and distribution. Baker echoes this view by providing the following example:

> Advertising is not an operating method to be considered as something apart, as something whose profit value is to be judged alone. An able management does not ask, "Shall we use or not use advertising," without consideration of the product or other management procedures to be employed. Rather the question is always of finding a management formula giving advertising its due place in the combination of manufacturing methods, product form, pricing and promotion and selling methods and distribution methods. (1987: 5)

While the 4Ps framework is the most popular framework, additional Ps such as partnership, people, packaging, and programming are also proposed by recent studies (Morrison 2002). People are defined as employees and managers. Packaging means assembling services and facilities to match market needs. Morrison maintains that:

a marketing plan should detail the continuing and new packages and programs for the upcoming twenty-four months or less. A financial justification for each package and program should be included, as well as an explanation about how these offerings will be tied in with promotional activities and pricing/revenue objectives. (2002: 250)

Next, partnership calls for cooperative advertising and other collaborative efforts. This book focuses on the standard classification of the marketing mix. What follows now is a detailed description of the traditional '4Ps': product, price, distribution (place), and promotion.

Product

Misiura (2006) describes a product as something physical, functional, and symbolic. Physical takes the tangible form such as a museum building. An example of functionality can be an experiential view of a bygone era, something that triggers memories or nostalgia. Symbolic means representation of something, "such as the shrine to Mumtaz Mahal in the shape of the Taj Mahal in Agra, India" (Misiura 2006: 131). The product operates at four different levels: core, facilitating, supporting, and augmented. Consideration of these levels is premised on the notion that a heritage tourist has several needs.

- Core level – generally signifies the intangible aspect of the product such as providing convenience and comfort or aiming to fulfill needs of self-esteem, belonging, and self-actualization.
- Facilitating level – further, the core needs are provided in a physical form using the facilitation level. In other words, the facilitating level of the product provides a tangible structure to the intangible form. For example, it can provide a stimulating learning experience through a well-planned historical interpretation of a heritage product.
- Supporting level – this level is meant to add to the overall experience. It adds a physical as well as a psychological layer to the facilitating level.
- Augmented level – the fourth level, called the augmented level, represents the totality of experience and benefits. In other words, it focuses on how the first three product levels are presented and often falls within the 'value added' realm. As explained by Misiura (2006), augmented can include numerous value-added attributes such as a brand name or being labeled a 'World Heritage Site.'

As is widely known, all products go through a life-cycle process. Commonly identified life cycle stages are: development, introduction, growth, maturity, and decline (Morrison 2002). Each stage needs a distinct marketing strategy. Table 3.1 provides a brief overview of the kind of marketing strategies that might be feasible at each life-cycle stage.

Table 3.1 Predictions at Each Life-Cycle Stage

Characteristics	Introduction	Growth	Maturity	Decline
Product mix	One basic model	Expanding product lines	Full product lines	Best sellers
Pricing	Generally lower prices – less range	Greater range of prices	Full line of prices	Selected prices
Promotion	Informative	Persuasive	Competitive	Informative
Customers	Innovators	Affluent market/ mass market gets interested	Mass market	Laggards
Competition	None or small	Some	Many competitors	Few competitors

Price

Price is also an important element of the marketing mix. Consumers often use price to gauge product quality (Yoo and Donthu 2000). Price is, in fact, often positively associated with the perceived quality of a product (Dodds, Monroe and Grewal 1991; Kamakura and Russell 1993). Both internal and external factors need to be considered when setting prices:

- Internal factors include marketing objectives (such as survival, current profit maximization market-share leadership, and product-quality leadership), marketing mix strategy (this implies that price must be coordinated with product design and life-cycle stage, distribution channel selection, and promotional mix decisions), and organizational considerations (such as selection of appropriate managerial personnel to set price and level of interaction with other functional managers).
- External considerations include factors such as the nature of the market and demand (which entails understanding potential and target markets, making decisions about cross selling, upselling, and different pricing strategies), competition (determining competitors' prices and their perceived rejoinder to the company's own pricing plan), and other macro environmental elements (such as political, economic, social, cultural, and technological).

A marketing manager also needs to understand general pricing approaches and other pricing strategies. Most popular general pricing approaches include cost-plus pricing (examples include adding standard markup to the product and break-even analysis), value-based pricing (perceived-value is the most popular version of this strategy), and competition-based pricing (the going rate pricing where a company decides to use the collective wisdom of competitors to set its own price) (Kotler *et al.* 2006). Pricing strategies can also be based on new products and existing products. New product pricing strategy includes prestige pricing (which focuses on entering the market at a high price to hold a prestigious position), market skimming pricing (which implies setting a high price in a price-insensitive market), and market penetration pricing (which suggests entering a price-sensitive market with a low price). Examples of existing product pricing strategies include (Morrison 2002; Kotler *et al.* 2006):

• Product-bundle pricing – this strategy combines several products and offers them at a reduced price;
• Price adjustment strategy – examples in this category include discount pricing based on volume purchased and time of purchase;
• Discriminatory pricing – this strategy is based on market segmentation and price elasticity techniques;
• Psychological pricing – examples include reference prices such as round figures, and ignoring end figures;
• Promotional pricing – this forms a special pricing approach centered on promoting visitations and a desired temporary image as per the market demand.

Pricing within the realm of heritage tourism is a complex phenomenon because traditionally most providers of heritage operate under the non-profit umbrella. Nevertheless, the past two decades have noted an increasing reliance on self-funding as government funds and donations become sparse. Added to this decreasing government subsidy, as noted by Fyall and Garrod, is "the increasing competition both from within and outside of the heritage sector, and a continually increasing demand for higher standards and more services from visitors" (1998: 215). Despite numerous functions of pricing, it has received limited management attention in the heritage sector. This can be partly attributed to its stereotype notion that it is solely driven by profit goals and hence often considered a stigma.

The scant attention to pricing in the heritage sector has mostly appeared in association with admission prices. This view is confirmed by Fyall and Garrod (1998). In their survey of heritage sites in the UK, the authors discovered that utmost importance in setting admission prices was given (in order) to: seeking revenue targets, maximization of end-of-year revenues, and market acceptance of the price. Rising admission revenues have thus served to offset the budget deficit and other related strategies have centered on increasing ancillary sources of spending such as the tea room and the gift shop. This is a somewhat commercial approach and has lacked research and long-term planning.

The pricing potential remains unabated in the heritage tourism field. Price can play a pivotal role in improving sustained use of a heritage property and controlling carrying capacity. To date, it has mostly been used as a revenue-making tool without any strategic planning. Although a body of views exist in literature on how right prices can promote sustainable development or promotion of tourism (Sinclair and Stabler 1997; Fyall and Garrod 1998; Garrod and Fyall 2001), strategic planning to reduce the commercial use of pricing in heritage tourism is still in its infancy stage. Laarman and Gregersen (1996) contend that a carefully crafted user fee can offer numerous benefits such as:

• Raise the revenue for effective protection and conservation of the site;
• Help to manage overcrowding at the site during heavy use periods;

- Generate funds for education, thereby enhancing the overall visitor experience;
- Provide evidence of economic viability to the public authorities.

Distribution (Place)

The distribution component of the marketing mix "consists of all channels available between the firm and the end user that increase the probability of getting the end user to purchase the product" (Shoemaker *et al.* 2000: 493). These channels can be of two categories: direct and indirect. Either the heritage institution establishes a direct contact with the consumer or arranges an indirect connection via an intermediary such as a travel agent, tour operator, meeting planner, incentive planner, or wholesaler. Distribution channel considerations usually depend on three factors: market coverage, level of intensity, and speed to the market. Based on the literature review, popular intermediaries of heritage attractions include wholesalers/ tour operators, travel agents, incentive planners or houses, representation companies, consortia, destination marketing organizations such as the convention and visitor bureaus and state tourism offices, and the Internet (Holloway 2004; Janes 2006; Kotler *et al.* 2006; Morrison 2002; Shoemaker *et al.* 2000):

- Travel agents – these offer numerous benefits and can help reach a geographically dispersed market. Heritage hotels interested in seeking business through a travel agency can list their names in the airline reservation systems and hotel guides. Direct communication with travel agencies in the form of information packages, updates, and familiarization tours can also help travel agents sell heritage products in an effective manner. Kotler *et al.* suggest that hotels relying on travel agents "must make it easy for agents to make reservations. Providing toll-free reservation numbers is essential to servicing travel agents" (2006: 120).
- Tour wholesalers – this indirect distribution channel, on the other hand, focuses on assembling travel packages which can include accommodation, transportation, entertainment, and/or meals. They secure an allotment, for instance, of hotel inventory to sell to the public. Tour wholesalers are considered a powerful distributor of international resort facilities. To capture wholesaler interest, a heritage tourism supplier should be willing to negotiate prices in exchange for volume and bulk in advance bookings.
- Incentive planners – these form another strong distribution channel. They are companies that offer travel incentives to their employees for good performance, productivity, or to boost employee morale etc. (Morrison 2002; Holloway 2004). Generally speaking, incentive planners are like wholesalers. They negotiate with tourism suppliers for best prices and blocks and then add markup commission to earn profits. Other indirect distribution channel examples include destination marketing organizations, consortia, and representation firms.
- Destination marketing organizations – this is also an important indirect channel. Examples within this bracket include convention and visitor bureaus that

can help disseminate information to travelers and potential travelers. To use their resources, heritage attractions should seek membership with them and establish an ongoing communication network.

- Consortia – this channel represents the leading hotels of the world. It can be effective for heritage hotels because hotels under this group belong to the elite category. Heritage attractions can indirectly relate to consortia through partnerships and coordination strategies with established hotels within the consortia.

- Representation firm – a representation firm is a channel of distribution that can help to market a heritage product to feeder market areas (Morrison 2002). This company can market the product in geographic areas from where there is demand for heritage tourism. Such companies charge a fee and have their own sales team in different geographically dispersed regions. They have a world-wide reservation network and are linked to the global distribution systems. Additionally, other services are offered such as printing promotional collateral material (such as special programs, postcards, newsletters, flyers, etc.). Although this distribution channel is generally patronized by all types of hotels including heritage hotels and resorts, its use can be extended to heritage attractions and facilities such as museums, historic houses, and handicraft shops. This is cheaper than establishing sales offices in feeder cities or traveling to distant areas for marketing purposes.

The aforementioned intermediaries can also be communicated in an appropriate plan which incorporates the sustainable requirements of the heritage industry. For instance, information on behaving responsibly and respecting the local community culture can be highlighted. As an example, the Arizona Office of Tourism website provides educational information about the Native Americans and guides the visitors in a responsible manner. It informs the visitors that each reservation operates under its own government and own rules. Also, alcohol and drugs are not tolerated. The site lets the visitors know that they should refrain from talking to the dancers until the dancing is finished. No applauding is recommended after the religious dances. Visitors are also informed that sacred areas and graveyards are restricted areas and are not open to the public. The site educates in a detailed manner. It says:

> If you plan to visit an Indian reservation, know that: each reservation operates under its own government and its own rules for visitors. Photography is a particularly important issue. Fees and restrictions vary. Contact each individual tribe regarding its policy. Do not attempt to take photos or make recordings or sketches without checking. Photographs are for private use only and are not to be reproduced or resold without written permission. Often, dances are part of religious ceremonies. Please observe them as you would a church service, with respect and quiet attention. Please refrain from talking to the dancers until they have finished performing. Please don't applaud after religious dances. Do not climb walls or other structures. Some are several hundred years old and damage easily. Sacred areas and graveyards are restricted areas and are not open to

the public. Alcohol and drugs are not tolerated. Like any village, a reservation is home to those who live there and should be respected as such. Although most reservations are open to the public during daylight hours, homes are private and should be entered only by invitation. Beware of purchasing arts and crafts that are not authentic. (Arizona Office of Tourism 2009)

Additionally, the Indian Arts and Crafts Association has posted a brochure that gives tips on how to be an "educated" buyer. Additional information on purchasing authentic arts and crafts is available from the Indian Arts and Craft Board.

Promotion

Next, the promotion aspect of the marketing mix consists of four elements: advertising, sales promotion, personal selling, and public relations and publicity. Promotional mix forms the company's complete marketing program. Each of its elements satisfies a different communication need and numerous combinations are needed, depending on the life-cycle stage. Regardless of the promotional tool used, six steps in developing effective communications and different budget strategies need to be taken into consideration. These steps involve one or multiple stages of the consumer purchase process and consist of:

1. Identifying target audience.
2. Determining the communication objectives such as awareness, knowledge, liking, preference, conviction, or purchase.
3. Designing the message in terms of message content, message structure, message format, and message source.
4. Selecting the communication channels, personal and non-personal.
5. Selecting the message sources.
6. Measuring the communications' results.

The promotion mix consists of advertising, sales promotion, personal selling, and publicity. An organization can use one or a mix of these tools to design promotion strategies. Advertising can be employed to construct a long-term image and to trigger quick sales. It is the most widely visible and well-organized element of the promotional mix. It is also the item in which most promotional dollars are spent. It is a paid form of communication. Personal selling, on the other hand, permits unparalleled opportunities to cultivate a long-term consumer. It involves oral conversations. These are held by telephone, face to face, or email, between salespersons and prospective customers. Sales promotion motivates purchase by providing incentives or contributions that bestow additional value to customers. It gives customers short-term incentives to make an immediate purchase. Examples include discount coupons, contests and sweepstakes, samples, and premiums. Public relations include all activities that a business engages in to maintain or improve its relationship with other organizations and individuals. Examples include relationships with the government, financial institutions, media, employees, travel trade, etc. Publicity is one public relations technique that involves non-paid communication of information about an organization's services. These are often third-party endorsements. As is noted by marketing scholars, all four present both advantages and disadvantages (Morrison 2002; Kotler *et al.* 2006):

- Advantages of advertising include low cost per contact, ability to reach customers where and when salespersons cannot, great scope for creative versatility and dramatization of messages, creates awareness and improves understanding, ability to create images that salespersons cannot, non-threatening nature of non-personal presentation, and potential to repeat messages several times. Disadvantages include inability to close sales, advertising clutter (thousands of advertisements compete for attention), customers' ability to ignore advertising message, difficulty in getting immediate response or action, inability to get quick feedback and to adjust message.
- Advantages of personal selling include ability to close sales, ability to hold customers' attention, immediate feedback and two-way communication, presentation tailored to individual needs, ability to target customers precisely, and ability to cultivate relationships. Disadvantages are high cost per contact (travel costs of sales people), inability to reach some customers effectively (customers may refuse a salesperson's help or presentation), and prospects may be unavailable for reasons such as geographic locations and schedules.
- Advantages of sales promotion include combination of some advantages of personal selling and advertising (can be mass communicated through mail or customers can clip them out of magazines), ability to provide quick feedback, ability to add excitement to a service or product, additional ways to communicate with customers, flexible timing – can be used on short notice or at almost any time, and efficiency (can be launched with modest initial investments such as printing coupons). Disadvantages are short-term benefits, ineffective in building long-term loyalty for company or brand – are very appealing for brand switchers, and inability to be used on its own in the long term without other promotional mix elements.
- Advantages of public relations and publicity are low cost, effective because they are not seen as commercial messages – services described by an independent party so becomes more believable, credibility and implied endorsements (for instance, has greater credibility than paid endorsements), customers feel that they are receiving the reporter's endorsement, prestige and impressiveness of mass-media coverage, added excitement and dramatization, and maintenance of public presence. Disadvantages include: difficult to arrange consistently – it is often a hit-and-miss proposition. Also, coverage is totally at the discretion of media people. Another disadvantage is lack of control (inability to ensure that what is covered and said is exactly what you want to say).

A review of literature suggests that print ads are a popular advertising tool in heritage tourism (Manfredo *et al.* 1992; Smith and McKay 2001). Extant

promotion-based research has focused on advertising and its effectiveness among lucrative market segments (Xiao and Mair 2006). Brochures and pamphlets continue to be heavily used (Hsieh and O'Leary 1993; Walters *et al.* 2007; Chhabra 2009), although recent studies have questioned its conversion rate. Contemporary focus has shifted to the examination of the effectiveness of external stimuli in stimulating consumers' visionary reaction to advertised material (Walters *et al.* 2007). In aggregate, the foregoing discussion demonstrates that the core purpose of heritage tourism marketing lies in designing promotional strategies and message content aligned with the existing or potential target markets. The messages are tailor made to appeal to these market segments to enhance revenue. As noted by Chhabra (2009), limited attention is given to the promotion of sustainable use of a heritage.

For instance, in a more recent study of select museums in the United States, Chhabra (2009) reports a major focus on public relations and personal selling. Increasing emphasis is given to trade shows and interaction with the tourism community and tour operators/travel agents. Sales promotion techniques are employed in conjunction with the local tourism community such as placing coupons with local businesses and restaurants (Chhabra 2009). These are offered as incentives to facilitate visitations. Other promotional strategies include cooperative marketing strategies and media relations to generate publicity through news releases and editorial coverage by offering interesting stories. Also, some employ 'impersonal' communication methods such as direct mail and advertising through the use of brochures, television, and/or radio. The advertising strategies mostly center on target markets and popular tools include TV and retirement magazines. Additionally, efforts on generating onsite sale of gift items and other ancillary products are report.

Determinants of the Marketing Mix

It is important at this stage to highlight the fact that the marketing mix cannot exist alone. It is influenced by numerous other functions such as service, market segmentation, research, environment analysis, consumer behavior, and organizational behavior. All these assist in planning a well-rounded strategic marketing plan for a heritage institution.

Service Function

The service function consists of the four characteristics: intangibility, variability, inseparability, and perishability (Kotler *et al.* 2006).

- Intangibility implies that a heritage tourism service is a promise because it cannot be touched, taken home, or consumed before the actual time. Tourism service has thus to be tangibilized using a physical form such as the physical features of the site, artifacts, promotional materials, etc.
- Variability means inconsistency because of the human element involvement. Service people have different personalities and the same message can be

communicated differently based on interactions between the consumer and the service person.

- Inseparability means that the employee and the consumer have to be present and the service is delivered in the presence of other consumers.
- Perishability implies that service cannot be stored. For instance, today's consumer space or seat for a heritage show cannot be sold tomorrow. Sustainable management strategies are suggested to address the intangibility, variability, inseparability, and perishability characteristics of services offered by the heritage institutions.

Additionally, service quality is important. The last few decades have developed several measures of service quality to address the gap between customer perceptions once at the site and their pre-visit expectations. SERVQUAL is one example of a popular service quality model. It consists of four features as illustrated by Misiura (2006: 132):

- Tangibles are the physical features of the attraction such as staff appearance and uniform.
- Reliability helps gauge delivery of promises associated with service quality.
- Responsiveness is a measure of the extent an organization or business is willing to go in order to assist a customer.
- Assurance is the level of knowledge obtained by the staff with the intent to benefit the customer. In a way, this measure is similar to the 'variability' characteristic of service. Standardization and consistency of staff attitude and behavior are essential to maintain service quality as they are a part of the heritage product itself.

Market Segmentation

The next function, market segmentation, helps understand current and potential markets. Market segmentation can assist in developing desired segment profiles. It is an organized process for recognizing homogenous groups. Four measures for identifying lucrative markets are suggested by Kotler *et al.* (2006):

- Measurability which measures size, purchasing power, and profiles of different markets;
- Accessibility determines if selected markets can be reached easily;
- Substantiality helps to determine if the markets are large and profitable enough to serve;
- Actionability measures if an effective program friendly to the mission statement and budget can be designed for the selected markets.

Consequently, the aforementioned measures can assist in designing market-appropriate coverage strategies such as differentiated, undifferentiated, and concentrated. Once target markets and appropriate market coverage strategies are identified, appropriate positioning is the next step. Positioning is the "way the product is defined by consumers on important attributes – the place the product occupies in consumers' minds relative to competing products" (Kotler *et al.* 2006: 280). The entire market segmentation process is akin to the 'buying proforma' technique. Buying proforma was introduced by Dibb and Simkin (1996) to aid marketers in developing a complete understanding of their customers so that an appropriate marketing plan may be developed.

Market segmentation has received abundant attention in heritage tourism literature. Numerous market segments are identified based on attributes such as demographics (Chhabra *et al.* 2002; Misiura 2006), motivation (Kerstetter *et al.* 2001), activities (Sung 2004), attitude (Poria *et al.* 2003), benefits (Frochot 2005), and spending propensity (Caserta and Russo 2002). Heritage travel is a popular family activity (Chhabra *et al.* 2002). Moreover, during the past two decades, psychographics have become a key factor in understanding consumer behavior and this characteristic has become increasingly relevant to heritage marketing (Poria *et al.* 2001; Misiura 2006). Extant literature has established that consumers in heritage tourism seek a symbiotic relationship with the heritage visited; and emotions are the most popular touchstone of this symbiosis (Poria *et al.* 2001). Nostalgia is often considered an important outcome of emotions which assists in engaging consumers and helps create a longing for the past (Lowenthal 2000).

Much of the foregoing research has focused on the superiority of one segmentation method over the other (Frochot and Morrison 2000). The objective of the segmentation task in heritage tourism has been mostly to design precise promotional strategies (Cooper and Inoue 1996) for meaningful market segments (Phaswana-Mafuya and Haydam 2005). But recently it has been argued that segmentation technique should be used to tackle marketing issues and not solely focus on revenue (Tsiotsou and Vasaioti 2006). Heritage market segment analysis on the basis of ethics have failed to appear on the academic radar.

Research Function

The research function falls within the broad framework of the management information systems which performs three functions: 1) interaction with managers to assess information needs; 2) development of needed information from internal company records, marketing intelligence activities, and the marketing research process and; 3) distribution of information to managers in the most appropriate form and timely manner to facilitate and enhance marketing planning, implementation, and control (Kotler *et al.* 2006: 43).

Information can be obtained from internal sources (such as company executives, front desk staff, service staff, etc.), marketing intelligence (macro market information, competitive information, and new innovation and trends), or marketing research. Marketing research is an important aspect of gathering information and helps identify and define marketing opportunities and problems. It also helps monitor and evaluate marketing actions and performance, and includes the task of communicating findings and its consequential inferences to the business managers. An effective research process for evaluation of programs and heritage products is needed. Seven basic steps for undertaking research are suggested by Mitra and Lankford (1999):

- Identify the problem and state relationships of variables;
- Review and analyze relevant literature and other studies;
- Specify hypothesis or research questions; develop a research plan;
- Study design and decide on research methods;
- Choose subjects, conduct study, and collect data;
- Conduct data analysis and report results;
- Discussion of implications of findings, make recommendations and generalizations.

Two broad categories of research exist: qualitative and quantitative. Qualitative research focuses on nature and essence of the product or issue in question, while quantitative research focuses on numbers in terms of how much and how many (Mitra and Lankford 1999). Mitra and Lankford (1999) provide a comprehensive view of these research methods:

- Qualitative research – philosophical roots for qualitative research are phenomenology and symbolic interaction, while quantitative research is underpinned on positivism and logical empiricism. Phrases most commonly employed in qualitative research are fieldwork, ethnographic, words, naturalistic, grounded, and subjective. Also, qualitative research makes use of inanimate instruments (such as scales, tests, surveys, questionnaires, observation computers) and is mostly deductive.
- Quantitative research – this type of research, on the other hand, uses axioms such as prediction, control, description, confirmation, and hypothesis testing. With regard to sampling, qualitative research mostly makes use of small, non-random, and theoretical designs. Quantitative research makes use of large, random, and representative samples. Data collection for quantitative research focuses on researchers' as primary instruments and is mostly interview based. The mode of analysis is generally inductive.

Today, a broader and mixed spectrum of research strategies is being suggested. It is argued that purely statistical modus operandi are enhanced with qualitative methods; quantitative/rigorous techniques need to be supplemented because they present an incomplete picture and single handedly are unable to deal with the crucial issues faced by marketing and tourism scholars (Walle 1997). Traditional research undertaken by scientists focuses closely on verifiable facts using meticulous techniques which limit areas of inquiry, restricting convenient populations and oversimplifying reality (Walle 1997). As a result, it has not been possible to scrutinize reality in all its complexity.

Consequently, during the last two decades a wide range of qualitative techniques have gained attention within the field of marketing research in the current era. As noted by Ritchie and Goeldner (1989), marketing has transcended its pure scientific focus and contemporary trends focus on increased eclecticism. Therefore, the recent paradigm focuses on the eclectic toolkit so that practitioner needs can be addressed. Contemporary tourism research needs to build an epistemological and methodological toolkit for fuller explorations (Hall 2005).

Mixed research methods address the limitations posed by each of the methods if used alone and can be extended to social, behavioral, anthropological sciences. According to Creswell and Clark, "because of the combination of both quantitative and qualitative approaches and the skills required to conduct both forms of research, mixed methods research is an advanced methodology" (2007: 180). Several topics for future advancement of mixed methods research are recommended by Creswell and Clark such as sampling procedures, procedures for mixing data, software needs, writing up mixed methods research, the philosophical foundations and worldviews of mixed methods research, validity and inference issues, applications of mixed methods research, and value of mixed methods research as understood by academicians and practitioners (2007: 187).

Environment Analysis

Environment analysis is important for strategic marketing. There are two kinds of environmental forces that require profound attention: micro and macro (Kotler *et al.* 2006). Micro forces lie close to the company such as suppliers, location, marketing intermediaries, and customers. For example, relationship with the customers is important to earn their loyalty. The suppliers are another important example as they provide resources. The location of, for instance a hotel, is a significant determinant of ease of access. Also, the marketing intermediaries can help in distribution and sale.

Macro environment pertains to outside forces such as competitive, political, economic, social/cultural, demographic, natural, and technological. Macro environmental factors (such as social, political, and economic) need to be taken into consideration because they can exercise significant influence on businesses operations. For instance, their mixed influence on tourism-related businesses can occur through crime, changing demographics, taxation, pension benefits, employment, interest rates, etc. Fall in revenue can lead to business decline. Competition can call for innovative marketing strategies. Political factors include information on laws and government agencies that can exert an influence on the tourism market. For instance, legislation is increasingly promoting ethical and socially responsible strategies. Economic factors include consideration of changes in consumer income and spending patterns. Social and cultural environments on the other hand refer to understanding of institutions that shape cultural values and enforce prohibitions. Cultural changes such as fashion and life style trends may or may not support an organization or firm's offering in the market.

Demography is the study of human populations in terms of size, density, location, age, gender, race, occupation, and other statistics (Kotler *et al.* 2006). Because demographics change over time, ongoing information is required of them.

Additionally, the hospitality industry is greatly affected by changes in technology such as the Internet and computerized systems. Although this factor is opposed by those who believe it threatens privacy, simplicity, and even the human race, it is the most dramatic force affecting tourism. One significant impact of the Internet has occurred on the pricing component of the marketing mix. Because of increasing pricing transparency, it is important to guarantee price parity, both online and offline. Another innovation is related to eLearning, which comprises of technology-assisted learning. This tool is extensively used for training, education and research. Virtual Learning Environments (VLEs) have become popular among tourism educators. The eTourism has become more and more focused on consumer-based technology innovations to enable organizations/agencies to facilitate interactions with their consumers (Buhalis and Law 2008).

Environmental factors assist to position the company in the marketplace. They help analyze market trends. Ongoing assessment of environment forces is thus required so that an organization or company may respond quickly and intelligently to both internal and external changes. This can assist in formulating proactive rather than reactive marketing strategies.

Consumer Markets

After research, the next important function is to understand different kinds of audience in heritage tourism. Heritage tourism markets can be broadly divided into consumer (local and tourist), organization, donor, and member markets (Prentice 2001). Under the consumer market, the consumer black box (where information is processed and transformed into a decision) forms a focal point for receiving and encoding information and making decisions. It offers information of utmost importance and relevance to marketing managers. The decision-making process of a consumer involves various steps: need recognition, information search, evaluation of alternatives, purchase decision, and post-purchase behavior. The heritage institution has the ability to influence the consumer at each stage. The objective is to channel the energies in a meaningful and sustainable direction. Furthermore, consumer characteristics such as psychological factors, social and cultural factors, and the influence of all the aforementioned characteristics on decision making are important to know.

Extending the consumer black box concept, some authors say that even though marketers try to understand what goes on in this black box, they can never understand it all. Kotler (2000) says that uncovering why people buy is an extremely difficult task. The author further says the buyer's psyche is a 'black box' whose workings can be only partially deduced. The human mind, the only entity in nature with deep powers of understanding, still remains the least understood.

The psychoanalytic model proposed by Sigmund Freud of id, ego, and super ego forms an important source of discourse on consumer behavior complexity (Freud 1961). According to Sigmund Freud, children enters the world driven by instinctual needs which they cannot gratify by themselves. Very quickly and painfully, they realize their separateness from the rest of the world and yet their dependence on it.

As they grows, their psyche becomes increasingly complex: A part of their psyche – 'the id' – remains the reservoir of their strong inner drives and urges. Another part – the 'ego' becomes their conscious planning center for finding outlets for their inner drives. And a third part – the 'super ego' – channels their instinctive drives into socially approved outlets to avoid the pain of guilt or shame. In other words, we might have inner needs such as recognition, need to show off, enhance self-esteem, but we will not express them in public (Kotler 2000). These needs are a part of the id. The ego will try to channel them through pretence or socially approved outlets – super ego.

The individual's behavior, is therefore, never simple. A person's motivational wellsprings are not obvious to a casual observer nor are they deeply understood by the actual individual (Kotler 2000). For instance, if a man is asked by a sales manager why he purchased an expensive foreign sports car. He may reply that he likes its maneuverability and its looks. At a deeper level, he may have purchased the car to impress others, or to feel young again. Now, as a marketing manager, if you accept his answer, you are going to be misled. In other words, you might come up with a promotional strategy which positions your cars in terms of smoothness and the exterior. Your positioning statement might never be effective for this type of market segment. Hence, thoughtful research methods are needed to gain an insight into motivations and behaviors. One example of prodding into someone's mind is to ask the customer to fill in the blanks. Or, show a picture and ask what kind of memories it evokes (Kotler 2000). So, when thousands and millions of dollars are at stake on advertising campaigns, a good psychological understanding of the consumer market is needed so that you can come up with effective messages and good positioning statements.

Next, it is important to heritage institutions to understand the consumer buying behavior process. Consumer buying behavior refers to the buying behavior of final consumers – individuals and households who buy goods and services for personal consumption. The central question for marketers is: "How do consumers respond to various marketing efforts the company might use?" The following steps in the consumer buying behavior process are suggested by Kotler *et al.* (2006: 220, 221):

- Need recognition – for the decision process to begin, a potential buyer must first recognize a problem or need. This can be caused by internal stimuli (social, hunger, etc.) or external stimuli such as attractive brochures, coffee aroma, etc.
- Information search – information can be obtained from: personal sources such as family, friends, neighbors, and acquaintances; commercial sources such as advertising, salespeople, dealers, packaging, and displays; and public sources such as restaurant reviews, editorials in the travel section, and consumer-rating organizations.
- Evaluation of alternatives – products are seen as bundles of product attributes. That is, you might go to a restaurant for attributes such as food, good service, and socialization. I might pay more attention to food while you might consider service more important for a satisfying experience. Hence, all of us see a tourism product as a bundle and may rank its attributes differently. Customers thus rank attributes differently which influence their purchase intentions.

- Purchase decision –at this stage, the consumer makes choice between various brands. As stated by Kotler *et al.*, "the consumer will buy the most preferred brand, but two factors can come between the purchase intention and the purchase decision: attitude of others and unexpected situation" (2006: 221).
- Post-purchase behavior – the smaller the gap between customer expectations and perceived performance, the greater the customer's satisfaction. Cognitive dissonance is buyer discomfort caused by post-purchase conflict. For example, after coming back from a Hawaiian vacation, you might see an advertisement for Alaska and wonder if you made the right choice. This explains why resorts/hotels/airlines etc. usually follow up with their guests/customers after their departure. They will send 'thank you' notes and try to convince them that they made a good choice and should come back.

Group Markets

Today, organizational markets offer substantial revenue potential for heritage tourism. Conventions, small conferences, and social, military, educational, religious, and fraternal organizations (SMERF) are interested in hosting their clients and members in heritage environments. Additionally, they have displayed a desire to utilize the same environments as a backdrop for training, meetings, and education sessions (McLean 2002). Organizational buying behavior involves several stages starting from problem recognition, general need description, product specification, supplier search, proposal solicitation, supplier selection, order-routine specification, and performance review. These eight stages are also called the buy phases (Kotler *et al.*, 2006). The organizational buying center also presents an interesting study. The buying center has been defined as "all those individuals and groups who participate in the purchasing decision-making process, who share common goals and the risks arising from the decisions" (Kotler *et al.*, 2006: 61).

From the perspective of heritage tourism, group business markets are of interest to museums, historic houses, and handicraft industries. For instance, museums have diversified their role using a neoclassical approach (maximizing utility in a benevolent way to cover operation costs) in the community by engaging in commercial activities such as offering their space to conference and event planners at a subsidized price.

Strategic Sustainable Heritage Tourism Marketing Model

Having presented different features influential on the marketing mix, it is now time to set the stage for the strategic sustainable heritage tourism marketing (SSHTM) model. As Figure 3.1 illustrates, six factors situated in the outer layer are crucial for sustainable marketing to happen and succeed. For effective results, these factors should be internalized into the marketing plan. These are: local community involvement and benefits; partnership and collaboration; authenticity and conservation; visitor mindfulness; interpretation; and economic viability.

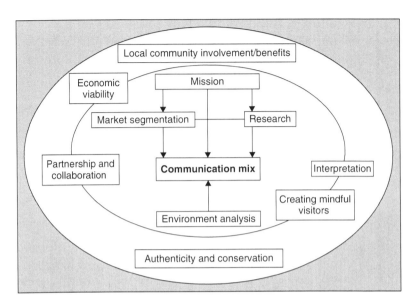

Figure 3.1 The Strategic Sustainable Heritage Tourism Marketing Model

Local Community Involvement and Benefits

Host communities have been repeatedly relegated to the status of a minor player in the tourism development and expansion deliberations (Pearce 1995). Often, perceptions and externalities in terms of socio-economic, cultural, and environmental costs are not taken into consideration. Recent tourism debates have centered on social exclusion issues. In a study by Hall (1994), several tourism development scenarios were noted in North America and Australia where heritage of the powerless or the minority has been ignored. Ashworth (1992) has referred to this situation as 'disinheritance' whereby some groups are erased from the chapters of history. Selective representation and interpretation examples can also be found in developing countries where the elite or the power groups decide what and whose heritage to include or discard (Timothy and Boyd 2003).

Emerging awareness of the aforementioned issues has generated the need to implement 'inclusive strategies' not only within the context of heritage presentation and interpretation but also involving local communities in the tourism planning and development process. Innskeep (1991) and Pearce (1995) describe the significance of involving the local community in decision-making processes pertaining to heritage tourism development. The authors maintain that this approach can provide inherent social benefits and facilitate sustainability. It is also important to note that the local community is not homogeneous and consists of diverse constituencies. Their views need to be included in the planning process. That is, to cultivate the entire community and decrease resistance, inclusion of a non-tourism audience is also crucial. For instance, the 'members only' policy poses inherent flaws because often memberships get restricted to Chambers of Commerce or to the businesses directly involved in tourism such as hotels, restaurants, and/or the attractions themselves. History and art activists are inroads to community support and their views are important. People who represent the root culture need to be reached (Cogswell 1996). Such an approach helps to take the community pulse. In this way, information can be exchanged and negotiated and protest, if any, mediated to obtain a desired response. Conflicts can thus be managed with outcomes such as reconciliation, compromise, and enhanced awareness (Timur and Getz 2008). This can also help dilute any negative perceptions locals hold about tourists; that is, cognitive dissonance can be minimized.

Although several pathways have been suggested by contemporary researchers, they have yet to be tested. According to Pearce (1995), a theoretical or conceptual framework is needed to gain an insight into how a local culture interacts and perceives tourists. Pearce (1995: 150) suggests seeking answers to the following questions to guide this line of query:

1. Who is actually having contact with the visitors?
2. How much contact is happening?
3. What are the type and range of situations involved in this contact?
4. What are the community attitudes and responses to the contact?
5. Are there any problems caused by the visitor–host contact?
6. Is the current level of contact desired and likely to continue or is there a preferred future tourism community interaction scenario?

Also, "provisions for buffering cultural contact, based on local preferences, are important ingredients in the development plan" (Cogswell 1996). Respect for privacy and acceptable host–guest contact zones has to be strategized. It has also been suggested that governments and the public sector involved in tourism should oversee host community education and participation in tourism (Tosun 2006). The objective is to facilitate and maintain existing public support for tourism and to reduce adverse social impacts on the hosts. Painter (1992) also suggests that communities can be educated by involving them in the tourism development process. But first, training and education needs need to be identified. Awareness of the human resource development needs of the community is required. In a study on local artists, Wells (1989) finds that they need assistance on technical aspects of taxation, marketing such as self-promotion and pricing, and other legalities related to the sale of arts and crafts. Furthermore, it is important to remember that finding an appropriate fit and making sure tourism brings economic and social benefit to local residents requires training local businesses. The training should inform businesses on how to take opportunity of changing markets, help them to seek grants for projects such as printed promotional collateral materials, and provide guidance on how to conduct research to understand the market (Caldwell 1996).

One of the pioneering experts in community participation techniques is Arnstein, who proposed a "Ladder of Participation" as an effective mechanism for citizen involvement. According to Arnstein, citizen participation enhances citizen power, defined as an attempt to redistribute power to enable "the have-not citizens, presently excluded from the political and economic processes, to be deliberately included in the future" (1969: 216). Through her ladder of participation model, she suggests gradations of participation in federal programs run by the United States government such as urban renewal, anti-poverty, and Model Cities. Figure 3.2 demonstrates eight rungs that form the ladder. These are broadly classified as non-participation, tokenism, and participation.

Non-participation includes manipulation and therapy. Tokenism includes informing, consultation, and placation, while participation encompasses partner-ships, delegated power, and citizen control. As the criterion indicates, the rungs of Arnstein's ladder represent the extents of citizens' power and level of involvement in the determination of the end product. Each rung represents a process by which the "have-not citizens can induce significant social reform which enables them to share in the benefits of the affluent society" (1969: 216). Arnstein also notes that the model dynamism differs from project to project and between developed and devel-oping countries. She reports more barriers when going up the ladder in a develop-ing country. In a similar vein, Pretty (1995) describes community participation on the basis of seven levels that stretch from manipulative participation to self-mobi-lization, with each level allowing different degrees of external involvement, local control, and power relationships.

Chogull (1996) presents a modified version of Arnstein's model when applying it to the developing countries. He proposes a modified eight-rung ladder and created four categories for the rungs: 1) support, which includes empowerment, partnership, and conciliation; 2) manipulation, which consists of dissimulation, diplomacy, and informing; 3) rejection, which includes conspiracy; and 4) neglect, which he equates with self-management.

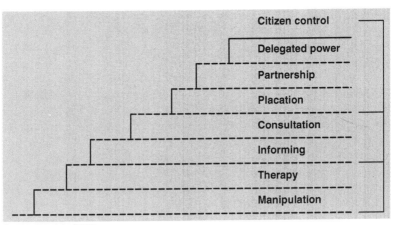

Source: Arnstein (1969)

Figure 3.2 Arnstein's Ladder of Participation
Source: Arnstein (1969)

- *Hierarchy Level 1: Empowerment* – at this level, the community members begin their own progress and demonstrate full control of the situation. They possibly partner with external organizations or allies to achieve desired goals.
- *Hierarchy Level 2: Partnership* – this position forms the second highest rung of the ladder. At this stage, the government is more intensely involved. There is a consensus among the community members and the outside decision-making bodies to split planning and decision-making responsibilities on development using structures such as joint policy boards and other informal devices for the resolution of problems and conflicts.
- *Hierarchy Level 3: Conciliation* – this stage comprises of situations where solutions and resolutions are crafted by the government and these are subject to ratification by the local community. It is more of a "top-down, paternalistic approach" (Chogull 1996: 437).
- *Hierarchy Level 4: Dissimulation* – this stage is focused on government's efforts or of those holding power to educate local communities and garner their support. A facade of participation is achieved at this level by placing local people on rubber-stamp advisory committee or boards.
- *Hierarchy Level 5: Diplomacy* – this stage is a manipulative stage. At this level, the government or the organization in power expects the local community to take charge of its own progress and be responsible for obtaining needed resources. This position can be attributed to disinterest, scarcity of financial resources or incompetence. However, the officials in power (for example, the government) can modify their policies and offer services in the form of consultation, attitude surveys, public hearings, and limited aid, if the community is able to show progress.
- *Hierarchy Level 6: Informing* – this stage comprises of a one-way flow from the officials to the community. Examples include discussion of local community rights, responsibilities, and options, without allowing for feedback or conciliation.
- *Hierarchy Level 7: Conspiracy* – at this level, the local community is not considered important enough to include them in the decision-making process. The poor people are often considered a liability and the government or the power groups are not interested in helping them.
- *Hierarchy Level 8: Self-management* – this is the lowest rung in the ladder. According to Chogull (1996: 440), "at this level, the government does nothing to solve local problems and the members of the community, by themselves, plan improvements to their neighborhood and actually control projects, not always successfully."

Arnstien's and Chogull's models can help community builders assess their performance. A more recent work by Tosun (2006) also warrantees attention. Tosun outlines typologies contextualizing community participation based on the degree of power distribution. His spectrum of community participation runs from spontaneous participation to coercive participation with the induced participation category in the middle. Table 3.2 provides a brief overview of Tosun's (1999) typology.

As the table shows, Tosun's spontaneous participation equates with Arnstein's degrees of citizen power. Induced participation runs parallel with Arnstein's degrees of citizen tokenism and Tosun's coercive participation is similar to Arnstein's non-participation category.

Table 3.2 Tosun's Typology of Community Participation

Spontaneous Participation	Bottom-up, active participation; direct participation; participation in decision making; authentic participation; self-planning.
Induced Participation	Top-down; passive; formal; mostly indirect; degree of tokenism, manipulation; pseudo-participation; participation in implementation and sharing benefits; choice between proposed alternative and interest in obtaining feedback.
Coercive Participation	Top-down, passive; mostly indirect, formal; participation in implementation, but not necessarily results in sharing of benefits; choice offered between proposed limited alternatives or no choice given; paternalism, non-participation, high degree of tokenism and manipulation.

Source: Tosun (1999)

All aforementioned typologies can serve as a valuable tool to ascertain the range of community participation in heritage tourism from the more common passive, manipulative or token toward more authentic and interactive rungs in the spectrum. According to France, "this spectrum accords well with the superimposed nature of tourism activity that is frequently grafted on to an economy and society in a 'top-down' manner" (1998: 224). For the purpose of this book, Arnstein's typology is employed.

Partnerships and Collaboration

Partnership is the next important ingredient of the SSHTM. It has been long recognized that a single organization or individual cannot command the future of the tourism industry. Collective power of collaborative action cannot be undermined whether the objective is conservation, economic development, or protected area management (Selin 1999). Most researchers accept that partnership is a term that implies devotion to a common cause among otherwise independent organizations and corporations. Selin maintains that partnerships can play a significant role by facilitating a sustainable development of tourism. He maintains that, "negotiation, mutually determined goals and actions, and monitoring resulting from cross-sector partnerships make it more likely that these initiatives will result in sustainable outcomes" (Selin 1999: 261). Additionally, contemporary forces in the economic, political, and social environment are compelling organizations to prioritize the need for partnerships. Common characteristics of partnerships and collaboration are popularly outlined as (Sitarez 1998):

- Defining collaboration as a process of joint decision making among key stakeholders of a problem domain about the future of that domain;

- Creating solution by constructively dealing with differences – involving joint ownership of decisions;
- Assuming collective responsibility for the domain's future;
- Making collaboration an emergent process. The key message of this formative work is that partnerships and collaborative arrangements are not static but dynamic.

To date, most partnerships are cross-sector initiatives that engage representatives from industry, government, and the voluntary sectors (Sitarez 1998). Examples include cooperative marketing initiatives (Witt and Moutinho 1989), intergovernmental coalitions (Selin 1993), public–private partnerships (Murphy 1985), and intersector planning (Gunn 1994). Regardless of the partnership type, all share similar assumptions:

- Tourism organizations operate in a complex and dynamic environment and multiple forces such as political, technological, economic, demographic, and socio-cultural influence the policy and direction of management (Trist 1977).
- A broader domain level focus is required among actors instead of an "organization-set perspective to help navigate through turbulent environments. This focus calls for collaboration between individuals, groups and/or organizations" (Gray 1985: 912). That is, "organizational and individual interests have to transcend traditional organizational boundaries" (Selin and Chavez 1995).
- Multiple outcome-based procedural approaches need to be adopted so that focus is shifted from individual actors to embrace a larger system dynamics (Rogers and Whetten 1982). Different models of partnership have appeared in tourism literature. Selin presents an evolutionary partnership model that involves different steps that evolve over time. Selin's spectrum encompasses partnerships across five primary dimensions: geographic scale (from homogeneous sector to multi-sector diverse sector organizations), grass roots to legal basis, locus of control (stretching from agency control to stakeholder control with other levels of control in the middle such as actively consulting, seeking consensus, negotiating agreements, sharing authority, and transferring authority and responsibilities), organizational diversity, and time frame (from temporary focusing on problem resolution and informal structure to long-term centered on permanent and formal structures). These can be plotted at the community, state, regional, or national levels. All these partnerships evolve in a dynamic manner. For instance, in regard to the locus of control dimension, Selin and Chavez (1995) suggest that tourism and natural resource management agencies are under compulsion to embrace more participatory planning and management techniques, which means sharing control with more stakeholders. That does not come without limitations such as loss of agency power and barriers to hard-fought laws outwitted by community-based collaboration. As feared by McClosky, collaborative processes can be co-opted or vetoed by industry and small local industries. That is, different stakeholders might have multiple and often conflicting visions. As a solution, Selin suggests that public

ownership and support for partnership outcomes can be enhanced by providing "meaningful opportunities for public involvement throughout the planning
process." (1999: 272)

Balance between private and public sector is an important factor as implied by
Augustyn and Knowles (2000) so that a representative selection of all members is
assured. Additionally, ongoing funds are needed to sustain collaborative activities
in the long-run. Augustyn and Knowles also suggest introducing a membership fee
but reasons and expectations need to be carefully laid out. Additionally, the authors
call for the involvement of ground-level staff in addition to managers and experts
in the collaboration process. The underlying premise is that the ground-level staff
are often directly in contact with issues. Finally a reward approach has been suggested. That is, "an internal reward system for 'better-than-average' contributions
to the attainment of partnership goals may make arrangements more dynamic but
strict criteria of what constitutes such 'better-than-average' contributions have to
be agreed between partners" (Augustyn and Knowles 2000: 350). Additionally,
ongoing evaluation of the partnership functions based on crucial success factors is
considered important.

   Moreover, clear direction and effective leadership are needed to drive issues forward (Aas *et al.* 2005). Different agendas of conservation bodies and the tourism
industry can hinder initiatives from either side to take the first step. Establishing
channels of communication has been found to be the most arduous task. Education
of user pays principles within the context of benefits and costs are needed.
Reconciliation of differences between various stakeholders is also a tedious task
and appropriate skills and understanding are required. There is also a need to raise
stakeholder capabilities. For instance, Aas *et al.* (2005) note that although local
community might be willing to get involved, lack of faith and knowledge can hinder involvement. According to Simmons (1994), raising capabilities will permit
stakeholders to participate as well as negotiate in the collaboration process. It might
not address the issue of power imbalances, but Arnstein's stages of 'manipulation'
and 'therapy' in the ladder of citizen participation might serve as a warning against
the pitfalls of involving local community at superficial or manipulative levels.
Other issues that offer possible hindrance to effective collaboration exist at the
macro level. External factors such as political, economic, cultural, and social at the
national level cannot be changed, but need to be seriously taken into consideration.
Thus, several inherent problems exist.

   Partnerships from a sustainable tourism perspective imply the need to partner
with various stakeholders to aim for sustained use of resources. Partners within the
heritage tourism environment have been broadly classified into the following categories: heritage institutions (heritage sites, attractions, events, and shops), the public sector (chamber of commerce, city or government who decides on tax
deductions), the ancillary sector (such as gasoline stations, restaurants, lodging,
gift shops, etc.), tourism organizations (such as the convention and visitor bureaus,
state tourism offices, national and regional tourism organizations), local community, and the academic community (the educational institutions).

Although constructing partnerships with the host communities is considered important by the supporters of sustainable heritage tourism, most studies have fallen short of
adding local community involvement/benefits to their marketing equation (Boyd
2002; Saarinen 2006). This is not to say that examples of success in non-marketing
contexts do not exist. For instance, ecomuseums are a product of sustainable development efforts and civic engagement. Fuller's concept of the 'ecomuseum' has a distinct
purpose to attract and build "deeper relationships with more diverse audience" (Spitz
and Thorn 2003: 3). Fuller (1992: 328) describes an ecomuseum as an "agent for managing change that links, education, culture, and power. It extends the mission of a
museum to include responsibility for human dignity." However, to date, this ideology
has not been applied to museums within the context of marketing strategies.

Partnerships also assist in embracing a multidisciplinary perspective and provide
a holistic view of a heritage environment. That said, partnerships can only be effective if good leadership and strategic vision is in place. Through partnerships, collective emphasis can be placed on intergenerational equity and intragenerational
equity. Although sparse, few successful examples of sustainable partnerships exist
in tourism literature. For instance, the 'Overhill' program in Tennessee (Caldwell
1996) (see Box 3.1). It enjoys a market identity because of harmonious relationship
between its various stakeholders.

Box 3.1 Tennessee's Overhill Program

Tennessee Overhill region is historically named after the McMinn, Monroe
and Polk counties. The first two years of the Tennessee Overhill program
were spent on research and training. Consultants from a variety of disciplines
assisted the local group with training in such areas as a museum development
and regional marketing. Surveys on site visitation were completed and a
three-year strategic plan drafted. Community education was a challenge.
There were people who thought tourism development should not be considered for economic development at all. There were old-line tourism types who
had little regard for or understanding of heritage tourism. The Overhill
Association's first brochure was designed to explain the project and the concept behind it to the indigenous population. A slide show and exhibit were
created and then taken to the civic club circuit by members of the Overhill
Community Education Committee. Support from the Tennessee Department
of tourism Development was especially helpful at this point. People who
thought of tourism development only in terms of billboards, brochures, and
paid advertising were more comfortable discussing broader approaches to
tourism development with a respected agency than with a new and untested
organization. The state agency reinforced efforts on several fronts.

From the beginning, Tennessee Overhill has followed the five principles
of heritage tourism that were set forth by the National Trust for Historic
Preservation:

1. *Focus on authenticity and quality.* We are convinced that true stories of the Overhill are far more interesting than any fictional commercialized version. The Tennessee Arts Commission has recently secured a grant from the National Endowment for the Arts to document and present the folk arts of the Overhill. A professional folk art specialist will work with local agencies and organizations to increase folk arts programming and will provide technical assistance to the Overhill organization and the artists themselves. In terms of tourism development, local culture is an underused accessible resource. Creating events or marketing existing events that showcase local culture can ultimately increase visitation and build community pride. Care must be taken, however, to ensure that local history and culture are presented with respect and sensitivity.

2. *Preserve and protect resources.* It is important to safeguard the future of tourism by protecting the unique elements that attract visitors initially. The Overhill Advisory Council believes that mismanaged tourism and inappropriate growth would produce a program amounting to another extractive industry. Slower growth, controlled by local amount to another extractive industry and is more desirable. There is a shortage of tools for local people to use for control. Zoning is an unpopular option, and an argument can be made that resistance to zoning is a local decision. Therefore, we are addressing such concerns subtly through education. Several exciting preservation projects are currently underway in the Overhill. One such project is in Etowah, where the city government and the Arts Commission are working together to restore the historic Gem theater as a public performance space. The city's strategy includes development of the programming that will attract visitors as well as local people. Both private and public efforts to preserve special places can be found across the region.

   Preservation means more than saving historic buildings or protecting open space – it also means identifying traditional culture and building an appreciation for that which makes our culture unique. There is a economic advantage to cultural tourism: travel and lifestyle writers appreciate story opportunities offered by folk artists, traditional craftsmen, and sites that reflect the uniqueness of a region.

3. *Make sites come alive.* Thoughtful interpretation can provoke visitors' interest in a region in a way that will result in return visits and opportunities to extend seasons. Many of our communities have taken advantage of the technical assistance offered through the Heritage Tourism Initiative, the Tennessee Humanities Council, and historic sites.

4. *Find the fit between the community and tourism.* Ensuring that tourism is of economic and social benefit to residents. Small local businesses must learn how to capitalize on changing markets. Capital must be found to continue local preservation efforts. For this reason the Overhill

has become involved in facets of economic development that are not normally associated with tourism development. Participation in the East Tennessee Community Design Center's Rural Connections II Program helped several small Overhill communities to launch projects designed to increase community income. The East Tennessee Foundation established a small grant program to help Rural Connections participants jump start projects. The Coker Creek Ruritan Club formed an economic development corporation that is reviving the strong crafts heritage of Coker Creek and helping others find ways to increase family income. The Community Action Group of Engelwood worked on a feasibility study and pro forma for its museum building and mounted a fund-raising campaign for bricks and mortar. Copperhill opened a new visitor center. The USDA Forest Service and the Cherokee National Forest targeted the Overhill for work through its Economic Recovery program, which was created to assist communities affected by timber sales. They provided grants for projects ranging from printed collateral materials to market studies and hospitality training.

One frustration is the absence of a state mechanism to provide more help to revitalization of small downtown areas. The National Trust for Historic Preservation's Main Street Program includes strategies that we think could help our towns. Successful Main Street Programs produce more than building refurbishment, paint, dress, and awnings. A good Main Street program can address numerous issues including business recruitment, market niches, retail merchandising, and cooperative marketing. However, most Main Street programs are geared for towns with populations greater than 5,000; most Overhill towns have fewer than 5,000 people.

5. *Collaborating.* Building cooperation between and among business people, operators of historic sites and museums, and governments was the guiding principle for forming the Tennessee Overhill Advisory Council and is the reason the council comprises such diverse people as forest rangers, museum directors, business people, real estate agents, preservationists, civic workers, craftsmen, and local residents.

Much of the success of the Overhill program is due to this group. Our partnership with the Cherokee National Forest and the US Forest Service has been very rewarding to our region. New government partners include TVA, Appalachian Regional Commission, and the Southeast Tennessee Resource and Development Council. Agencies with which we have long-standing relationships, including the Tennessee Arts Commission, Tennessee Humanities Council, Tennessee Department of Tourist Development and the Southeast Tennessee Development District, continue to help us plan for the future.

The local government partnership that was created when McMinn, Monroe, and Polk Counties agreed to jointly fund the Overhill project is critical. Without basic support for the office and staff it would be difficult to function productively.

The work of the National Trust for Historic Preservation and the Tennessee Department of Tourist Development with McMinn, Monroe and Polk Counties has been even more important than we initially realized. There are new printed materials available to market the Overhill. A new hospitality curriculum is being developed. The Overhill is beginning to enjoy a market identity that is evident in the increased inquiries about the region by name. A study grant from the USDA Forest Service was used to contract for the assistance of the National Trust for Historic Preservation in developing a market plan for 1995–1996 that could best capitalize on the 1996 Olympics on the Ocoee River. A new regional organization exists with an expanded mission that will continue to work towards a holistic approach to economic development. We will continue to consider our past as we plan for the future in the Overhill.

Source: Caldwell (1996: 127–131)

A multidisciplinary expertise is thus required. For instance, anthropologists can assist in the identification, documentation, and interpretation of those elements of history and traditional culture that have the potential to attract visitors. Therefore, it is important to remember that setting the sustainable heritage tourism bandwagon in motion is an arduous task. Partnership is a crucial sustainable marketing tool.

Authenticity and Conservation

It is an established fact that authenticity and conservation of heritage are crucial for sustained use of resources and intergenerational equity. A detailed discussion on the authenticity discourse is provided in Chapter 2. At the center of heritage sustainability lies the need to promote the objective and essentialist ideologies of authenticity (McKercher and du Cros 2002). Hence sustainable marketing of heritage is premised on efforts to maintain the 'past as it is.' Several tangible indicators exist in literature to gauge the level of authenticity at heritage institutions.

Next, conservation of heritage is important. The primary basis of conservation includes protection of heritage resources. It emphasizes the purposeful use of resources in a manner that it is appreciated and used for recreational purpose while at the same time striving to sustain the core value of heritage for future generations (Pearce 1997). Conservation comes to the fore when efforts are made to prevent the decay of heritage resources over time (Ashworth and Tunbridge 2000). Several conservation approaches have been suggested by literature: preservation, restoration, renovation, and regeneration:

- *Preservation* – Timothy and Boyd (2003: 94) describe preservation as an effort "to maintain the site in its existing state." Retaining the present form is an arduous task (Wall 1989). As maintained by Pearson and Sullivan, preservation is necessary for sites where there is a danger that "cultural significance will be diminished by a higher degree of intervention, where the present state of the site is itself significant" (1995: 233).
- *Restoration* – is an act of returning a property to a previously set criterion. It implies that new materials ruin the authenticity of a heritage property. According to Pearson and Sullivan (1995), restoration comprises of two activities: putting together dislodged pieces of a building, site or object and removing the impression of time on them. This situation is possible only if ample evidence of the previous state exists. This entails a great amount of research to determine the original version of the property or object. Hence such tasks are tedious, time consuming, and costly.
- *Renovation* – on the other hand, renovation refers to the act of making changes to a site while at the same time retaining its historical character. Examples of renovation in heritage tourism include those historic buildings which retain their original façade but are modified in their interior (Wall 1989). In this case, emphasis is on adaptive use of the site in a manner that respects the original character.
- *Regeneration* – conservation can happen in the form of urban renewal and regeneration when "decisions are made not to demolish obsolete buildings, but to be utilized in urban renewal and regeneration projects" (Timothy and Boyd 2003: 96). Examples include cities all over the world that are changing to create post-industrial ambience. This extends the use of discarded historic buildings and urban centers.

While the sequential steps suggested above can be applied universally, modifications are needed to fit local situations, requirements, and mission. Another important point to remember is that heritage conservation is not without challenges. As Tiesdell, Oc and Heath (1996) state, challenges include:

- Clash of policies on new developments and conservation;
- Modernization versus maintaining traditional forms;
- Balancing the needs of tourists and needs of local residents;
- Maintaining high-quality environments as tourist arrivals increase;
- Difficulty in measuring the success of renewal;
- Viewing historic centers in isolation from the city while planning;
- Tourism left out or ignored in urban planning strategies.

Different countries enforce conservation guidelines using different regulations. Some are an extension of guidelines crafted by the UN charter. Conservation bodies are responsible for listing and protection of heritage properties. These range from being full government agencies to quasi-governmental agencies that resemble non-profit organizations and associations. Examples include: Council of Europe,

English Heritage, Getty Conservation Institute, ICCROM (the International Center for the Study of the Preservation and the Restoration of Cultural Property), UNESCO, and ICOMOS International. As pointed out by Timothy and Boyd, "in the developing world, heritage is usually listed and protected at the national level by government agencies (e.g. ministries of culture, environment and tourism). In the development world, the tendency is more towards quasi-public forms of guardianship through various associations and conservation groups" (2003: 112).

Moreover, several international agencies operate beyond the national realm that serve as guardians of the world's heritage. The most widely recognized agency is the United Nations Educational, Scientific and Cultural Organization (UNESCO), whose World Heritage List strives to guard and bestow international prestige to properties/sites of unique historic and natural value. Through a series of conventions, UNESCO has facilitated widespread interest and commitment from national governments and agencies to toil toward protecting the world's unique heritage. Box 3.2 provides guidelines for World Heritage Listing. The purpose of World Heritage Listing is twofold:

1. The List is a means of recognizing that some places are of substantial significance as cultural or natural sites for the entire international community to feel responsible for them.
2. The list is a tool to promote conservation of unique and fragile sites. By joining the convention, a nation promises to take care for its site.

Box 3.2 ICOMOS Criteria for World Heritage List Inscription

*   Represent a masterwork of human creative genius.
*   Exhibit an important interchange of human values over a span of time, or within a cultural area of the world, or development in architecture, monumental arts or town planning and landscape design.
*   Bear a unique or at least exceptional testimony to a civilization or cultural tradition which is living or which has disappeared.
*   Be an exceptional example of a type of building or architectural ensemble or landscape which describes significant stages in human history.
*   Be an outstanding example of a traditional human settlement or land use which is representative of a culture or cultures especially when it has become vulnerable under changing conditions.
*   Be directly or tangibly linked with events or living traditions and with ideas, beliefs, artists and literary works of outstanding universal value (The Committee considers that this criterion should only be included in exceptional circumstances).

Source: ICOMOS (2004)

The World Heritage List was established by the World Heritage Convention of 1972. The World Heritage Convention is overseen by WHC (World Heritage Committee and is serviced by UNESCO). The World Heritage Center houses the Convention and was set up in Paris in 1992. The Center and the Committee are governed by three non-governmental bodies. The International Committee on Monuments and Sites (ICOMOS) deals with cultural sites and publishes operational guidelines for the implementation of the World Heritage Convention. In particular, guidelines establish criteria for judging outstanding universal value and provide advice on the submission of WHS nominations (ICOMOS 2004). While not all applications are successful, since the inception of WHS in 1972, 878 properties around the globe comprising of 679 cultural, 174 natural and 25 mixed properties in 138 States Parties have been successful in their applications (Lyon 2007).

World Heritage Sites are registered on the UNESCO listing and are judged by the World Heritage Committee. Gaining WHS status is a strenuous and lengthy process, with a number of organizations, such as ICOMOS, providing expert advice to the World Heritage Committee. Sites that are successful in their application have to progress through a number of stages before they are given WHS status. Sites are first placed on their own State Party's (i.e. country) Tentative List, then placed on the World Heritage Committee's tentative list, and finally granted World Heritage Listing. From a strategic marketing perspective, benefits associated with the listing include a prestigious title, global attention, government interest (more funding opportunities might be tapped because of national interest), economic benefits if leakages are minimized and local people benefit (Timothy and Boyd 2006). Issues include increased visitation. WHS often serves a sightseeing role and attracts visitor to its site and the surrounding areas. Moreover, heritage and tourism are strange bedfellows. Conflicts arise because the approach of heritage organizations is to protect and preserve, while the overriding aim of tourism is often to be profitable.

Interpretation

Interpretation can be defined as a process that explains to visitors the significance of the place visited (Moscardo and Woods, 1998). Tilden (1977) refers to interpretation as an educational activity that communicates meanings and relationships through hands-on experience and instructional media. Some heritage institutions assume that visitors know everything and do not require any comprehensions. However, this assumption is flawed (Timothy and Boyd 2003). Visitors require appropriate information and their behavior needs to be managed to minimize misuse and disrespect of heritage resources. Literature has extensively referred to Tilden's guiding principles of interpretation to achieve effective interpretation. As Box 3.3 illustrates, these suggest inclusion of personality and life experiences of the visitors, inspiring qualities, need to be provocative, holistic, and follow a fundamentally different approach when addressing different groups.

Box 3.3 Tilden's Guiding Principles

1. Any interpretation that ranges from no relation with what is being displayed or described to something related to the personality or experience of the visitor.
2. Information, as such, is not interpretation. Interpretation is revelation based upon information. However, all interpretation includes information.
3. Interpretation is an art, which unites many arts, whether the materials presented are scientific, historical, or architectural. And art, to some degree, is teachable.
4. The primary aim of interpretation is provocation not instruction.
5. Interpretation should strive to present a whole rather than a part.
6. Interpretation addressed to children (say up to the age of 12) should not be a dilution of the presentation to adults, but should follow a fundamentally different approach. To be at its best, a separate program for kids needs to be designed.

Source: Tilden (1977)

Good interpretation should also take special needs into consideration such as bilingual and multilingual (Light 1992), cultural difference (Upitis 1989), and disability (Harrison 1994). Four categories of people with special needs were suggested by Harrison (1994): 1) those who are wheelchair borne; 2) the blind and partially sighted; 3) people with hearing problems, and the elderly; and 4) those who have mobility issues. Next, success of interpretation rests on the effectiveness of the media selected. Two major types of media have been identified by literature (Timothy and Boyd 2003):

1. Personal – this type of media includes guided tours, trail hikes, and train and stagecoach trips and information attendants offering living history and cultural demonstrations, role playing, and living history performances such as re-enactments.
2. Non-personal – this category includes written material (such as brochures, guidebooks, labels, and maps), self-guided tours, and signs. Self-guided tours serve as a useful non-visual medium while signs offer a visual medium. Most challenges to interpretation relate to interactivity and the diverse needs and interests and perceptions of the audience. Also, resource issues and interpreter issues (such as people-related skills and content knowledge, communication skills, friendly disposition, and dynamic personality) pose challenges.

For interpretation to be sustainable, it should not be driven by economic goals. Information should be neither over-simplified nor excessively interpreted (because it can ruin the spontaneous connection with the site) to cater to visitor needs. And it should not become a commodified show to the extent that the original message is compromised for entertainment and history is falsified (Bernard and Lane 1993; Urry 1990). The inherent objective of interpretation is to seek a compromise between education and entertainment and to instill respect for heritage and responsible behavior among the visitors (Knudson, Cable and Beck 1995).

While crafting interpretive material at the micro level, a clear overview of the local heritage story encompassing themes and topics is needed. It is likely that the visitors have already encountered some aspects of local heritage in the community; hence, a connection to the local environment can enhance visitor experience. This view is echoed by Cogswell, who explains that contents in "brochures, guides, and other interpretive materials should contain good general explanations balanced with concrete local references or illustrations. Exhaustive display of collections, uncaptioned photographs, and disorganized 'show-and-tell' strategies often detract from the key goal of interpretation" (1996: 9). Sustainable heritage devices can also include the following:

- Careful designing of walking and driving tours;
- Thoughtful planning of maps;
- Focus on vernacular life to help feel 'sense of place' such as cemetery practices;
- Sites where agricultural activity is taking place.

Additionally, inclusion of the local manpower needs to be promoted to help visitors understand and respect what they see and experience. Examples include local guides, people with local dialect, and tours hosted by local businesses (Cogswell 1996). Events such as staged shows and festivals can help visitors to witness local culture without being intrusive. Sustainable planning also requires inclusion of living bearers of local cultural traditions and their products (McKercher and du Cros 2002). These include folk music and dance actors, native craftsmen, and heritage goods such as clothing, decorations, etc. Folk people and cultural artisans need to be cultivated through long-term planning and investment in relationship building.

Previous studies point out conflicts between commercial representations and accurately showcasing the "local" way of life. In the case of festivals, Cogswell argues that fundraising should not be confused with interpretive programming (1996: 11). As explained by Caldwell (1996), careful and sensitive interpretation can facilitate visitors' interest in a region in a manner that they are thoughtful to the host community. Interpretation can thus play a crucial role in promoting conservation and sustainable development and can be used as an effective visitor management tool. Careful planning can stimulate economic and environmental benefits, facilitate community involvement, and enhance sustainable and harmonious attitudes and values among hosts, tourism professionals, and tourists.

This view is confirmed by Timothy and Boyd who point out that "from a conservation perspective, the underlying value of the educative and entertaining roles of interpretation is to enhance awareness, create a sense of ownership, and instill a desire to interact with relics of the past in a sustainable manner" (2003: 204).

Pearson and Sullivan (1995) also argue that quality interpretation raises the value and appreciation of heritage sites among both the hosts and guests. This enhances the need to protect the site. As mentioned earlier, the significance of host community involvement should not be underestimated. By allowing local residents to promote and support selected elements of their heritage, greater potential for sustainability success can be triggered. For interpretation to reinforce sustainable behavior in visitors, care has to be taken to create strategies that facilitate visitor mindfulness. The next element of sustainable marketing focuses on this topic.

Creating Mindful Visitors

Literature extensively refers to the need of creating mindful visitors in heritage tourism and suggests multiple ways to accomplish this task. Reference to this topic is mostly found within the realm of visitor management. The 'mindful' term was coined by Moscardo (2001). It is defined as a state of being receptive and a willingness to learn, see, appreciate and understand the past from various perspectives (McIntosh 1999; Chhabra 2009). The underlying premise, within the context of sustainability, is that mindful visitors are more sensitive and attentive to the environment around them. Langer (1989) posits that such attitude can lead to better decision making, enhanced health and self-esteem, self-actualization, attention restoration, and better quality of life. Moscardo (2001) crafted a list of features, conditions, and outcomes for heritage managers to understand how mindfulness can be effectively instilled. According to Moscardo (2001), main features of visitor mindfulness include:

- Receptivity to learning;
- Awareness of the setting;
- Development of new routines;
- Conditions that support visitor mindfulness are new and different settings, control and choice, different and changing situations, and personal significance.

Outcomes of the aforesaid mindfulness attitude include feelings of control, achievement, fulfillment, ability to tackle problems, and ability to learn and recall (Langer 1989). It is basically a restoration of the mind. Additionally, for successful mindfulness, Moscardo (1999: 61–74) suggests the following communication methods:

> Inclusion of variety and innovation (such as appealing to different senses, providing different social experiences, using multiple physical settings and media), use of multisensory media, uniqueness/controversy/astonishment, use of questions and curiosity, visitor control and helping them find their way around (examples include simple paths, comprehensive orientation system using signs and maps), interactive exhibits, connecting with the visitors (engage them, allow them with some degree of control by offering choices,

encouraging participation), knowing the visitors (conduct research and understand their socio-demographic characteristics, perceptions, behavior, and motivations) and effective orientation at a physical level.

Moscardo (1999) argues that the aforementioned communication tools can help visitors understand the outcome of their action and enable them to behave in a manner that generates minimum negative impacts on the heritage site, the hosts, and the overall environment. In this way, conservation efforts can be promoted. Hence, an appropriate visitor management framework has to be in place to promote and generate effective visitor mindfulness so that sustainable goals of the attraction can be achieved.

By taking the aforesaid sustainable factors into consideration, heritage tourism can be strategically planned for the future and carefully processed through contemporary goals. Strategic planning in sustainable marketing requires a long-term vision and a harmonious blend of the multiple elements featured in the outer and inner layers of the Strategic Sustainable Heritage Tourism Marketing model. A balanced and carefully planned convergence of all sustainable marketing components is thus required. This cannot be accomplished without a strategic vision.

Strategic Planning

Strategic planning requires well-planned distribution strategies which can link heritage resources to selected group of consumers who are predisposed to genuine interest in the host community. Long-term planning can help develop a vision so that the health and viability of the heritage resource can be protected. This can be done through ongoing efforts to strengthen the overall heritage environment of host communities. As Cogswell warns, "short-sighted approaches to seizing cultural tourism opportunities may risk 'killing the goose that lays the golden egg'" (1996: 13). This also includes safeguarding the protection of cultural intangibles. Proactive planning is needed to ensure intergenerational equity of a heritage resource is maintained. Mere lip service and promises need to convert into actions. Overall, a holistic and well-rounded planning and development strategy can guide sustainable marketing efforts. Finances need to be distributed equally among promotional strategies and development of local cultural interpretation and programming. Earmarking some funds to sustain local heritage can go far in demonstrating the commitment of heritage tourism institutions to a long-lasting and genuine partnership with the host community.

The philosophy of social marketing or relationship marketing should consider the benefits to the host community in addition to focusing on the target markets. Also, thoughtful "targeting and prioritizing of tourism funds can ensure thematic distinctiveness and consistency in the heritage tourism product" (MacDonald 1992: 368). It is important to understand that "the meanings to be derived from any heritage attraction are neither static nor inherent but must always be arrived at" (Harvey 1996: 53). For instance, in the case of Northern Ireland with its disputed history and watchful present, and where public generally is so highly sensitized to any suggestion of misrepresentation, sectarian bias or hidden agendas that even a consensual level of neutrality is almost impossible to achieve. In this sensitive cultural and political context, heritage enterprises must proceed with a keen awareness of the possibilities for creating or reinforcing dissonant heritage. (Harvey 1996: 53)

Similar views are maintained by Urry (1990) who states that an endless struggle has emerged between viability of the market and authentic representations of local heritage. And this has resulted occasionally in a "commercial (and political) screening and packaging of reality. What tourists are guided through are often not profitable 'pseudo-events' reflective neither of past or present realities" (Urry 1990: 98).

Fundamental imbalances of power in the heritage tourism industry exist and heritage can be promoted in a sustainable manner only if issues of inclusion and empowerment are addressed. Heritage tourism should not become another extractive industry. Using South Africa as an example, Khan and Kilian raise a fundamental question: "how can tourism be promoted in order to promote a more integrated society and economy?" (1996: 78). South Africa has undergone a major transition to democracy, heralding a new era of potential peace and stability. Nevertheless, Khan and Kilian point out that "the country's past continues to limit its development potential today" (1996: 82). Selected non-black heritage is often presented to tourists. Another issue likely to be encountered in developing countries is the neo-colonialism issue. This problem can be tackled by actively involving host communities and diminishing the distance between the center and the periphery. As Petford tries to demonstrate in his study (of Wales, England), power "structures and relationships can, through internal neo-colonialism, allow the imposition of cultural and economic programs for tourism in peripheral areas which lack the political and economic power to control the development" (1996: 99). Petford further notes that this does not reflect the complete picture. He found that Wales "is slowly reclaiming its own heritage, and, on the margins of the tourist industry, is carving a new, less stereotypical, image for itself" (Petford 1996: 99).

Therefore multiple perspectives, elements, and frameworks have to be considered in strategic sustainable marketing of heritage tourism. Traces of this view exist in the principles set forth by the National Trust for Historic Preservation for sustainable development of heritage tourism (Caldwell 1996: 127):

1.   Focus on authenticity and quality.
2.   Preserve and protect resources.
3.   Make sites come alive.
4.   Find a fit between the community and tourism.
5.   Collaborate.

The Strategic Sustainable Heritage Tourism Marketing Model

Figure 3.1 presents a modified version of the sustainable marketing model proposed earlier by Chhabra (2009). As the figure illustrates, strategic planning of the integrated sustainable marketing heritage tourism paradigm is centered on a long-term, collaborative and multidisciplinary holistic approach. To conclude, the following elements are crucial for the successful sustainable marketing of heritage tourism:

- Local community involvement within the context of Arnstein's participation ladder;
- Collaboration between stakeholders in terms of marketing together or managing the tourism flow and impact and local community benefit to promote intra-generational equity;
- Preservation and conservation emphasis and promoting objective authenticity of tangible and intangible heritage;
- Strategic planning in marketing with a long-term focus – ongoing SWOT analysis of the macro and micro environments to promote intergenerational equity;
- Creating mindful visitors;
- Careful interpretation content and communication of other educational tools;
- Ongoing research on how best to sell a sustainable heritage product and promote responsible behavior;
- Economic viability.

Summary

The purpose of this chapter is threefold: first, to introduce marketing mix and its primary components within the context of heritage tourism; second, to offer an insight into other functions which play a crucial role in providing a broad and holistic approach to the marketing mix frequently planned by heritage institutions – these include service, market segmentation, research, environment analysis, consumer behavior, and organizational behavior; and, finally, to consider elements key to the sustainable marketing of heritage tourism such as local community involvement/benefits, partnership/collaboration, authenticity and conservation, and interpretation and visitor mindfulness. Thereafter the strategic sustainable heritage tourism marketing model (SSHTM) is proposed.

Central to the consideration of the SSHTM is the notion that strategic sustainable marketing does not simply happen. A well-rounded long-term schemata is required which employs a multidisciplinary perspective and a diverse group of stakeholders. Prior consideration is required of issues such as dissonance of heritage, marginal communities, overt commodification, glocalization, emerging markets, and adequate local host community involvement.

Questions

1. Describe the primary elements of the marketing mix as they apply to heritage tourism.
2. What are the crucial agents that exercise dominating influence on marketing mix strategies?
3. Describe Arnstein's and Tosun's community involvement paradigms.
4. Describe the SSHTM. What features in the model ensure sustainable considerations toward the heritage tourism marketing plan?

4   Museums

This chapter examines the marketing strategies pursued by selected museums across the globe using the proposed sustainability paradigm. First, an insight is offered into ongoing issue (repatriation) faced by museums across the globe. This is followed by a description of the contemporary museum culture, which is crucial to know so that marketing managers can be vigilant toward cultural sensitivities of native communities. The chapter later provides a universal insight into marketing strategies of museums by examining the marketing techniques of Heard Museum (United States), Gandhi Memorial Museum (India), Tibet House Museum (India), and the Freud Museum (UK).

A museum is a complex heritage phenomenon. Its function has expanded in recent years in response to the changing environments. McLean succinctly expresses the evolution of museum purpose:

> Whereas in 1904, museums were collections of objects which were arranged and displayed, now they also document and preserve. As scientific methods have improved, so equally have the methods of preservation and conservation. Whereas the objects were displayed 'in accordance with scientific method' now they are interpreted; and significantly, where museums were 'interesting to the scholar and the man of science,' now they operate 'for the public benefit.' (1997: 10)

A late twentieth-century definition by the UK Museums Association interprets a "museum as an institution which collects, documents, preserves and interprets material evidence and associated information for the public benefit" (Museums Association 1984). Museums of today function as complex institutional missionaries and serve varied audiences through their programs (Suarez and Tsutu 2004). The code of ethics for the American Association of Museums states that contemporary museums in the United States mirror the scope of human vision and its commitment to the public (AAM 2009). The core mission includes "collecting and preserving, as well as exhibiting and educating with materials not only owned but also borrowed and fabricated for these ends" (AAM 1996: paragraph 1). A yet broader vision, extending the scope and boundaries of museums, is presented by the international museum community. According to the International Council of Museums (ICOM):

a museum is a not-for-profit making, permanent institution in the service of the society and of its development, and open to the public, which acquires, conserves, researches, communicates, and exhibits, for the purposes of the study, education, and enjoyment, material evidence of man and his environment. (1987)

In sum, museums are heritage institutions that aim to educate the public, collect and conserve objects (AAM 2009; Alexander 1996; Chhabra 2008; McLean 1994), facilitate research, serve as cultural centers (AAM 2009), and provide entertainment (Burgers 1992; Chhabra 2009). From a European perspective, a museum, "as cabinet of curiosities is also the storeroom of a nation's treasures, providing a mirror in which are reflected the views and attitudes of dominant cultures, and the material evidence of the colonial achievements of the European cultures in which museums are rooted" (Simpson 1996: 1).

Several issues have adorned the museum performa and insight. Of paramount focus in the contemporary era is the past neglect of minority communities and its subsequent recognition leading to renowned efforts. For example, an insight into the history of African American Museums provides the progressive stance embraced by marginalized ethnic communities in the United States. The African American Museums were the result of the Civil Rights Movement, which served as a catalyst for new developments in the 1960s. As noted by Simpson (1996), the political fervor of the Civil Rights period motivated the African Americans to pull the reins of their lives together, dispel stereotype myths, and promote their culture and heritage. The desire to provide the Black community with "a powerful forum for self-expression, education and cultural control" motivated many African Americans to establish African American museums and cultural centers (Austin 1982). One of the best-known museums dedicated to the authentic interpretation of African American heritage and culture is Anacostia. It is operated by the Smithsonian Institution and is the first African American museum to receive federal funding.

Parallel to the African-American developments, Native Americans in the United States also began searching civil rights and greater self-determination. An examination of Native American history reveals that during the colonization era of the Americas, the native population was mistreated and subjected to biased policies with an attempt to delete their cultural practices. However, as Simpson noted, simultaneous with the discriminatory treatment, the material culture of the Native American was "studied, admired, and collected" (Simpson 1996: 135). A special advisory body, the North American Indian Museums Association (NAIMA) was established in 1978 to support the work of Indian museums throughout North America and to assist in their further development, including resources, collections, marketing, research, and interpretive programs. According to Article III of NAIMA by-laws (NAIA 1980):

An Indian museum is defined as an established non-profit institution essentially educational or aesthetic in purpose, with professional staff, that provides exhibits, research, or programs in North American Indian subjects. In addition, the institution must meet the following requirements: 1) a majority of either, the Board of Directors or the staff members, must be North American Indian, Eskimos, Aleuts, Inuit or Metis; 2) the institution must serve a local Indian population.

The Repatriation Issue

This discussion on museums will be incomplete without reference to the repatriation issue encountered by most of the Western museums across the globe. According to Simpson, repatriation is the "most difficult issue seeking resolution by museums in the post-colonial era. Emerging nations and indigenous peoples in western nations are calling for their cultural treasures and the remains of their ancestors to be removed from display and many are demanding their return" (1996: 171).

Ghastly methods and fanatical collection techniques were used earlier by those who hunted bodies and skeletal remains for personal research or to sell to researchers (Hinsley 1982; Cole 1985). Collections of mementoes from human bodies made this act even more gruesome. Associated acts of display have received increasing criticism from indigenous communities across the world and legal actions have attempted to secure repatriation and reburial (Uberlaker and Grant 1989). According to Simpson:

> The practice of publicly displaying human remains demonstrates a total disregard for the rights and concerns of peoples of other cultures, particularly non-western and fourth world peoples; those who were subjected to the political control of European nations. Subjected to repression and cultural domination under colonial administration, their religious beliefs have been disregarded by researchers and collectors excavating burial sites in their search for human remains and cultural artifacts. (1996: 178)

In 1979, the Archaeological Resources Protection Act was passed in the United States which made the excavation, removal, and trafficking of artifacts from federally owned or administered land punishable by up to five years in prison and $250,000 in fines (Simpson 1996: 181). Opposition to museological practicism, which places Western values upon dissemination of knowledge and education before the beliefs and sensitivities of descendents or culturally affiliated groups, has led to the current controversy over the continued holding, research, and display of human remains. Criticism and debate about the continuing display and retention of human remains in museums has influenced museological practices: Australian museums no longer display Aboriginal remains and museums in New Zealand have removed the tattooed heads, or moka mokai, from display. In the United States, circumstances have undergone a dramatic change with the passage of the Native American Graves Protection and Repatriation Act (NAGPRA) in 1990. Under the NAGPRA, "ownership of Native American material is given in the first instance to lineal descendants; second, to the tribe upon whose land the objects or remains were discovered; third, the tribe with the closest cultural affiliation. Excavation and study of such material can only be undertaken with a permit and with appropriate tribal consent" (Simpson 1996: 182).

Contemporary Museum Culture

It is thus crucial for the marketing managers of contemporary museums to be vigilant toward cultural sensitivities of native communities. As heritage tourism continues to grow, Henderson (2005) argues that contemporary museums have become a piece of the innovative and creative industries that regard culture and heritage as important forms of popular entertainment. However, Chhabra (2008) claims that there has been a recent function shift from connoisseurship to emphasis on social inclusion. In fact, today's museums perform a tripartite role:

- As agents of social change;
- As focal points of cultural activity;
- As repositories of heritage and knowledge.

It is known that the museums are an important part of the heritage tourism industry. This can be largely attributed to their ongoing financial situation. According to Tobelem:

> the weight of ever greater financial constraints following a reduction in state funding and/or need to find new financial resources in order to allow for museums to expand, forces museums to find ways to generate supplementary funds and to establish the means for better communications directed toward various target groups. (1998: 342)

Tobelem (1998) goes on to write that museums, in the company of the entire heritage sector, have become progressively engaged in business apprehensions such as concern about costs, financing, evaluation, growth, and profits. Marketing is a new term, added to their vocabulary. Kotler and Levy (1969a) present one of the first testimonials to the need for museum marketing. Regarding ongoing disinterest of a large section of population, the authors wonder if this lack of interest is due to inappropriate presentation of museum's offerings. They illustrate how the 'manner of presenting' doubt "led a new director of the Metropolitan Museum of Art (Met) to broaden the museum's appeal through sponsoring contemporary art shows and 'happenings' which led to sustained increases in the Met's attendance" (1969a: 11). The Met museum example thus set forth the need for museums to embrace marketing.

Today, regardless of the reason of emphases on the audience (such as public funding and accountability, need to produce revenue, compulsion to embrace marginal groups), museums are hunting for ways to access a broader public, build community relationships, and compete successfully with other suppliers of tourism, leisure, and educational activities. This invasive change has blurred the boundaries which had once alienated museums from other recreational and educational agencies. The contemporary modus operandi has asserted that significance of marketing be recognized within the museum realm.

Tobelem identifies four factors that have propelled the introduction of marketing into museums and their relative significance varies by country and nature of the organization:

- Phenomenal growth of museums over the past few decades;
- Fiscal constraints;
- Competitive environment;
- Need to fully understand the visitor needs.

The last factor seeks to gain an insight into the perceptions and preferences. Benefits of marketing, thus, are many, but it still remains a poorly understood term with the majority of the museums across the world. It is the task of contemporary researchers to dispel the negative myths associated with marketing.

To date, most of the marketing initiative has been driven by the need to increase or manage membership database (Wilson and Jones 1984), raise admissions (Lovelock and Weinberg 1989), fund raising in terms of donations (Ames 1988), and sell museums as a service product (McLean 1994). A more recent study by Chhabra (2009) examines the marketing plans of heritage museums in the United States to determine if sustainable promotion of the heritage product is pursued. The author reports only subtle traces of sustainability focus in the marketing strategies, as the main attention still remains focused on audience needs.

As described in the second chapter, marketing has evolved from being product-centered to consumer-centered. The contemporary marketing environment accords a high degree of importance to the individual consumer and focuses on relationship-building efforts. Transposing this schema to the museum world, one can note that the object-centered approach of museums parallels the product-centered philosophy as the museum focus was earlier on collections and the wishes of the public were ignored. Since then the museums priorities have also shifted along the spectrum to focus on the quality of visitor experience and augmented attendance. They now remain in a state of alert attendance to the visitor needs (Tobelem 1998).

Nevertheless, more recent studies indicate traces of shifting from the consumer end of the spectrum to a more controlled environment to achieve sustainable objectives. According to Tobelem and a recent study conducted by Chhabra (2009), "museums are not in a position to use marketing for what it is today: a tool for analysis and a means for action to achieve its objectives" (Tobelem 1998: 339). These unique heritage institutions have complex, and often conflicting functions to perform. The challenge lies in their tripartite purpose as custodians, providers of public service, and revenue seekers to meet economic exigencies. This conflict is succinctly reported by Chhabra (2008) when she found that the museum mission and curators' ideology were not analogous to each other.

The central question worrying museum directors is: would the emphasis on market-driven programs place at risk their professional standards, the integrity of the institution, and their core purpose of authenticity and conservation? Would it not, after all, by trying to attract the mass market and entertain the greatest number, diminish the core value of the institution (Tobelem 1998; Suarez and Tsutu 2004)? To this, the advocates of marketing respond that:

> marketing is not an end in itself; it can only be a means at the service of the organization, intended to allow it to attain its defined objectives efficiently. Marketing is then one branch of administration among others and it is the responsibility of the leaders of the institution to determine in which area or areas it is to be applied. (Kotler and Andreasen 1987, quoted in Tobelem 1998: 351)

A discussion of the marketing techniques employed by the Heard Museum (United States), Gandhi Memorial Museum (India), Tibet House Museum (India), and the Freud Museum (UK) provide a universal insight into the marketing management function employed in different countries and help gauge the extent to which sustainability remains the focus of attention. The four selected museums are both similar and dissimilar to each other. For instance, the Gandhi Museum is focused on a political icon 'Mahatma Gandhi' and the Freud Museum is centered on Sigmund Freud and his daughter. The other two museums, Tibet House Museum and the Heard Museum, focus on minority ethnic communities. The founder of the Tibet House Museum is His Holiness Dalai Lama, who is actively involved in museum management. In the case of the Heard Museum, Native Americans from different tribes in Arizona lend an ongoing active ear and voice to the content display and management. Whereas at the Freud Museum, Freud's belongings are displayed in an old house. While the Tibet House Museum and the Heard Museum draw essence and interest on the basis of their association with living cultures, the Freud Museum and the Gandhi Museum act as repositories of what is a large part of historical past today.

Heard Museum, Arizona, United States

The Heard Museum was founded in 1929 and is located in downtown Phoenix in the State of Arizona (United States of America). It displays Native American culture and art. It has grown considerably since 1929. Today, it houses over 25,000 works of art in its permanent collections which are displayed in five galleries. The museum has five more galleries called the 'changing galleries.'

The museum is owned by a private non-profit group and managed by a board of directors. It provides a wide variety of facilities and services. It offers numerous exhibitions (at one point of time), an art gallery, museum shop, café, artist studio, library, archives, administrative space, a theater, amphitheater, auditorium, education center, and multiple courtyards. Adjacent to the museum shop is the Berlin Gallery, which features Native American art that is for sale. A variety of activities are available in each gallery for visitors. These include art projects, matching games, movies, and sound bytes. Several restrictions are imposed on visitors to these galleries. For instance, flash photography is prohibited.

Plate 4.1 The Heard Museum

As education is the core purpose of the museum, several educational tours are offered, including tours for schools. The Museum also offers guided tours, hands-on activities, and a Bonus Tour guided by an American Indian instructor. In addition, the Museum provides group tours that are tailor made to match audience needs and preferences.

The Billie Jane Baguley Library and Archives is a research facility housed on the museum premises which presents a range of information on indigenous art and cultures from around the world. The library also houses a great collection of resource items on more than 23,000 American Indian artists. These collections include American Indian art and culture of the Southwest, American Indian fine arts, and general anthropology and art history. This library is a donation and is overseen by volunteers. Library tours are also offered.

The Heard Museum hosts a variety of events and festivals throughout the year. These include the Heard Museum Spanish Market, which is a marketplace built in the central courtyard of the museum offering visitors a chance to view and purchase works of art from more than seventy-five Native American artists from Arizona and New Mexico. Membership incentives include visitor benefits, such as free admission for two adults, and 10 percent discount in the gift shop and bookstore for all Heard Museums. Levels of memberships are based on visitor donations. For instance, $60 is a 'Friend' all the way to $10,000 to receive a 'Gold Circle' membership which offers great benefits. Volunteers are both young professionals and retirees. They are trained to maintain the museum's commitment to excellence, leadership, and the core purpose of the museum mission. Entrance fees are charged with the sole purpose to pay for the museum maintenance and not to earn profits.

The mission of the Heard Museum is to provide education about the heritage, living cultures, and arts of native peoples, with an emphasis on the Southwest community. The mission statement states that the museum is "meant to be a place of learning, discovery, and an opportunity to share native traditions that will touch your heart" (Heard Museum 2009).

The Heard Museum follows a tripartite philosophy with regard to marketing: marketing, relationship, and social. According to the staff, the needs and satisfaction of their target markets is their top priority and interpretive techniques and exhibit text are sometimes modified to suit the audience. Mutually satisfying long-term relationship is another important objective of the museum. Both these focuses are guided by the purpose to safeguard the interests and wellbeing of the Native American Society.

The majority of the visitors are from within the state, such as the local people, families with children, American Indian art collectors, and event goers. Additionally, visitors from adjoining states such as Utah, New Mexico, Nevada, and California remain a target market. The museum hosts many bus tours and these comprise mainly of international visitors who include museum visits in their itinerary as a part of the regional tour package. More specific statistical records on the museum visitors show that gate visitors are 88 percent Caucasians. Also, 92 percent have earned some college education, with 68 percent having college degrees, and 72 percent are non-locals.

Environment Analysis and Research

The strategic marketing plan is based on the examination of both micro and macro environment factors. The economic and political are considered important while designing marketing strategies. According to the marketing director, economic factors affect tourists' travel and spending behavior at the museum's gift shop. Monitoring of social and cultural changes is important as they influence visitor views of Native Indians, which in turn can affect their interest in the museum.

Significance of demographic factors lies in the fact that education level guides some of the marketing strategies. Other factors include geographic locale, age, and family make-up, depending on the program or activity being marketed. Technology, on the other hand, poses both opportunities and threats. As more people are able to access information via the Internet, they have the opportunity to find information on matters that previously could only be learned through onsite visits. On a positive note, various technological innovations are used now to offer virtual tours and electronic information on exhibits and programs. This serves as an effective educational tool, thereby facilitating knowledge and understanding before the actual visit.

Both primary and secondary research is used to enhance marketing strategies, such as surveys, observations, and visuals. Research agenda includes focus on understanding visitor behavior and preferences. Surveys are also given to onsite visitors to understand their demographics, reasons for visiting, and satisfaction.

Distribution and Promotion Strategies

Main distributional strategies are the museum website, e-commerce, presence of Pueblo Spirit (gift, novelty, and souvenir shop focusing on Native American products) at the Sky Harbor Airport, and other Heard Museum locations in Arizona. With regard to promotional tools, the museum employs all four promotional mix elements (advertising, sales promotion, personal selling, and public relations and publicity). Promotional collateral includes e-communiqués, member newsletters, postcards, brochures, and flyers. The brochure is in fact the most popular form of promotional collateral used by the museum to inform the audience about the current programs. Other promotional techniques consist of various advertising tools such as television commercials, tourism campaign print-outs, radio, and occasional ads in various magazines and newspapers.

Care is taken to align promotional messages and themes with the overall purpose of the museum. According to the museum staff, message themes focusing on testimonials, word play, trick photography, or slice-of-life promotional formats are not used because of authenticity constraints. Examples of public relations activities include establishing strong associations with the local convention and visitor bureaus (Scottsdale and Phoenix) and the local media professionals. The public relations team is also responsible for ongoing environment analysis and setting priority events aligned with what is happening in the community. Sales promotion techniques are also used, including 'sizzling summer' Saturdays and ticket premiums and vouchers. Merchandising consists of onsite sales through the gift shop.

Local Community Involvement and Partnerships

The Heard Museum Board consists of entrepreneurs and representatives from the Native American Community. From the local community interactions, focus is on selected geographic regions where population meets the museum's demographic criteria of interest. Of special interest is what these people read and where they get their news from. Interactions within the local community are mainly centered on travel industry, community leaders, art marketers, and the media. From a marketing standpoint, tokenism perspective is used as the museum is interested in working with others in the community to create mutually beneficial programs.

Additionally, a participation approach is used when educational programs are planned. According to the Director of Education, participation from the local Native Americans is critical for the museum to enable creation of authentic and appropriate exhibits and programs. Participation at the regional level is considered equally important. Training and education programs are provided to the local community. For instance, the museum frequently plans programs that teach teachers to effectively relate to American Indian topics. School-based activities and weekend and scouting programs are also designed to educate the local community.

Important marketing partners from the private sector are corporate sponsors, including APS (Arizona's leading producer of electric power), Salt River Project, JP Morgan Chase (Bank), and Target Stores. Among the public sector, partners of interest from a marketing perspective include the City of Phoenix, Phoenix Convention and Visitors Bureau, Scottsdale Convention and Visitors Bureau, Arizona Office of Tourism, Phoenix Office of Arts and Culture, Maricopa Partnership for Arts and Culture (MPAC), and libraries. The core purpose of partnering is to seek financial support. Other aims include efforts to build overall visitor attendance to Phoenix, promotion, provide diversity of programs, and extend audience reach. Future partners of interest are corporations and funders and Arizona State University. According to the Director of Marketing, this interest is being driven by the objective to reach a broad spectrum of visitors and to enhance financial support. A variety of incentives are offered to partners such as event tickets, recognition through advertising and other promotional programs, and discounts on private use of the museum. Benefits are determined by the level of support provided to the museum.

Authenticity and Conservation

According to the Director of Collections, Education and Interpretation, the object version of authenticity is crucial. Most important is to represent the past, have real objects not manufactured, represent the local community, and have materials verified by historians. The next level of importance is given to market demand, documented history, true versions of the original object, and from the actual period. Modifications to reflect global culture were considered neutral.

The ability to provide a place of learning, interest and enjoyment, self-enrichment, social interactions, and opportunities for contemplation are considered among the most important roles. The next level of importance is given to conservation, a place to find out about the past, interpretation of the past, and education. The most important conservation approach for the long-term heritage health of the Heard Museum is renovation. Items posing crucial challenges to the general conservation process are modernization versus maintaining the traditional forms, balancing the needs of tourists with those of the local community, and maintaining high-quality environments as museums get crowded. Other points of concern include the museum being viewed in isolation from the city in the city planning and development process, and tourism left out or ignored in urban planning strategies.

Interpretation and Creating Mindful Visitors

The purpose of interpretation at the museum is to value add and better position the museum product, attract markets that provide the maximum revenue, and reflect personal and organizational ethics. Popular forms of interpretation include organized talks and discussions, guided tours and walks. Interpretive materials include exhibit labels, docents, and demonstrators. Special needs are accommodated by providing wheelchair-accessible electric door openers, elevators and lifts, ramps, and captioned video. Interpreters are all locals.

Once inside the museum, adequate signs are available to guide the visitors from one exhibit to another. The best resource of the interpretive media is the personal guided tour. Other forms of interpretation include brochures, story telling, labels, maps, signs, visual media, and audio. Voice variations are used whenever necessary. Care is taken to offer authentic interpretation through the appropriated training and education of the tour guides.

Based on Tilden's guiding principles of interpretation, a review of interpretation techniques at the museum shows that museum uses carefully designed strategies and relates to the personal experience of the visitor. Inspiring techniques used by the museum offer to stimulate visitors' interest and provide an overall positive view of the exhibits. The good communication skills of tour guides enhance the overall experience and learning. Additionally, it is also noted that the interpretive contents take into consideration the characteristics of the visiting audience. For instance, bigger font texts are used for elderly people. Additionally, the museum includes at least one member from the Native American community to ensure authentic information and ambience is provided.

By offering relevant and authentic artifacts that demonstrate Native American lifestyles, Heard Museum creates mindful visitors. Additionally, trained and educated tour guides capture audience attention by offering different interpretation perspectives. The first-person voice of American Indians is used to narrate the past. Receptivity to learning is encouraged by providing multiple ways to learn and read, listen to guides and ask questions, hands-on demonstrations, video, interactive computer, etc. While presenting the heritage of native peoples, considerable focus is also given to contemporary living American Indian cultures.

Several students from a Southwestern university in the United States visited the museum to examine its effectiveness in creating mindful visitors. Their comments have been supportive of the museum's efforts. It is noted that most visitors are interested in learning about the site's historical background and the Native American culture. The term 'shared heritage' is recurrently used by interpreters; it helps to connect the audience with the community and local environment, and offers a sense of nationalism as a whole. Also, hands-on participatory activities such as making paper flowers and interactive puzzles appear to enhance visitor engagement. Somewhat similar but limited marketing efforts are noted in the Gandhi Memorial Museum.

Gandhi Memorial Museum, New Delhi, India

The Gandhi Memorial Museum is a history museum and focuses on a historical icon of India: Mahatma Gandhi. Its aims and objectives are presented in Box 4.1 and its history is articulated as follows:

The origin of this Museum goes back to the period soon after the assassination of Mahatma Gandhi on the fateful evening of January 30, 1948, when the slow process of scouting for, collecting and preserving the personal relics, manuscripts, books, journals and documents, photographic and audio-visual material, all that could go into a Museum on the life, philosophy and work of Gandhiji began in an unostentatious way in Mumbai. Later the work was shifted to Delhi and in early 1951 the nucleus of a Museum on Gandhiji was set up in the Government hutments adjoining Kota House. Later still, in mid-1957, it was shifted to the picturesque old mansion at Mansingh Road. It was finally brought to its present new and permanent home, most appropriately built opposite the samadhi of Mahatma Gandhi, India's most revered place of pilgrimage site at Rajghat, New Delhi, in 1959. The imposing two storey Museum was formally inaugurated by Dr. Rajendra Prasad, the President of India, in January 1961. (Gandhi Memorial Museum 2009)

The museum today contains a rich collection of memorabilia closely connected with Mahatma Gandhi. These include relics, books, journals and documents, photographs, audio-visual materials, exhibitions, and art pieces. It has become a popular site sought by scholars for Gandhian and allied literature. The museum consists of the galleries and other displays for visitors, library and publications section, photo section, audio-visual section, Gandhi Literature Center, and special exhibitions.

It is managed by a registered society (a non-government organization). From 1971 to 1996, the main financial support was being provided by Gandhi Smarak Nidhi (a non-government organization) in the form of a corpus fund of rupees 3.13 million, the interest on which the day-to-day operation depended. However, with time, the financial position of the museum has deteriorated due to inflation and other economic downturns. It was in 1996 that the Government of India decided to offer a corpus fund of rupees 50 million. Since that time, the main financial sources for the museum are: interest on Government of India's corpus fund and Gandhi Smarak Nidhi's reduced corpus fund of rupees. 2.08 million. In summary, the main funding source today is income from financial contributions and donations.

The aims and objectives offered in Box 4.1 form the core purpose (mission) of the museum. As Box 4.1 illustrates, preservation, education, and fund raising are

Plate 4.2 Mahatma Gandhi Memorial Museum

Box 4.1 Aims and Objects of the Gandhi Memorial Museum

(i) To collect, preserve and display Gandhiji's records consisting of his letters, correspondence, books, cine-films, manuscripts, photographs, voice records, personal effects and mementos etc.

(ii) To promote the study, diffusion and understanding of Gandhiji's life and message through the establishment of Sangrahalayas, Libraries, Auditoriums, Study Centres, Archives, Gandhi Bhavans in Universities, Gandhi Galleries, Gandhi Shelves etc. in places of public interest and through other media of communication.

(iii) To take proper and necessary steps to preserve and protect various places associated with Gandhiji's life and work.

(iv) To acquire by private negotiations or through the machinery of the Land Acquisition Act immovable properties wherever situated connected with Gandhiji's life for carrying out the objects mentioned above.

(v) To undertake and execute schemes of memorials at the places associated with significant memories of Gandhiji with Columns and Tablets.

(vi) To publish literature, periodicals, books, brochures, booklets to propagate ideals, thoughts and teachings of Gandhiji or in the aid of the memorials and to arrange film-show etc. in furtherance of the objects.

(vii) To prepare and distribute audio-visual material or replicas thereof as a means of propagating teachings of Gandhiji's life.

(viii) To undertake, organize and facilitate Study Courses, Conferences, Lectures, Seminars and the like to promote the aforesaid objects.

(ix) To train men and women for carrying out any of the aforesaid activities.

(x) To do all such things as are conducive or incidental to the attainment of the above objects, inter-alia: (a) To invest and deal with funds and moneys of the Samiti; (b) To issue appeals and applications for moneys and funds in the furtherance of the said objects and to raise funds or collect funds by gifts, donations, subscriptions or otherwise, of cash and securities, and of any property either movable or immovable and to grant such rights and privileges to the donors, subscribers and other benefactors, as the Samiti shall consider proper; (c) To acquire purchase or otherwise own or take or lease or hire in the Union Territory of Delhi or elsewhere, temporarily or permanently, any movable or immovable property necessary or convenient for the furtherance of the objects of the Samiti and other benefactors, as the Samiti shall consider proper. (d) To draw, make, accept, endorse, discount, execute, sign, issue and otherwise deal with cheques, hundies, drafts, certificates, receipts, Government Securities, promissory notes, bills of exchange or other instruments, and securities whether negotiable or transferable or not.

(xi) To undertake and accept the management of any endowment or trust fund or donation to further the objects of the Samiti, etc.

Source: Gandhi Memorial Museum (2009)

the main points of focus. The next few paragraphs provide information elicited from the museum staff.

Environment Analysis and Research

Approximately 75 percent of the visitors are Indian and the rest are foreigners. Indian visitations include organized school trips. The museum does not conduct environment analysis to guide its marketing strategies. In fact, environment analysis is not considered a priority for the museum management. Research emphasis is to publish and design literature to "propagate ideals, thoughts, and teachings of Gandhiji" (Box 4.1). Research to understand the visiting audience, its motivations, and preferences is non-existent.

Distribution and Promotion Strategies

The key distribution sources comprise of books, a website, and the audio-visual material available on the website. The book counter in the library sells books and encourages visitors to take the museum tour. With regard to promotion mix, it appears that personal selling is used at the bookstore to entice visitors to take a tour of the museum. Advertising and sales promotion techniques are seldom used. The museum is often mentioned by public media (in newspapers), and hence gets publicity to some extent from external sources.

Community Involvement and Partnerships

Community engagement in the decision-making process is non-existent, although the staff are all local. No special training and education programs are designed for the local community. Also, the museum does not have partnerships, either with the local community or with other tourism stakeholders in the region such as lodging and restaurants, etc.

Authenticity and Conservation

With regard to authenticity criteria, the museum considers the following elements crucial: represent the past, documented history, and from the actual period. Additionally, the museum places emphasis on the history version of the donors. Utmost importance is given to the following items associated with the museum role: conservation, education, interpreter of the past, place of learning, self-enrichment, and social interactions. The museum also aims to enhance the self-esteem of visitors and to help provide conceptual grounds to discover oneself. The long-term heritage health of the museum is based on effective preservation, restoration, and renovation.

Interpretation and Visitor Mindfulness

Interpretation forms include organized talks and discussions, guided tours, and walks. The multicultural needs of the audience are met by using two languages:

Plate 4.3 Mahatma Gandhi Memorial Museum (exhibits)

Hindi and English. All interpreters are local. Mindful visitors are created through interactions and film shows. The major challenge encountered in the mindfulness process is lack of awareness among the audience of Mahatma Gandhi's contribution to India. The museum is trying to engage the visitors by connecting and providing information on the historical significance of Mahatma Gandhi.

Tibet House Museum, New Delhi, India

His Holiness the Dalai Lama founded the Tibet House Museum in 1965 to preserve and propagate the cultural heritage of Tibet and to bestow a center for Tibetan and Buddhist studies. Since 1959, Tibetan refugees fleeing from the political turmoil in their native soil have traveled across the Himalayas to India. Many brought with them treasured objects and books of religious and cultural importance and these laid the foundations of the museum and the library.

The museum is located in New Delhi (India) and is housed in a five-storey building. The facility includes valuable Tibetan art and artifacts, a library (which contains nearly 5,000 volumes of manuscripts and books), a resource center, a conference hall, a gallery and a bookshop. The Tibet House provides incentives and resources for research and translation projects and publishes important texts and research results. It also serves as a host for lectures, and organizes conferences, exhibitions, film shows, and events. The main theme is Indian and Tibetan Buddhist history, religion, philosophy, art, literature, and culture. It stands to bear witness to the crucial and growing heritage of the Tibetan people.

The Tibet House has curated several major exhibitions centered on Tibetan art. These have mainly focused on Thangkas, statues, and handicrafts:

> Thangkas are scrolls with paintings of Buddhas, of deities or teachers and mandalas. They are used as objects of veneration and meditation often seen in temples, monasteries and private homes. The art of Thangka painting is a unique Tibetan contribution to the history of art. Exhibitions provide an opportunity to display some of the holdings of the Museum to a wider audience in India and abroad. (Tibet House 2006)

The museum has housed some historical exhibitions which have strengthened the historical links between India and Tibet. For instance, an exhibition of Tibetan art and handicrafts was held at Rabindra Bhavan in New Delhi to commemorate the Gandhi Centenary in 1969. The exhibition themes were embedded in the Thangkas which depicted the key events of Lord Buddha's life. His former lives as narrated in the Jataka Tales, were also put on view. Tibetan refugee craftspersons made the exhibit handicrafts.

Other programs include Dharma Discourse. On the advice of His Holiness the Dalai Lama and to satisfy the growing interest in Tibetan Buddhism, the Tibet House has organized formal religious discourses by prominent Tibetan masters of the four traditions of Tibetan Buddhism. Seminars are also provided which are a kind of monastic dialogue. Additionally, other programs are associated with music and dance, conferences and workshops centered on Buddhism and history of Tibet, art, language, heritage, environment issues, and peace education.

The museum mission is not only to preserve the past but also to explore opportunities in which Buddhism can promote peace and harmony and help alleviate global suffering. His Holiness the Dalai Lama stresses universal interdependence and advocates a sense of harmony and compassion as the cure to suffering. His vision guides the activities of Tibet House and also guides its dual purpose of promoting universal harmony: encouragement of cross-cultural and inter-religious dialogues and exploration of the relationship between science and religion; and ecological responsibility for the fragile from a Buddhist perspective. The information on marketing was obtained through a visit to the museum and preliminary interviews with museum staff. The museum later did not extend their formal response to the marketing-related queries with an answer that it does not pursue marketing. This is akin to the conventional notion that marketing is all about promotion. However, adherence to several components of the sustainable marketing model was observed and the museum is to be commended for that. For this reason, the author decided to include a description of this unique museum.

Environment Analysis and Research

The key markets are tourists, scholars, and local residents. Several environment factors are taken into consideration on an ongoing basis. For instance, a Buddhist literature-friendly software has been designed enabling reprints. Political environments stay in focus and associated discourses are reflected in the exhibition and conference themes. Research has not been the focus so far in the marketing strategies, although visitor characteristics are documented based on the observation of the museum staff.

Distribution and Promotion Strategies

The museums operates on a small budget and uses mostly personal selling and publicity and public relations techniques to promote programs and awareness. Its main promotional collaterals are its monthly newsletter and brochures. Because of its association with the Dalai Lama, it enjoys the prestige of a celebrity endorsement and is given free publicity by the mass media such as the newspapers, television, and radio.

Local Community Involvement and Partnerships

It has members from the local community. With regard to partnerships with the locals, a tokenism approach is used. It offers educational programs to the local community in Delhi such as a special course on Buddhism. For example, an introductory course on Buddhism was offered in 2004. The course was planned in congruence with the needs of educated people who sought to obtain a general understanding of Buddhist history, art, culture, philosophy, and practice. A range of dialogue was offered on different aspects of Buddhism, such as the figure of the historical Buddha, early Buddhism and the transition to Mahayana, Buddhist art and culture in India and other parts of Asia. The program also included some meditation sessions to enable the audience to experience first hand the techniques needed to seek harmony within oneself. As the website and interview with Tibet House personnel indicates, partnerships exist on a limited basis with the local community and other non-profit organizations such as the India International Center.

Interpretation and Creating Mindful Visitors

Creating mindful visitors is brought about by involving them in activities such as active discussions and meditation sessions. Meditation also helps create a mindful state of mind. Additionally, signs of silence are posted all over the museum. Educational talks and interpretation are conducted by experts. For instance, Mr. Gene Smith gave a talk on "Tibet House and its role in Tibetan Literary and Cultural Preservation since 1959 to the Present" at the Tibet House Conference Hall and released a book titled *Gyal-bai Chos-tshul*, which is a collection of writings in Tibetan language by Lama (monk) Doboom Tulku. The credentials of Mr. Smith are:

> In 1965 he came to India under a Foreign Area Fellowship Program (Ford Foundation) grant to study with living exponents of all of the Tibetan Buddhist

and Bonpo traditions. He began his studies with Geshe Lobsang Lungtok (Ganden Changtse of Tibet House), Drukpa Thoosay Rinpoche and Khenpo Noryang, and H.H. Dilgo Khyentse Rinpoche. He decided to remain in India to continue serious studies of Tibetan Buddhism and culture. He travelled extensively in the borderlands of India and Nepal. In 1968 he joined the Library of Congress New Delhi Field Office. He then began a project which was to last over the next two and a half decades, the reprinting of the Tibetan books which had been brought by the exile community or were with members of the Tibetan-speaking communities in Sikkim, Bhutan, India, and Nepal. (Tibet House 2006)

Authenticity and Conservation

Tibet House has played a vital role in spearheading Tibetan cultural preservation and advocating the unique role of Tibetan culture for the world. Tibet House's early activity in publishing encouraged many other publishers. This has resulted in over 8,000 volumes of publications and has spearheaded an initiative by state publishers in the People's Republic of China.

In addition, international festivals organized by the museum provide a platform to display the authentic art accomplishments from the Buddhist cultures of Sri Lanka, Japan, Korea, Thailand, Nepal, Mongolia, Vietnam, and Tibet. Another example of preservation and authentic interpretation efforts is offered in Box 4.2.

Box 4.2 Preservation and Interpretation Efforts of Tibet House Museum

Once upon a time, in Tibet, the capital city of Lhasa used to come to life twice a year to celebrate two major Buddhist festivals: the Monlam Chenmo or great prayer festival and the Tshokcho with Sedreng (Golden Procession). Pilgrims would come from all over the nation to attend the festivals which combined religious practice with entertainment; these are the two aspects of Tibetan culture that have not failed to arouse interest regardless of where they have been recreated in the world.

Tibet House, in its mission to introduce Indian audiences to authentic Tibetan culture and traditions, had a mini Monlam Chenmo festival in 1999. Customary prayers were conducted at Buddha Jayanti Park and a traditional invocation to H.H. the Dalai Lama was performed by the Chant Master of Drepung Monastery who walked at slow pace on a ramp while intoning the invocation in a traditional deep undertone style. It was a grand event, and was patronized not only by H.H. the 14th Dalai Lama but also by the former President of India, Shri R. Venkataraman.

Source: Tibet House (2006)

Tibet House honored the 250th anniversary of Buddha's Mahaparinirvana in 2006 with a major cultural event, an International Festival of Buddhist Chanting and Ritual. This festival lasted for three days and saw the participation of groups from most Buddhist countries. The Festival was inaugurated on October 8, 2006 by HH the Dalai Lama at Buddha Jayanti Park (New Delhi) – also marked thriteen years of the installation of the Buddha Statue at the park. On this occasion, Tibet House recreated the atmosphere of the second great festival, the Tshokcho, by organizing a Golden Procession. As many as 108 monks and nuns belonging to the four major traditions of Tibetan Buddhism participated and paraded at the park in their ceremonial apparel, each carrying a different kind of offering. The Golden Procession confirms object authenticity as it consists of indigenous participants. For instance, monks are joined by eight nuns from the Shugsep nunnery, Dharamsala. Numerous monastics form the Golden Procession and, in addition, each monastery is represented by four monks who add to the ambience by chanting during the event. Each monk carries a banner, representing Buddhas and their respective wisdom qualities. However, there are concerns of the negative effects of staged authenticity on the Buddhist culture itself since everything is showcased and divorced from its original setting (the monasteries).

Freud Museum, London, United Kingdom

Freud was a refugee from the Nazi occupation. He left his home in Vienna in 1938 and took exile in England. He brought his belongings with him and these included antique collections, his library, furniture, and couch (which later became world famous) where he was born. This couch was used to treat his patients. His working environment was a reflection of a unique laboratory of his mind. He curated his own collections. The emigration of German and Austrian scientists and intellectuals in the 1930s left a permanent impression on Europe and America. Their influence on global culture has softened but several visible commemoratives of these vital changes have survived. The Freud Museum remains today not only as a memorial to one man's exodus but also to the facilitator of intellectual freedom.

> The Freud museum has recreated Freud's environment. The museum is also filled with memories of his daughter, Anna Freud, who lived forty-four years of her life in the house. The museum is now being developed into a cultural and research center to provide exemplary value to local community and academicians. It also provides educational programs in the forms of seminars and conferences. It offers its property for meetings, buffets, and formal dinners and filming. Over the last 10 years the Public Program of the Freud Museum has organized a number of innovative public conferences. It offers several exhibitions at any one point of time. One famous exhibition is titled "Interpretation of Dreams" [see illustration in Box 4.3]. (Freud Museum 2009b)

Box 4.3 Exhibit – The Interpretation of Dreams

Daughter in a box

"A woman patient dreamt that she saw her only fifteen year old daughter lying dead 'in a case'. In the course of the analysis she recalled that at a party the evening before there had been some talk about the English word 'box' and the various ways in which it could be translated into German. ... She had guessed that the English 'box' was related to the German 'Büchse' and had then been plagued by a recollection that 'Buchse' [receptacle] is used as a vulgar term for the female genitals ...

It might be presumed, therefore, that the child lying in the case meant an embryo in the womb. After being enlightened up to this point, she no longer denied that the dream-picture corresponded to a wish of hers. Like so many young married women, she had been far from pleased when she became pregnant; and more than once had allowed herself to wish that the child in her womb might die. Indeed, in a fit of rage after a violent scene with her husband, she had beaten with her fists on her body so as to hit the child inside it. Thus the dead child was in fact the fulfillment of a wish, but of a wish that had been put aside fifteen years earlier."

One exhibition theme is centered on 'Freud's Wanderlust'. This new exhibition presents Freud as a traveler and the travel accounts are based on information derived from multiple sources (such as archive, maps, prints, photographs, letters, postcards, books and objects assembled by Freud during his travels). Another exhibition is titled 'Promised Lands: Freud's Exiles':

This exhibition, first shown in 1996, has been brought back as a counterpoint to *Freud's Wanderlust*. The two exhibitions face each other in the same exhibition space, as two contrasting aspects of travel. *Wanderlust* shows Freud as a passionate traveller: *Exiles* shows him as a refugee and sketches the cultural background and historical forces that determined his fate and that of his family. It covers their history beginning with their economic emigration from Freiberg to Vienna in 1859 and ending with the flight from Nazism to England in 1938. (Freud Museum 2009a)

The museum's mission statement focuses on efforts to celebrate the life and work of Sigmund Freud and Anna Freud. One of the far-reaching objectives of the Freud Museum is to heighten public awareness of the applications and ramifications of Sigmund Freud's work, and to do this in as imaginative a way as possible.

Environment Analysis and Research

Approximately 65 percent of the museum visitors are foreign tourists. Fifty percent of all visitors are students and 15 percent come in groups. The museum is striving to attract more British visitors. The museum actively involves the local community by offering volunteer placements to local schoolchildren and by working with a local community college on a project. To keep upbeat on exhibition themes, ongoing focus is placed on environment analysis especially associated with the technological, social, demographic, and economic trends.

Local Community Involvement and Partnerships

Not much information is provided on local community involvement. It appears that it is not of paramount significance in the marketing strategy. Partnerships, however, receive significant attention. Examples of stakeholder partnerships and collaborations include sharing exhibitions with a local gallery and a nearby library. According to the Director:

> We seek partnerships for our conferences and our exhibitions first to widen our range and audience, and second because we lack resources to manage them effectively totally independently. The partners are varied and include independent curators, art galleries, universities, art colleges, and professional associations.

Authenticity and Conservation

With regard to authenticity, the museum guarantees this by preserving Freud's study as it was in his day. Museum standard guidelines are used for the preservation of the collection and documents. As stated earlier, the Freud Museum houses the possessions that Sigmund and Anna Freud brought with them to London at their emigration in 1938. These include their personal papers and photograph albums.

The museum research center thus offers original documents and exhibits to researchers and scholars. The research library specializes in the history, theory, and culture of psychoanalysis. Its holdings include the working library bequeathed by Anna Freud and books left by Dorothy Burlingham. The letter and document archive consists primarily of copies: most original documents were transferred to Washington to form the Sigmund Freud Archives in the Library of Congress. At present, the archive catalogue lists around 6,000 letters to and from Freud, 1,500 others and over 1,000 miscellaneous documents. The Freud Museum archive continues to receive material from various sources and the catalogue will continue to be updated at intervals. Freud's set of monochrome photographic prints was probably collected around the turn of the nineteenth century. Most are reproductions of works of art but a significant minority consists of photographs of primarily Italian scenes. Probably these prints were souvenirs of Freud's travels. The conservation focus mostly rests on restoration. For interpretation of Freud's work and his house, the following sources are used: the guidebook, signage, and an audio guide.

Discussion

It appears that legacy is an important characteristic of the Tibet House, the Heard, and the Freud museums. The Tibet House Museum is unique because it represents legacy in progress since its founder, His Holiness the Dalai Lama is actively involved in shaping its core emphasis and imaging. The Freud Museum and the Heard Museum represent bygone legacies, although they differ in that the Freud is centered on a famous literary icon whereas the Heard's focus is on an ethnic community with marginalized heritage representation in the United States. Location, historic documentation, original artifacts, nature of the patrons, and endorsement by founders or owners of the artifacts bestow objective authenticity to each of the museums under study.

As stated earlier, a good interpreter needs to share or unveil different perspectives. For instance, for Native Americans, the arrival of Columbus in the Americans marked the beginning of five hundred years of cultural conquest and disenfranchisement (McMaster 1990). Whereas, for the mainstream population, his arrival on the American soil is commemorated by words such as 'discovery' and 'time for celebration.' Inviting criticism from the community whose culture is being represented is one step in this direction. For instance, the Heard Museum occasionally invites Native Americans as speakers and delegates and their group tour is performed by one of them. Authorship power has to be given. For instance, the Burke Museum in Seattle gives a great deal of authority to its Native American Advisory Committee. Also, as noted by Simpson, "an increasing number of indigenous curatorial staff in museums creates opportunities for the native perspective to be heard, not just in the exhibition planning process, but in management and policy making as well" (1996: 58). Community-based partnerships require funding support.

Partnership efforts associated with marketing in all museums represent the tokenism level. Research focus is more on current markets and the edutainment needs of visitors. Product-driven philosophy is only followed by the Indian museums (Gandhi Memorial Museum and the Tibet House Museum).

For decades, the policy in the United Kingdom and the United States of America had been to assimilate all ethnic groups into the mainstream Anglo-American or British culture, using the 'melting pot' concept. However, the American bicentennial in 1976 brought to attention the more recent years of American history within the context of immigration. Greater awareness of cultural diversity was thus fostered. Distinctive qualities of each culture needs to be preserved as they can enrich the shared culture. Ethnic museums have seen an unprecedented growth in Canada and North America. They serve a crucial purpose. For instance, formerly silent historical record of ethnic lives can be unveiled. The Museum of Chinese document Chinese American history in Manhattan and across America and help offset degrading stereotypes of Chinese Americans and of Chinatown and to give a sense of pride and reverence to the Chinese Community (Yu 1990: 4).

Democratization of museums began in the UK and the United States at about the same time. For instance, a museum in the City of New York introduced a series of community-based projects in 1971 so that the local population was adequately represented. The developments in the American museums spearheaded parallel community-oriented initiatives throughout the international museum community. For instance, in 1986, the British Museum in London (UK) played host to an international conference titled 'Making Exhibitions of Ourselves: The Limits of Objectivity in Representations of Other Cultures' (Simpson 1996). It is because of the growing awareness and the need to include the history and cultures of minority communities, several museums were established and considered eligible for federal funding. As noted by Simpson, "there has been a tremendous blossoming of cultural expression among the indigenous peoples and other ethnic minority groups, resulting from a growing awareness of the importance of cultural heritage and the desire for free expression and civil rights" (1996: 7). This trend is evident in the marketing strategies of the Heard Museum. However, the museums in India and the Freud Museum do not reflect this trend. Much needs to be accomplished in terms of interaction and partnerships with the local community.

European-style museums have served to establish and promote traditional cultures as they experience a process of cultural renaissance. That said, politics and ideologies in cultural representation remains a contemporary issue which is still being tackled by museum communities. As demonstrated by Truettner (1991), political and social needs often prejudice the manner in which the Native American population is treated and represented. Another prevailing controversy is about the museum failure to present minority cultures as living and dynamic (Simpson 1996). Instead, they are represented as unchanging, frozen, or still primitive based on the notions of many Europeans. When looking at the museum case studies, it appears that both the Heard and the Tibet House museums are particularly sensitive to the way the culture in focus is portrayed. This is not a complex task for the Tibet House, as the pioneer leader of the Buddhist culture is one of the governing bodies. The Heard Museum, however, is not run by Native Americans although their participation and views are actively sought.

Distribution and promotional strategies of each museum are dictated by limited budgetary allocations and the respective marketing philosophies. All select museums place emphasis on object authenticity connotations. Conservation emphasis is on preservation and restoration while traces are visible with regard to adaptations toward the reconstruction. Heard Museum leads other museums in terms of effective and sustainable interpretation and visitor mindfulness strategies. The Indian museums depict a somewhat relaxed stance with regard to these important functions.

Marketing Museums in the Future

Evidently, today, Western trends show that the non-profit organizations compete for consumers' discretionary time. Most museum studies point to market-driven ideologies being increasingly embraced by the contemporary museums. To this effect, several frameworks and paradigm dominate discussion on how to better serve museum audience, broaden their appeal, improve accessibility, and enhance their experience. For instance, Geissler (2006) proposes a service convenience model based on focus group interviews of customers attending an art museum. The key facets of the service convenience underscored by the author are decision, access, and transaction convenience. Geissler also lays stress on the need to develop museum brands. According to the author, "developing and maintaining a unique and appealing brand image seems just as important for art museums as for other types of organizations, both for profit and non profit" and key factors that influence branding are "permanent nature of the collection, changing exhibits, facilities, and perceptions of accessibility" (Geissler 2006: 83). The underlying rationale for this argument is that brand images influence perceptions and favorable, well-thought-out brand facilitates word-of-mouth promotions.

The audience characteristics have moved beyond socio-economic demographic models. It is the lifestyle information that is more relevant for museums today and is more likely to help determine what people prefer or want to do. Modern market segmentation techniques have to be identified not the conventional ones based on socio-demographic profiles. Importance of consumer surveys and mystery shoppers is being asserted today. It is hoped that these will aid in improving staff relations and customer care. Societies today are time poor, hence well-thought-out marketing strategies are needed. A recurring slogan across tourism institutions is "create high value visits and market well." A visitor or non-visitors to a museum today is least influenced by the free-admission tag. This calls for an organized research plan. Using a market-driven approach, delegates at a non-profit conference concluded that because "the choice of things to do in leisure time is growing. Delegates had to face the fact that museums and galleries will have to diversify, develop strong brands, and compete harder for a share of the market, while delivering the expected social agenda" (Geissler 2006: 31).

Although market and relationship-driven philosophies predominate, the emerging middle class in the West demands authenticity, education, and uniqueness. It is probable that museums will take note of such preferences and restore their emphasis on research, authenticity, and conservation. The Southeast part of the world, however, presents somewhat of a mixed picture. Although traditional product-based emphases is tantamount for stand-alone museums, other museums are adapting to changing environments. Consequently, the later ones are modifying some aspects of their offerings such as programs, events, etc. to suit audience needs. This part of the world is likely to shift its focus toward more consumer-friendly strategies. From this perspective, it is lagging behind the West, which now is in need of transforming its brand.

Summary

The aforementioned discussion should serve the purpose of stimulating further discourse on marketing and museum functions. By no means is this discursive presentation a conclusion. Ongoing monitoring is needed. Nevertheless, a lens is provided through which sustainable efforts can be gauged. The marketing measures should serve as barometers to detect shifts and future direction. All the case studies are unique and can serve as role models because of the successful extent to which they have sustained their traditional purpose. Yet, these studies also show a universal need for extensive local community involvement, revisit of the research focus, a broader spectrum of partnerships, and more emphasis on strategic planning instead of being carried over by short-term goals.

Contemporary museums have a duty to the society while having to meet commercial objectives and targets because of ongoing budget squeezes. Additionally, they have their own performance and revenue bottom lines to accomplish. Contemporary museums should pursue dichotomous objectives: modify and promote heritage to promote civic engagement and, at the same time, maintain the traditional purpose by promoting objective authenticity. In sum, something close to the new 'ecomuseum' paradigm needs to be the blueprint for the civic engagement portion of the museum function today.

Questions

1. Compare the purpose of different museums discussed in this chapter. Which one adheres the most to the sustainable model criteria?
2. Briefly explain the key issues pertaining to minority representations and repatriation. Have these been addressed by contemporary museums?
3. Did democratization of museums begin at the same time in the UK and the United States? Provide examples in support of your answer.
4. Why are museum brands suggested today?
5. What is an eco-museum? Provide at least two examples of eco-museums.

5 Historic House Museums

The focus of this chapter is on historic house museums. It begins first by reviewing the core purpose of various organizations across the world which are entrusted with the task of promoting the conservation and public use of historic houses. Next, numerous classifications of historic houses are presented. Specific challenges to the successful and sustainable use of historic museums are later discussed. An overview of current research focus is also informed. This is followed by an illustration of the marketing strategies employed by historic houses situated in four different countries: United States, United Kingdom, Switzerland, and India. The chapter concludes with a discursive summary using the SSHTM lens.

Historic house museums are known to focus on the maintenance, care, and interpretation of either a single, historic residential structure or a set of building structures allied with and including a single residence that functions as the main center. A historic house museum can be defined as an earlier residential building whose enormous significance as an artifact and as a setting has commanded its protection as an important resource for the benefit and enjoyment of society (Kanawati 2006). Such structures are endorsed by the National Register of Historic Places (USA) for the following reasons:

- They are associated with an important historical event;
- They have at some time housed a significant historic personality;
- They represent certain periods or styles of architecture;
- They provide a view of the past.

English Heritage (UK) and the Historic Houses Association (UK) also provide a somewhat similar emphasis (see Box 5.1). They support historic built environments with an aim to raise awareness of the unique characteristics of the historic structures and to influence decisions about the sustainable management of historic buildings and landscapes while at the same time indulging in promotional efforts to enhance enjoyment of the heritage. Looking beyond Europe, the National Trust of Australia performs parallel functions to protect and promote historic houses (see Box 5.2). As is evident from the descriptions in Boxes 5.1 and 5.2, the public sector interest in historic houses is stimulated by the economic potential and conservation needs of these unique structures.

Box 5.1   Primary Functions of English Heritage and the Historic Houses Association

English Heritage

English Heritage is the government's statutory adviser on the historic environment. Officially known as the Historic Buildings and Monuments Commission for England, English Heritage is an executive non-departmental public body sponsored by the Department for Culture, Media and Sport (DCMS). Its powers and responsibilities are set out in the National Heritage Act (1983) and today it reports to the parliament through the Secretary of State for Culture, Media and Sport.

English Heritage works in partnership with the central government departments, local authorities, voluntary bodies, and the private sector to:

- Conserve and enhance the historic environment;
- Broaden public access to the heritage;
- Enhance people's understanding of the past.

Its 'Heritage for All' theme states: English Heritage works to promote enjoyment of our shared heritage to the widest possible audience. The historic environment is a resource from which everyone can benefit and is a fundamental tool for regeneration, sustaining community pride, supporting small businesses, creating a sense of identity and belonging, and connecting with and educating the next generation. It works hard to ensure that everyone can access the built heritage in England, and gain something meaningful and inspirational from the interaction.

Historic Houses Association (HHA)

The HHA represents privately owned historic houses, castles, and gardens. These structures offer conference and accommodation facilities, unique venues for weddings, civil partnerships, dinners, and other special events. These houses are an integral part of the national life for the following reasons:

- They attract visitors from abroad and generate income for the local and extended community.
- Their new market, which comprises of 72 percent Russians, states that historic castles and houses are one of their key reasons for visiting Britain.
- They constitute a rich and unique cultural heritage, as Britain's historic houses still contain art and other treasures that have disappeared from their counterparts elsewhere in Europe – and most are still family homes.
- The places inspire learning outside the classroom.

Sources: English Heritage (2009) and
Historic Houses Association (2009)

Box 5.2 Primary Functions of the National Trust of Australia

The National Trust of Australia is a community-based, non-government organization, dedicated to promoting and conserving Australia's indigenous, natural and historic heritage through its advocacy and custodianship of heritage places and objects.

The Australian National Trust movement was set up in New South Wales in 1945 and other states in Australia quickly embraced it and established National Trust offices in the 1950s and 1960s. Each State and Territory National Trust is a completely autonomous entity and exercises its own right for managing its affairs.

The Australian Council of National Trusts (ACNT) was formed in 1965. It advocates the interests of the National Trust at the federal level, provides a forum for exchange of information and coordinates the work of its constituent bodies.

Source: National Trust of Australia (2009)

Boxes 5.3 and 5.4 trace the history of historic house museums in the United States in chronological order. Similar developments across the world have occurred which lay foundations for the support and popularity of these unique structures.

Box 5.3 History of Historic Residential Structures (Nineteenth Century)

1847   Residents of Deerfield, Massachusetts, attempted to save the Hoyt or 'Indian House' but their efforts were in vain. However, they preserved the door of the house and later they were able to reconstruct the entire structure. The event provided the much-needed impetus for preservation in Deerfield. This led to the creation of the Potcumtuck Valley Historical Association and the Historic Deerfield.

1850   Caldwell, one of the loan program commissioners, endeavored to save the Hasbrouck House in New York. While appealing to local residents, Caldwell found support from the New York Governor, Hamilton Fish, whose 1850 rationale for saving the structure remains current in the early twenty-first century. Fish and Caldwell were successful and the New York Legislature appropriated $2,391 to pay off a loan and acquire the property, plus offered another $6000 for additional land to protect it. A flag was raised at the structure to mark the first dedicated house museum in the United States.

1853–1874	Ann Pamela Cunningham's work to make Mount Vernon a public museum remains a landmark effort in the field of house museums. The creation of Mount Vernon and the Mount Vernon Ladies Association were the most important single-handed efforts to create and support Mount Vernon by raising support and funds. The establishment of Mount Vernon is significant because it created a pattern for the development of many historic house museums, particularly by volunteer groups; it is also an early example of a national major effort carried out primarily by women and it was duplicated many times at different house museums and historic sites. For many who have sought to save historic structures, a critical element of the rationale has been the almost mystical experience and connection with the past build through the experience of a historic object.
1880s 1890s	Awareness of decorative arts and material culture of early Americans expanded as individuals sought to identify and collect pieces to remind them of their past.

Source: Butler (2002: 19–32)

Box 5.4 History of Historic Residential Structures (Twentieth and Twenty-First Centuries)

1907	Congress acted to protect important historic, natural, and scientific resources of national significance by passing the Antiquities Act.
1910	A notable organization during this era was the Society for the Preservation of New England Antiquities (SPNEA) led by William Summer Appleton from Boston, who began his career in 1905 by participating in efforts to preserve and restore the Paul Revere House. The Massachusetts Legislature granted SPNEA the right to property tax fee. Across the country, similar groups appeared. These were sometimes assisted by patriotic or genealogical organizations such as the Colonial Dames and the Daughters of the American Revolution.
1916	The National Park Service became a bureau of the Department of the Interior, and gradually started acquiring historic sites administered by other agencies.
1935	Congress passed the Historic Sites Act, establishing new research and inventory programs and provided continued

	assistance to the Historic American Buildings Survey estab-lished in 1933.
1940s	Colonial Williamsburg became the single most important private preservation, historic site of the era. Established by John D. Rockfeller Jr. in the late 1920s and 1930s, Colonial Williamsburg served as both a model example and a resource for the development of historic structures and historic house museums.
Late 1940s	The federal government took steps to enforce preservation and education.
1947	Delegates from different museum and preservation organizations met at the National Gallery of Art to plan for a national private agency with an aim to bridge the gap between government and private interests. Two entities were the outcome of this meeting: the National Council for Historic Sites and Buildings and the National Trust for Historic Preservation. Consequently, within a few years, the functions of the two entities became confused and overlapped. In 1953, the Council merged with the Trust.
1964–1965	National Arts and Cultural Development Act and National Foundation on the Arts and Humanities Act (1965) were introduced as a result of the Report of the Commission on the Humanities. The purpose was to provide support for the humanities with a special emphasis on programs grounded in local history and preservation. Following this legislation, Congress established the National Endowment for the Arts and the National Endowment for Humanities (NEH). The endowments, particularly the NEH, provided support to local history museums, including historic houses. Federal funding was now made available.
1966	National Historic Preservation Act was passed. Also, the Transportation Act established the Department of Transportation, which had in its mandate the duty to preserve natural and historic sites impacted by new highway construction. Also, this era saw an upsurge of volunteer support for historic structures.
1970s 1980s	The number of academic programs expanded, offering degrees in museum studies or historic administration. The notion of history became inclusive in class, race, and ethnicity perspectives and Americans came to recognize that the 'past' included events more recent than the American Revolution.

Source: Butler (2002: 26–33)

Historic houses received huge impetus on a global level in 1998 when the International Council of Museums (ICOM) created an International Committee for Historic House Museums. Emphasis was placed on the fact that these structures constitute a special museum category because they are conserved in their original state and contain furnishings and collections made by the people who used to live there (Pinna 2001). In fact, the historic houses have some unique 'fossilized' characteristics which make them different from many other type of museum and bestow in them a high symbolic value. They instill feelings and memories in visitors and offer a special ambience which takes the visitors to the previous era and have them wonder about old lifestyles, etc. They put visitors in direct contact with history itself. Gorgas writes that "more than a monument that celebrates a lost past, a historic house is seen as a place where people have lived out their life" (2001: 10). In sum, such structures are significant for two main reasons (Pinna 2001: 4):

- They are used to conserve, exhibit, or reconstruct real atmospheres which are difficult to manipulate if one does not wish to alter the very meaning of 'historic houses.'
- A historic house museum is unlike other museum categories because it can grow only by bringing together original furnishings and collections from one or other of the historic periods in which the house was used.

Several types of historic house museums exist, ranging from royal palaces to residences of famous people, artists studios, "rich bourgeois houses and even modest cottages" (Pinna 2001: 4). Pavoni and Selvafolta (1998) present the following categories: royal palaces, houses devoted to famous men, houses built by artists, houses dedicated to a style, period, or era, houses of collectors, historic houses with a distinct socio-cultural character. Although no exhaustive classification of historic houses exists, an initial categorization proposed by Butcher-Younghans (1993) is the most widely used classification:

- The Documentary Historic House Museum;
- The Representative Historic House Museum;
- The Aesthetic Historic House Museum.

The Documentary Historic House Museum is by far the most popular type of historic house museum. As described by Butcher-Younghans, "it commemorates a rich or famous individual or family – a town's founding father, a celebrated writer, a former U.S. President, or an industrial magnate. The primary interpretive aim is to chronicle the life of an individual or relate an important historical event" (1993: 184). Examples include the grand estate of Thomas Jefferson and Betsy Ross's urban artisan-class brick home in Philadelphia, USA, and the Freud Museum, UK.

Representative Historic House Museums are those historic houses that have been restored to "interpret a particular style of architecture from a particular period. The focus is on a way of life rather than on a particular individual or family" (Butcher-Younghans 1993: 185). Examples include Plymouth Plantation in

Plymouth, Massachusetts (USA), the Old World Wisconsin in Eagle, Wisconsin (USA), Carisbrooke Castle (UK), and Maison Tavel (Switzerland).

The Aesthetic Historic House Museum serves as a setting for special collections where decorative and fine arts, furniture, and antiques from various periods are displayed. The house serves "as a backdrop for the objects, with no particular attention paid to former residents or the events that took place there. Houses of distinctive architectural design also fit into this category" (Butcher-Younghans 1993: 185). Examples within this category include the Henry Francis du Pont Winterthur Museum in Wilmington, Delaware (USA).

Of renowned fame are the historic country houses in England. According to the Gowers Committee (report commissioned in 1948 from a Committee on Houses of Outstanding Historic or Architectural Interest under the chairmanship of Sir Gowers), "these houses represent an association of beauty, of art, and of nature – the achievement often of centuries of effort – which is irreplaceable, and has seldom, if ever, been equaled in the history of the civilization" (quoted in Butler 1980: 13). The Historic Buildings Council in the UK was set up in 1945 and the Historic Buildings and Ancient Monuments Act was passed in 1953 to facilitate grants and loans for the preservation, restoration, and maintenance of exceptional buildings of historic candidature. Butler (1980) provides the broad classifications of historic houses in the UK based on: private ownership, public ownership, educational establishments, and National Trust-classified country houses based on ownership (both private and public).

Challenges

Regardless of the country which houses these unique structures, commonalities of issues and challenges exist across all borders. These include security-related issues, management of public visits, and protection of the exhibited heritage. Moreover, their interior space or the furnishings and objects cannot be subject to any alterations. Also, such unique structures emphasize the "whole set of objects and its interaction with the spirit of the people who lived in the house which poses special problems in terms of communication with the public" (Pinna 2001: 4). Another big issue pertaining to historic houses is the fear that when objects are displayed and commodified, they get altered and obtain new connotations (Gorgas 2001). The transformed museum's perspective is not history or life per se, but portrayal of history or life; not the past per se, but its representation (Gorgas 2001: 11). Other key challenges specific to the Historic house museums include (Butler 2002: 24–40):

- *Technological changes* – ongoing advancement in technology presents continuing opportunity as well as poses an encumbrance. Also, "while offering some opportunities to better control data, the computer is not a panacea for all administrative problems" (p. 35). As systems become updated, data has to be transferred in the event that the old system becomes redundant. Systems used for audio and visual programs also evolve. Interpretive techniques need to be based on stable systems and have flexibility to adapt to updates. Similar concerns apply to conservation technologies. For instance, treatments currently regarded as best tactics to improve the impact of light on an artifact might not be feasible as new technological innovations take place.

- *Changing demographics* – changes in the visiting population also pose a challenge as museums struggle to adhere to the needs of new and diverse groups of visitors. It has become increasingly important to place the museum in the context of time and relate a complete picture of how it has evolved with times. This calls for ongoing creative and diverse interpretive strategies based on the needs of different market segments.
- *Funding* – this remains an arduous issue and is needed in an ongoing manner to keep this unique category of museums afloat. Butler suggests that admission or gift shop revenues are not enough for museum survival. According to him, "financial support from the community, the development of an endowment, and grants from charitable foundations and from government on all levels" are collectively crucial for existence (Butler 2002: 37). Financial resources from local agencies such as businesses, foundations, and the public sector can be possible if community support exists for the local museum. A friendly tax structure is another important element that affects fiscal management of the museum. Moreover, augmented competition for philanthropic funds also poses a challenge.
- *Age of the museum* – a young museum which is only one generation old can face a doubtful future. Standards of performance, acceptable a generation ago, are no longer adequate in the contemporary era. To raise standards of good performance, ongoing updates on the knowledge of management, history, collections and care, and interpretation techniques are required.
- *Relevancy* – another challenge is the need to be relevant to the contemporary world. An emerging approach to history argues that house museums cannot exist in isolation from the present. The past has to be molded in relation with the present and the future. That is, it has to have meaning in the contemporary world. Needs of the society and civic engagement need to be taken into consideration.

Other problems are associated with the museology concept such as: social and political significance of these structures, issues associated with restoration and conservation, ethical problems allied with reconstruction and with the falsification of original essence of the house-museum, management of exhibits, visitors, and staff, fiscal constraints, security issues, and usage of the site for non-museum events.

In comparison with museums and art galleries, historic houses have been a product of less attention in academic literature. Limited research that is available, however, has significant marketing implications due to their focus on service quality, consumer behavior, market segmentation, story narrations, and authenticity. For instance, Frochot and Morrison (2000) explore service quality issues associated with the historic house museums, using HISTOQUAL, a modified version of the SERVQUAL scale. Five dimensions represent HISTOQUAL: responsiveness (such as staff assistance, their friendliness and knowledge, convenient open hours, etc.), tangibles (property characteristics such as cleanliness, attractiveness, authenticity, signs, interior, garden, and the parking lot), communication (in the form of interpretation and information), consumables (for instance, restaurant food and goods offered at the shop), and empathy (reflected in facilities for people with special needs and children). The authors report that tangibles receive highest rating in terms of service, followed by communication and responsiveness.

Few studies have focused on examining the effectiveness of interpretation techniques within the context of consumer preferences, application, and learning outcomes (Light 1995; Mitsche *et al.* 2008). Others have scrutinized tales and narrations offered by docents and tour guides within the context of heritage dissonance and power influences (Butler 2001; Eichstedt and Small 2002; Modlin 2008; Rosenzweig and Thelen 1998). Modlin examined tales told at the historic house plantations and reported that "many plantation house tours commonly refer to a specific year – the frozen moment" (2008: 265). Such narratives are far from complete and just and are dominated by prevailing power relations. Eichstedt and Small (2002) find that most historic houses in the states of Virginia, Louisiana, and Georgia (USA) fail to narrate a fair picture of the enslaved. In support of this view, Butler (2001) examines promotional brochures from the southern plantations in the United States and reports evidence of a brainwash of the history associated with slavery. According to Modlin, "when plantation museums do a poor job of retelling the story of slavery, they fail to engage in socially responsible tourism" (2008: 266).

Authenticity has also been the topic of discussion in research related to historic houses. For instance, Cameron and Gatewood (2000) explain that historic houses are popular for visitors seeking an authentic experience because their frozen past forms an attractive appeal (Pinna 2001). Institutions such as historic houses have social functions to perform and it is their responsibility to portray a holistic and fair account of history. Modlin identifies several myths employed by docents and offers suggestions on how best to challenge these myths to provide a socially responsible product and experience. Another study worthy of note due to marketing relevance is by Jewell and Crotts (2009), who explore the underlying motivations and needs of visitors to a historic house. The authors employ a technique known as the hierarchical value map (HVM) based on means-end theory. Such a method can help design effective communication messages desired by the visitors. An examination of a prior study by the authors (Jewell and Crotts 2001) reveals that authenticity and preservation (rather than restoration) emphasis are considered important attributes for a satisfying experience by visitors. As reported by Jewell and Crotts, preservation enables "visitors to see how a house was built, as well as providing historical evidence of the public and private life of the family" (2009: 245). Based on motivations, visitors can also be placed on a continuum with the 'general leisure traveler' category at one end and heritage tourists at the other end. In the middle of the spectrum are visitors seeking a relaxing leisure experience with preference for attributes such as nice weather.

What follows now is a description of marketing strategies employed by four historic houses: Dickinson Homestead (USA), Maison Tavel (Switzerland),

Carisbrooke Castle and Dickens Historic House (England). To a large extent, information is elicited from the marketing staff to gain an insight into their marketing strategies. Another core purpose is to determine if the select case studies embrace or accord primacy to the key elements of the Srategic Sustainable Heritage Tourism Marketing model. While Dickenson Homestead and Dickens Historic House are independent non-profit entities and fall into the category of the Documentary Historic House Museums. Maison Tavel is owned by the City of Geneva and managed by Musée d'art et d'histoire and the Carisbrooke Castle is managed and marketed by the Southeast Chapter of English Heritage. The later two belong to the category of the Representative House Museums.

Dickinson Homestead, Massachusetts, USA

The Emily Dickinson Museum is situated in the United States. It consists of two historic houses in the center of Amherst, Massachusetts. These houses were closely associated with the poet Emily Dickinson and members of her family during the nineteenth and early twentieth centuries. The Homestead was the birthplace and home of Emily Dickinson. The Evergreens, next door, was home to her brother and his family. The Emily Dickinson Museum was created in 2003 when the two houses merged under the ownership of Amherst College. The museum is dedicated to educating diverse audiences about Emily Dickinson's life, family, creative work, times, and enduring relevance, and to preserving and interpreting the Homestead and the Evergreens as historical resources for the benefit of scholars and the general public.

Facilities include the museum shop, exhibits, tour center, and the library. Tour guides accompany beyond the tour center and tour sizes are limited for visitor comfort and safety of the collections. Hence a carrying capacity threshold is used. Several interesting programs are offered daily. For instance, a 90-minute exploration is offered of the world of the Dickinson family, with a main focus on Emily Dickinson's life and work. This tour includes both the houses. Additionally, 'This was a Poet' program is offered daily. It provides an introduction to Emily Dickinson and her poetry. The tour takes place at the Homestead and concludes with a poetry reading. Free admission is give to students from the local colleges.

Other tours include the 'Exploring the Museum's Landscape: Audio Tour' and the 'Grounds of Memory' tour. For the first tour, visitors are welcome to explore the museum grounds on their own during the museum's open hours. The museum's audio tour, 'Grounds of Memory,' is recommended to enhance the overall experience. Visitors who purchase a house tour ticket receive a coupon for a complementary audio tour which is valid for one month. The second tour is a self-guided audio adventure around the museum's grounds. It features more than thirty of Dickinson's poems and surveys the Dickinson family's fascination with landscapes and the natural world. Additionally, the Dickenson library offers a program called 'Replenishing the Shelves.'

With regard to the mission, the museum is dedicated to educating diverse audiences about Emily Dickinson's life, family, creative work, tomes, and enduring relevance, and to preserving and interpreting the Homestead and the Evergreens as historical resources for the benefit of scholars and the general public.

Research and Environment Analysis

Primary methods of conducting research include surveys and observations and visual experiments. Routine environment analysis is conducted to identify opportunities and threats. For instance, political environment is important because Democrats tend to support arts and hence a Democratic government is more likely to be supportive of the museum. Economic factors also exert a huge influence on marketing and management decisions at the museum. According to the staff, if the United States continues with the downward trend in economy, it will be difficult to raise admission fees or charge a fee for programs. Limited funds imply that more creative ways are required to market an event.

Distributional and Promotional Strategies

The museum uses online listings, calendars, announcements, and employs local organizations on a short-term basis to distribute posters and programs. Electronic marketing techniques such as emails are heavily used. Press releases are also frequently utilized. Print advertising is employed when funds are available and it includes tools such as newspapers, brochures, postcards, and posters.

Local Community

Visitors represent the local community and their opinions are actively sought. Other local community interactions are with the local and regional chambers of commerce. The relationship with the local community follows the 'participation' approach. Training and education programs are frequently provided to the local community and the aim is to satisfy the educational needs of students, and teachers.

Partnerships and Collaboration

Partnerships and collaboration are sought with other museums in the area and the local banks. The public sector partnerships mostly center on the chamber of commerce. The purpose of partnering is to seek help in marketing to feeder cities which are either inaccessible or expensive to reach. Future partnerships are being sought with large financial institutions and historic/cultural organizations. The purpose is to establish a broader outreach of visiting audience. The museum offers incentives to partners such as web presence on all programs and/or advertising depending on the benefits obtained from the partner. No reward programs are offered.

Authenticity and Conservation

For the museum, the following adherence to authenticity is of utmost importance: representing the past, having a documented history (from the actual period), being a reproduction of the original, being true to the original object (based on the history version of the donors, verified by historians), and representing the local community, region, and donor values. The museum is neutral toward authenticity being modified to represent globalized culture. However, it considers adhering to the market demand important.

The museum accords the highest level of importance to the following tasks: conservation, offering a place to find out about the past, interpreting the past, education, enhancing self-esteem, and providing a place of learning, interest, enjoyment, enrichment, social interactions, contemplation and opportunity to discover oneself. The biggest challenge to conservation is the effort to maintain high-quality environments as tourist arrivals increase. Other challenges next in level of significance are accommodating the need for modernization while at the same time maintaining traditional forms, balancing the needs of tourists and local residents, historic centers are often viewed in isolation from the city while planning, and tourism is either ignored or left out in urban planning strategies.

Interpretation and Visitor Mindfulness

The purpose of interpretation is to appease the heritage management organization responsible for the property on which heritage is offered to the public. Forms of interpretation include organized talks and discussions, guided tours and walks, and theatrical performance. Interpretive materials include actors, curators, education materials, and books. Each guide is trained to be alert and sensitive to the needs of their multicultural visitors. Interpreters are both local and non-local. Mindful visitors are created by learning from a guide's familiarity with Emily Dickinson, her poetry and/or the museum itself. Once the guide has that information, he/she can modify the tour to meet the visitor needs. Receptivity to learning is encouraged through handouts and materials. Challenges encountered in the visitor mindfulness process include time management. For instance, in a guide's desire to meet the needs of the individual visitor, sometimes the conversation can ramble on and as a result the tour can get inadvertently disrupted. Guides are trained to handle each unique instance with professional mindfulness to the whole group and not just one individual.

Maison Tavel, Geneva, Switzerland

Maison Tavel is situated in the Old Town of Geneva, Switzerland. Because it is the oldest dwelling in the city, it is considered a tribute to the medieval period. Maison Tavel represents the lifestyle of the bygone era. Although it was destroyed by fire in the thirteenth century, a noble family called the Tavels later reconstructed its edifice. They transformed the house into a fortified palace. Over the years, the ownership of the building was passed to many influential families of Geneva. The city of

Plate 5.1 Maison Tavel

Geneva acquired this building in 1963. As elegantly articulated by the Musée d'art et d'histoire, this unique historic structure:

> stands as an exemplar of the civilian architecture of the city. It features cellars, where the erstwhile traders exchanged their belongings. The palace also has apartment and kitchen areas. The inhabitants of the city are known to have worked and lived in the apartment areas of the Maison Tavel of Geneva. Furthermore, the attics and the basement of this building are consecrated to the urban history of this Geneva attraction. (1998: 1)

Prints, drawings, coins, photographs and silverware form the rich display of Maison Tavel, which bear witness to the eventful past of the city. The museum office was only able to give an approximate breakdown on the type of visitor market that Maison Tavel attracts. The majority of the tourists are from Europe. Some are Japanese and few are from other Asian countries. Another major market is the local school groups.

Environment Analysis and Research

For the most part, environment analysis is not conducted, although there are ongoing plans to develop a detailed marketing plan which will include many long-term strategic planning tools. The political environment is, however, an important factor to consider as the institution relies on government funding. Hence, close watch and association with political authorities is maintained. Research is included in the overall marketing strategy and it is mostly focused on seeking visitor information, such as their socio-demographic characteristics, preferred activities, interests, and travel behavior. Questionnaires are distributed occasionally at the entrance point of the historic house.

Distribution and Promotion Strategies

The primary indirect distribution channel is the Geneva Tourism Office. Due to a lack of human resources, the market potential of other intermediaries, such as travel agents and tour operators, has not been tapped. The institution is planning to develop their website in the near future so that it can serve as an important direct distribution channel.

With regard to promotion, Maison Tavel heavily relies on advertising. It makes use of multiple tools such as wall posters, brochures, and regular newsletters. Temporary exhibitions serve as an important promotional tool to lure visitors to the Maison Tavel. Also, public relations and publicity are extensively used. Local media contacts are maintained and information on new events and exhibits is frequently shared with them. Sales promotion is not extensively used, although free admission tickets are offered to some newspapers and magazines who advertise for Maison Tavel. The newspaper advertising offers these on 'first come, first serve' basis and, as a result, the whole process generates much hype and interest among the readers.

Local Community Involvement and Partnerships

Local community is actively involved in the marketing process of the exhibition or exhibits have a local theme. Invitations are extended to seek their views and knowl-edge so that an accurate picture is portrayed. For instance, at an exhibition on the archeology of Gaza, accuracy and authenticity of information was ensured by seek-ing the views of the Arab community and key diplomatic officers. Partnerships are maintained with the Geneva Tourism Office, the political authorities, and the media. Members are regularly informed through newsletters. They are mostly local followed by non-local Swiss, and then Europeans. Geneva is surrounded by France on three sides and hence the French language is heavily used.

Conservation and Authenticity

With regard to conservation, primary emphasis is on restoration. Efforts are made to keep as much of the historic house intact as it was during the ancient times. The ren-ovation is based on the fifteenth-century trends. However, for preservation purpose some parts, such as sculpted heads, have been removed and these are displayed inside a showcase. In such situations, care is taken to inform the visitors of the

Plate 5.2 A Maison Tavel Exhibit

change. Challenges associated with conservation include clash of policies on new developments and conservation, modernization versus maintaining new forms, balancing the need of tourists and the local residents, and maintaining high-quality environments by being attentive to the carrying capacity of Maison Tavel. Also, another issue is associated with being isolated in other events planned by the city.

With regard to authenticity, the following criteria are given the highest level of importance: representation of the past, documented history from the actual period, history version of the donors and verified by historians (whenever possible). Market demand and adaptation to modify global culture receive a somewhat mixed response as these versions of authenticity are needed to attract contemporary markets. However, the institution treats these criteria carefully as it puts to risk the core purpose of Maison Tavel.

Interpretation and Visitor Mindfulness

The purpose of interpretation is to value add and better position Maison Tavel within the minds of the visitors seeking a heritage experience. That said, apart from guided tours, interpretive material is not extensively employed. On guided tours, forms of interpretation include organized talks and discussions, guided tours and walks, and theatrical performances. All tour guides are local. Multicultural issues seldom arise because the majority of the visitors speak French. A few visitors know only German and so tours are conducted in German for them. With regard to visitor mindfulness, there is no set agenda to facilitate receptivity to learning, awareness of the setting, or development of new routines. However, visitor behavior is constantly monitored by the surveillance team, who are trained to deal with situations where visitors touch or stand too close to the artifacts or brush their bags too close to the wall paintings.

Carisbrooke Castle, Isle of Wight, UK

Carisbrooke Castle is a historic castle situated in the village of Carisbrooke, near Newport on the Isle of Wight, United Kingdom. From 1100 to 1293, the castle was in the possession of Richard de Redvers family. In 1293, the last Redvers resident sold it to Edward I, after which the government was entrusted to warden the castle as representatives of the Crown. Charles I was imprisoned here for fourteen months before his execution in 1649. From 1896 to 1944, it became the home of Princess Beatrice (daughter of Queen Victoria). She was the Governor of the Isle of Wight. It is now under managed by English Heritage.

Plate 5.3 Carisbrooke Castle

In 2008, a new building to handle admissions and a shop were added to the castle site to improve visitor experience. In June 2009, the Princess Beatrice Garden was inaugurated. It is an Edwardian-style garden and offers a place for visitors to relax and be enthused.

The mission of the south-east chapter of English Heritage is to help and encourage people to nurture their historic environment as an integral part of life today and as a foundation for tomorrow. Their strategy for 2005–10, titled "Making the Past Part of our Future," lays out a plan regarding how they seek to create places where people want to live, work, and visit, and where the rich past is a vital and living part of the future. It is believed that:

- By understanding the historic environment people value it;
- By valuing it they will want to care for it;
- By caring for it they will help people enjoy it;
- From enjoying the historic environment comes a thirst to understand.

Approximately 20 percent of Carisbrooke Castle visitors comprise school children and these are offered free admission. Carisbrooke Castle has a dedicated education room which has been furnished with various education aids. Bespoke literature and information packs are provided for all school visits. During the summer months, Carisbrooke offers a program of events and trails which aim to involve family visitors in the history of the castle. It holds regular donkey demonstrations which are popular with the young visitors. Its new film, introducing the history of the castle in a fun way, helps to engage visitors and brings to life the story of the past. It also provides hands-on interactive armor, and cross-bow and cannon activities to engage all types of visitors. The new Princess Beatrice Garden is intended to be a place to inspire and relax, and it reminds visitors of the pleasures of the natural world.

Environment Analysis and Research

Carisbrooke Castle was once a royal home; therefore, it is of historical significance to the nation. This has limited its marketing functions when serving as an attraction. It is only recently that English Heritage changed its strategy from rigid confinements and tradition to being more adaptive to the contemporary environment. English Heritage routinely conducts environment analysis to identify strengths, weaknesses, opportunities, and threats for the Carisbrooke Castle. Box 5.5 offers an insight into the environment factors considered by English Heritage. Research agenda is not included in the marketing plan.

Distribution and Promotion Strategies

- English Heritage works closely with the Isle of Wight Chamber of Commerce and other community organizations on the island. It advertises events in *Visit Britain*, *County Life* and other general more affluent high-end magazines, as well as local community newspapers to reach their family demographic.

Box 5.5 Environment Factor Consideration by English Heritage

The free admission to schools is a political factor because we are a government advisory board. From a marketing perspective as an attraction this is difficult because we lose a huge percentage of 'paying visitors' to this group. From a historical perspective our children should have free access to the country's history to learn.

The drop in the British pound has had a massive effect on the country's OSV (overseas visitors). Earlier, England was far too expensive to visit, but now the euro is nearly level, this has increased the amount of visitors. We are government funded – nevertheless the new strategy in fact is in place so that one day the properties will become self efficient. The properties are becoming more of an attraction than an historical preservation – there is a fine line.

Recession saw a drop in visitors – people do not have as much expendable money. To combat this there was an influx of vouchers onto the market, which has kept the numbers of paying visitors to a good level. However research suggests that people are not loyal – they are in fact only interested in offers and this ultimately decides where a family goes on a day out.

Cultural environment is one of the biggest factors – we provide knowledge of English History. The organization's main focus is to preserve the country's incredible historical properties and the information that is linked with them.

Ageing demographic needed to be addressed. English Heritage has always been perceived as an older, stuck-up traditional company – the new strategy developed was to target the youth of today so when they grow up it will have a sustainable target market and they will not lose touch with the country's legacy.

The organization has had a drastic profile change over the last few years to try and promote that history can be fun and also a great way to learn. Carisbrooke is off the main land and has a totally different demographic – families travelling down to the coast for the summer. From July to the end of August there is a massive increase in ferry crossings. The rest of the year we only promote on the island to locals. The website allows more information to be delivered to a bigger target audience.

Source: Jones, M. Personal Communication (July 12, 2009)

•   Customer retention marketing strategies are occasionally used. Other advertising strategies include advertising events in magazines and local regional newspapers and joint tickets with the local ferry companies (joint tickets are a ticket sold on the ships that give cheaper admission to the properties). English Heritage hires external companies to provide a form of guerilla advertising (they dress in costumes and hand out leaflets in public places when events draw near).

- With regard to public relations and publicity, the castle always receives coverage in the local press and English Heritage relies heavily on this promotional tool. It also uses local radio stations on the island to inform about competitions and forthcoming events, which is considered an effective strategy. The biggest promotional strategy that has accomplished wonders is cross-selling at sister sites; this requires an internal focus on the current visitors. Through internal advertising techniques such as membership research and surveys, English Heritage reports that people take more notice of other member sites.

Local Community Involvement and Partnerships

Close associations are maintained with other attractions on the Isle of Wight (IOW). Interactions are also maintained with the IOW Chamber of Commerce, the City Council and local trade and hoteliers. Non-participation category of engagement is used with the local community. As stated earlier, this is a top-down, formal, passive or indirect participatory approach. Local community involvement or views are mostly not considered while planning marketing strategies.

Training and education programs are also offered to the local community, such as free guided tours for schools. In addition, interactive learning facilities exist for schools groups. The history of the local area is also provided by Carisbrooke Castle. More partnerships are being sought with television to provide nationwide coverage. No incentives are offered to partners. Members, however, have free entry to all English Heritage attractions.

Authenticity and Conservation

Authenticity is considered a crucial element at Carisbrooke Castle. The most important criteria are objectivity-based and include representation of the past, documented history, reproduction of the original (real not manufactured), representing local values of the region, verification by historians, and modifications to reflect global culture. The next level of importance is accorded to the following items: being true to the original object and based on the history version of the donors. A neutral response is given to the following criteria: represent market demand, should be from the actual period, and should represent the local community.

Different kinds of roles define the Carisbrooke Castle's purpose. These include offering a place to find out about the past, being an interpreter of the past, providing education, offering a place of interest and enjoyment and self-enrichment, supplying opportunities for social interactions and contemplation, and being a place to discover oneself. Another primary task is to seek profits. Multiple conservation approaches are employed by English Heritage for this, which include preservation, restoration, renovation, and regeneration. The most important challenges associated with conservation include the clash of policies on new developments and conservation, maintaining high-quality environments as tourist arrivals increase, and tourism left out or ignored in urban planning strategies. The next level of importance is given to issues related to modernization versus maintaining traditional forms and balancing the needs of tourists and local residents.

Interpretation and Visitor Mindfulness

The purpose of interpretation is to add value and better position the product, attract markets that provide the maximum revenue, reflect personal and organizational ethics, and appease the heritage management organization responsible for the property on which heritage is offered to the public. Popular forms of interpretation include guided tours and walks, and electronic audio guides in multiple languages. Both print and audio materials are utilized. The multicultural needs of the audience are addressed by distributing leaflets and audio guides in different languages.

Special care is taken to accommodate visitors with special needs. All employees are required to regularly participate in health and safety training modules. Risk assessment training is also given and many receive training on first aid. The core purpose of this training is to ensure that an exceptionally high level of customer service is offered to augment the visitor experience. Mystery shoppers are frequently used to examine all aspects of the welcome experience, as well as service and catering delivery in the shops. In sum, overall customer experience is regularly monitored. Formal sessions are held to report the results and training needs are identified and acted on. A model of the castle 'circa 1600' is set up in the courtyard and is designed to allow close access to wheelchairs and to cater to the needs of those with visual impairments. Also available is an introductory video subtitled to benefit those with hearing impairments. In addition, Carisbrooke offers wheelchairs to visitors in need and welcomes special-assistance dogs.

Dickens Historic House Museum, London, UK

Charles Dickens's historic house is a national historic site in London, United Kingdom, and has served the purpose of a museum for many decades. Charles Dickens is Britain's most famous novelist and this house was his former London home. Dickens moved into the house in 1837 after he married and his first child was born there. Dickens lived at the house until 1839 and then moved to a larger property. It was here that he completed some of his famous pieces of work: *Pickwick Papers*, *Oliver Twist*, and *Nicholas Nickleby*.

The Dickens House is part of the 'Museum Mile' program centered on the theme to reveal a 'mile of discovery.' This program suggests a walk by London's thirteen exclusive museums and art galleries. The purpose is to offer a nostalgic (and fascinating) view and reflection of London in its past and present era. The 'Museum Mile' program stretches from Euston Road to the River Thames. The program brochure provides the following description of the Dickens House: "Visitors can see paintings, rare editions, manuscripts, original furniture and other items relating to the popular Victorian novelist Charles Dickens. Highlights include the original monthly parts of the novels, manuscript fragments, and the desk designed by

Dickens for his reading tours." In 1905, the Dickens House founded a journal titled *Dickensian*. Included among other published text are articles of literary criticism written by authors from around the world. The house also hosts an annual conference which takes place in selected venues across the globe. For example, in 2007 the conference was held in Philadelphia, USA and Durham, England was the venue in 2008. The historic house also offers a Dickens Fellowship to those who share an interest in the life and works of the writer from 1812–1870. Another program, 'Friends of the Charles Dickens Museum,' is offered to provide unlimited access and discounts at the gift shop.

A pocket guide titled *Dickens' London: A Geographic Tour* is an interesting communication piece aligned with the 'Obsessed with the City' campaign. The purpose is to highlight the significance of Charles Dickens to London's history and his relationship with the nation's capital. It is the only surviving home of the author and is important in the sense that it inspired him.

The authenticity of this house is endorsed by its original location and physical connection with the author. Also, it houses original artifacts belonging to Dickens or donated by the Dickens family. The core purpose of the Dickens House is: to keep alive the spirit of Dickens in London as a master wordsmith, an entertainer, a witness of Victorian life and a model of conviviality.

Education of the public drives the main goals, which is evident from the leaflet titled "Please Sir, I want some more." The following narration is provided on the back page: "Discover the world of Britain's greatest novelist in his former London home. On four floors, you will see reconstructed period rooms, galleries with artifacts from Dickens's life as well as the impressive library with many beautifully bound editions of his works." The exhibition themes provide a subtle connection between Dickens's work and the contemporary environments. For instance, a recent exhibition theme was "Ignorance and Want: The Social Conscience of Charles Dickens." The exhibition narrated stories of poverty through Dickens' works and connected them to contemporary poverty issues.

Although basic information was obtained by a primary visit to the museum and the website, detailed information could not be elicited from the museum personnel to verify certain facts. Nevertheless, the existing information suggests similar strategies to the ones employed by the Freud Museum. These museums use objective authenticity as their brand to endorse their historical narrations. At the same time, they rely on exhibitions based on the negotiated authenticity themes to engage the contemporary visitors and build a bridge between history and the current trends in the country and the world. Both share budgetary constraints and funding issues.

Summary

Historic houses are a complex phenomenon as they serve as both 'objects' and 'museums.' They offer a unique heritage environment by evoking feelings and memories in visitors, thereby transforming them into time travelers. In the words of Gorgas, "the impacts on the public along with a particular type of mental and emotional reaction are produced by the presence of the people who once lived in the house" (2001: 10). However, what needs to be remembered is that what is offered is not history per se but its representation using the dominant perspective. The entire setting is captured and narrated based on a theme. Hence the issue associated with the politics of history and power of narration applies to these structures. A national level support and advocacy reinforce the significant role they play as paradigms of national unity.

As pointed out by Pinna, historic houses are unique in that "they are used to conserve, exhibit or reconstruct real atmospheres which are difficult to tamper with" (2001: 4). They put visitors directly in contact with history. Historic houses managed by the public sector follow standardized policies are more prone to standardized narratives.

Organizations such as the HSA also work with private houses of unique historic value and offer their services to promote conservation of such sites. Programs such as the 'Friends Membership' program garner support and donations from advocates of local and national heritage. Also, examples of successful campaigns such as 'History Matters' and 'Pass It On' demonstrate that people care. Advantages of knowing history are multifold: generates a fascination with the world, helps understand oneself, structures individual and collective identities of human beings, and creates a connection with the surrounding community. Heritage is an important educational resource. Children who visit heritage sites grow up into advocates and ardent visitors. Engaging new audiences with campaigns such as your heritage or mine also helps to promote both national and local heritage.

A few commonalities emerge between the case studies presented in this chapter. All can be commended on pursuing active conservation programs. Also, all are on the same page with regard to their emphasis on objectivist authenticity, although they are treading a fine line in their efforts to adapt to the diverse audience. In all cases, financial stress is a common issue, with the exception of Maison Tavel where human resources is the big issue. Active partnerships with local communities are lacking across all of them. A range of research techniques is pursued from observation and surveys to mystery shopping. Lessons can be learnt from all as each one presents distinct marketing features.

Questions

1.   What are the primary functions of English Heritage and the Historic Houses Association (UK)?
2.   What is the most widely used classification of historic house museums?
3.   Describe some of the primary challenges faced by historic house museums today.
4.   Briefly explain the distribution and promotion strategies embraced by Dickinson Homestead and the Carisbrooke Castle.
5.   Which one of the four case studies presented closely follows the guidelines laid down by the SSHTM model?

6   Heritage Hotels and Resorts

Adaptive use of old buildings is one way that cultural and historical elements are appropriated by the leisure and tourism industry. As urban conservation sites (Chang 1997), heritage hotels and resorts have become important cultural, historical, and ethnic symbols of unique ethnic environments. The heritage hotel concept also serves as an important mechanism to facilitate preservation and restoration of unique buildings. Also, heritage hotels are now a part of the 'International Hotels Environment Initiative' which aims to address some of the sustainability inspired issues such as eco-efficiency, cultural management, ecolabels, and best practice guidelines.

Because of their economic value, heritage hotels have captured the interest of both the private and public sectors. Additionally, they have garnered the support of the local community because of their rich heritage and cultural values. Heritage hotels as a tourism commodity have many uses such as:

*   Being used as a tool to promote civic pride, local identity, and cultural capital;
*   Helping bridge the gap between locals and tourists by projecting an "attractive image for investors, tourists, and local residents" (Chang 1997:47).

It is therefore surprising that, to date, literature on historic or heritage hotels is meager. Of the few studies that have appeared, research focus has centered on monumental aspects of historic hotels in urban South-East Asia (Peleggi 2005), challenges associated with the conservation of built colonial heritage (Henderson 2001), renovation of a historic hotel and the issues associated with its authentic identity (Hart 1994), a discussion of literary lodging concept (Chernish 1998), and economic impact of heritage hotels (Dincer 2003).

This chapter offers an interesting account of marketing strategies pursued by four unique hotels/resorts situated in different parts of the world. Each hotel/resort offers a distinct heritage setting. The resort in the United States is situated on an Indian Reservation. Because of its authentic location and tribal engagement, the resort ambience is distinctive with regard to the portrayal of tribal culture and art work in the lobby and its various corridors. The hotel in India has a rich colonial heritage and is now branded as a museum hotel. It houses many colonial and pre-colonial murals, artifacts, and relics. The hotel in Scotland (UK) is a built on a historical site and the hotel in Japan is situated inside a temple and managed by monks.

Sheraton Wild Horse Pass Resort, Arizona, USA

The Sheraton Wild Horse Pass Resort (SWHPR) offers 'Warm Comforting Connections' and serves the needs of luxury and upscale business and leisure travelers. The SWHPR was designed to represent the Gila River Indian community's heritage and culture. Gila River Indian community comprises Pima and Maricopa tribes. The Wild Horse Pass prides itself as a destination resort where the natural and living culture surroundings define the atmosphere, and the history of the land is attributed to a pioneering Native American tribe, 'Gila River.'

A large part of the development of the resort had to be approved by the elderly in the community to ensure that the Gila tribe was being portrayed in an accurate and authentic manner. For example, at the entrances of the resort and its Aji Spa, guests enter through a rounded frame which follows the 'The Man in the Maze' theme, an important part of the Pima creation story. The man passing through the maze symbolizes the life cycle. According to the SWHPR website, its Aji Spa is:

> The world's leader in authentic Native American Healing offerings, is more than a place where the stresses of daily life are released. It's a place where lives are changed ... the lives of guests who transcend the barriers of discomfort by Healing the Body, Mind and Spirit ... and the lives of the children of the Gila River Indian Community who directly benefit from every guest that passes through our doors. Embark on an experience – unlike any other – that is closely overseen by Tribal Elders and is conceptualized and implemented by Pima and Maricopa Tribal members with generations of past spirits guiding their actions. (Sheraton Wild Horse Pass Resort 2009)

The resort is managed by Starwood Hotels and Resorts. Its specific aim of 'offering warm comfortable connections' is nested within the corporation's mission statement. A close examination of the mission statement shows that the property follows a mixed orientation to manage the resort: social, marketing, and manufacturing/product:

> We succeed only when we meet and exceed the expectations of our customers, owners and shareholders. We have a passion for excellence and will deliver the highest standards of integrity and fairness. We celebrate the diversity of people, ideas and cultures. We honor the dignity and value of individuals working as a team. We improve the communities in which we work. We encourage innovation, accept accountability and embrace change. We seek knowledge and growth through learning. We share a sense of urgency, nimbleness and endeavor to have fun too. (Sheraton Wild Horse Pass Resort 2009)

As Box 6.1 illustrates, social marketing emphasis is evident in the numerous sustainable activities pursued by the resort. The Sheraton Wild Horse Pass strives to increase its total sales and popularity within the hospitality industry. Because of economic recession, they want to make sure that their sales do not decline. In summary, their core objectives include:

Indulge The Spirit

The Sheraton Wild Horse Pass Resort & Spa, a 500-room resort was designed to be an authentic representation of the Gila River Indian Community's heritage and culture. It is conveniently located 11 miles from the Phoenix Sky Harbor International Airport on the ancient Gila River Indian Community. The AAA Four Diamond resort offers its guests a recreational, educational and inspirational experience never before available in a resort setting. The architecture, design, art and legends of the Pima (Akimel O'otham) and Maricopa (Pee Posh) tribes are celebrated in every detail imaginable, indoors and out.

Plate 6.1 Sheraton Wild Horse Pass Resort, 'Indulge the Spirit'

- Bring more meetings/conventions to the resort;
- Increasing the resort's popularity in the industry;
- Keeping frequent contact with previous guests and future guests;
- Getting the resort's name out more through advertisement;
- Communicating Native American heritage in an authentic manner;
- Indulging the spirit by an authentic representation of Gila River Indian Community's culture and heritage (see Plate 6.1).

Sheraton Wild Horse Pass Resort offers two restaurants, a resort lobby bar, a poolside grill, and a golf course. The resort also has a large amount of meeting space. The resort participates in various sustainable activities as is shown in Box 6.1.

The resort hosts a wide range of conventions and meetings. Although the main emphasis is on group markets, families on leisure visits also frequent the resort. The current target markets include weddings, meetings/events, golf players, families, and people just looking to relax. The majority of Sheraton Wild Horse Pass guests are business travelers (who attend meetings and conferences) and families who are taking a short vacation.

Environment Analysis and Research

The SWHPR routinely conducts an analysis of its competitors and takes economic, demographic, natural, technological, and cultural factors into consideration when formulating promotion strategies. Detailed information on this aspect of strategic marketing, however, could not be obtained from the resort. With regard to research, the SWHPR used both in-house and follow-up surveys, which invite guests to comment on their overall stay experience, facilities, and the quality of service. The resort also asks individuals to fill out questionnaires to evaluate conference facilities and services. Additionally, it maintains information on repeat guests and local guests through in-house databases.

Box 6.1 Sustainable Activities Pursued by the Sheraton Wild Horse Pass Resort

The Sheraton Wild Horse Pass Resort and Spa, Arizona's only Native American-owned, GeoGreen designated luxury resort, was pleased to announce its participation in Earth Hour 2009.

As the lights went down and the Sonoran Desert darkens, the Sheraton Wild Horse Pass Resort and Spa came alive with the energy of Earth Hour 2009. The Resort became 'dark' in observance of Earth Hour from 8:30 p.m. to 9:30 p.m., local time, by powering down all interior/ exterior lighting within reason, to continually ensure the wellbeing of their guests. With those environmentally conscious guests in mind, the Sheraton Wild Horse Pass Resort and Spa decided to turn Earth Hour 2009 into an evening of celebration with activities sure to supply the most discerning of guests with luxury while together protecting the Earth's precious resources.

The festivities began at 6:00 p.m. with the Sheraton Adventure Club's Earth-oriented family activities including glow stick tag, Earth-ball games, glow-in-the-dark face painting and craft demonstrations which promote Earth preservation. Following the family activities portion, all guests were invited to enjoy a poolside viewing of *Planet Earth*, beginning at 7:15 p.m. The movie led into the big Earth Hour event from 8:00 p.m. to 10:00 p.m. featuring songs, stories and stargazing. Venerated Tribal Elder Emmett White was at the outdoor fire pit to discuss the Gila River Indian Community's respect for the environment in the GeoGreen lecture series entitled, 'Verbal Journeys through Mother Earth.' And the activities will continue with Mr. James Ashley, of Arizona State University's Mars Space Flight Facility. He was the evening's guest astronomer and provided telescopes and shared classification and description of phenomena in the sky.

Throughout the evening AAA Five Diamond/Mobil Five-Star Kai restaurant and Ko'Sin restaurant featured Earth-inspired menu items made from locally grown ingredients including a composition salad with a blue corn-meal scone, mesquite meal brittle, local Arizona petite greens and a small artisan cheese. The Resort's lobby bar featured a wheat grass Jell-O serving for the children and a Green Geopolitan Martini for Resort and Restaurant guests aged 21+.

The Resort's activities were a reflection of its commitment to cultural sustainability, environmental responsibility and community involvement. It was proud to join the ever-growing list of participants, currently more than 1,672 cities and towns in 80 countries across the world have signed on to cast their vote for action on climate change.

Source: Sheraton Wild Horse Pass Resort (2009)

Plate 6.2 Sheraton Wild Horse Pass Resort

Distribution and Promotion Activities

Compared to some other resorts in the area, the SWHPR does not mainly concentrate on the elites. Distribution and promotion strategies focus on the upper middle class in order to obtain more sales. Because a lot of the bookings today are made using online sources, travel agencies form an important distribution channel. One primary source of advertising is travel magazines. With regard to local community involvement, a participation approach is evident. As stated earlier in Chapter 3, this is a grass roots kind of participation category which stresses community empowerment and citizen control. Local residents are given the opportunity to self-plan events and the resort exhibits that represent their culture and region. Decision-making processes related to the marketing of heritage actively take local community views into consideration. Since the resort is owned by the Native American tribe, the tribal community exercises a key influence on the representation of their culture and heritage in the resort. For instance, ceiling murals (Plate 6.3) are painted by the tribal artists. Drawings made by tribal children are displayed on a wall. The entrance of the resorts is marked by welcome panels on each side. On the right side, the following words are written in Pima language (see Box 6.2): Friend, welcome to my house. It is good to see you. The creator be with you.

Box 6.2 Welcome in Pima Language

NOVOCH IVAKIE
ENKI ETSAPEN
THAK EM NIE
JIOSH ATH OM
VEMVHK

Plate 6.3 Lobby and Native American Ceiling Murals

Interpretation and Creating Mindful Visitors

Brochures, signs, murals, panels, and guided cultural tours are the main interpretation techniques used by the resorts. The guided cultural tours are conducted by a member of the tribal community. The resort also uses an interpretive trail guide to lead its visitors through the 2.5 mile-long trail on the reservation. Along the trail are signs describing the indigenous flora and fauna species on the reservation. The core purpose of interpretation is to communicate and reflect personal and organizational ethics of the Gila River Community. A variety of techniques are used to encourage visitor mindfulness such as the use of oral presentation, information offered next to each panel, and a display of pictures, drawings, artifacts and handicrafts on the resort premises. Also, engagement activities with the tribal community are offered which include opportunities to weave baskets with the tribal people.

Authenticity and Conservation

The resort culture and heritage represents a blend of objective and negotiated versions of authenticity. Objective is endorsed through the murals, language, and handicrafts. Negotiated stance is evident in the use of wood inside the resort premises, since the woodwork tradition started much later as an alternative source of income to farming and basket-weaving profession when the Gila River waters were diverted by non-tribal farmers which led to a forty-year famine-like situation. Although alterations were made with the changing environment, adapted practices remained in harmony with the core cultural values of the tribe. The ceiling murals reflect this mixed approach. An information sheet helps interpret the message and history of each mural:

- One mural panel shows 'different periods of time- from the early 1900s to now.' The Elders are passing on the Creation Story to the next generations. They are also passing on the ancient customs and traditions in the hope that the priceless heritage will not be lost.
- Two murals depict the pottery-making and basket-making traditions. One of them shows Maricopa woman making pottery and the other one portrays Pima women making baskets.
- Another mural shows children listening to the tales of the Elders and learning the Creation Story – the 'way of life.'

With regard to conservation, based on the personal visit made by the author to the site and interactions with the cultural manager, it appears that both preservation and regeneration strategies are employed. Some artifacts are displayed and preserved in their original condition. For instance, a calendar stick is on display with an information tag stating: "Prior to written language, all Pima and Maricopa historical events and legends were passed down orally. The only written history was recorded on a calendar sticks such as these. Each notch represents a time frame and each symbol represents a significant occurrence that took place during that time."

Culloden House Hotel, Scotland, UK

Culloden House Hotel was originally a Jacobean castle. It was here that Bonnie Prince Charlie (a well-known Scottish hero) was stationed prior to the tragic historic battle on Culloden Moor on April 16, 1746. The entire site is of great historic importance in Scotland. The hotel interior features a living room with Adamesque plasterwork, several magnificent antiques, and a huge open fire. The site's history is articulated on the hotel website (see Box 6.3).

The hotel property offers a range of facilities including forty acres of parkland, twenty-eight bedrooms, the Garden Pavilion, and four luxury suites. The Culloden House was awarded the 'Most Outstanding Scottish Country House Hotel 2004' at the Scottish Incoming Golf Tour Operators Association's (SIGTOA) annual dinner ceremony held in St. Andrews. The mission statement of the hotel is:

> In class by itself ... where Highland hospitality has been elevated to the highest art form, without being 'stuffy' nor too 'proper' or reserved. After all you deserve without compromise, the very best. (Culloden House 2009)

Box 6.3 History of Culloden House Hotel

- Culloden House stands as part of Scotland's past. The nearby site close to the Culloden House is the battlefield of Culloden. This is a site that changed more than the history of Scotland. It has been estimated that there are some 20 million people of Scots descent living in other countries as a result of this huge diaspora as the aftermath of this one battle. The battle itself was fought on flat marshy moorland, part of the Culloden estate, and less than two miles from the house. Here, an army of some 4,500 Jacobites, tired, hungry and ill equipped met a Government force of 9,000 strong, well fed and rested troops under the command of the Duke of Cumberland.
- This was the last battle pitched by a foreign force fought on British soil, and was over in less than an hour. Out gunned and out fought by the better trained troops of the Government army, the Jacobites were utterly defeated. They lost some 1,500 men during the battle.
- The site has been restored and on a still spring day, it still speaks eloquently but silently of the clansmen who died for the Jacobite cause. The site is now owned in perpetuity for the nation by the National Trust for Scotland. This 180-acre piece of boggy ground has become a place of pilgrimage for the many millions of Scots, both in Scotland as well as those scattered abroad.
- Culloden House therefore stands out as a symbol, both of Scotland's past, and her present. Its name and situation are redolent of a turbulent and romantic history; its present that of a welcoming Scotland, welcoming to her sons and daughters making the pilgrimage back home, providing the finest of modern accommodation within a superbly historic setting.

Source: Culloden House (2009)

As the mission statement states, the core aim of the hotel is guest satisfaction. It is a small Georgian country house property which specializes in upscale accommodations. Most of the guests are from the UK or Europe and North America. Additionally, new target markets are noted to emerge from India and China. The marketing plan does not have a research agenda. Most research on visitors is gathered from secondary sources such as reservation records and in-house guest observations. Environment analysis is not included in the marketing plan.

Promotional tools employed are public relations and direct mail to UK citizens. Local community is considered important during the shoulder (off peak) season. The Highland location makes the hotel seasonal and it relies on the local market during off peak season for functions, dinners, and weddings. The hotel emphasizes preservation strategies to conserve its historic structure and facilities. The hotel does not have any marketing partners. No additional interpretation techniques are used to educate the guests about the hotel's history beyond the information provided in the hotel brochure and the website. The hotel, however, has an established reputation for being mindful to its guests by attending to their needs. The core purpose is to earn profits by providing good service and creating satisfied guests.

Imperial Hotel, New Delhi, India

Hotel Imperial in New Delhi, India, is based on the '1911' theme which is the year the capital of India was moved from Calcutta to Delhi. This year was a landmark in Indian history and the '1911 Coronation Durbar' is commemorated by the hotel in the form of a restaurant, a bar and a verandah (patio). The hotel was built in 1934 and its founder, Lady Willingdon, is often referred to as the 'spiritual mother of the Imperial.' Lady Willingdon also decorated the hotel interior, using multinational material such as fabric from Europe, marble from Italy, chandeliers from Austria, teak from Burma, and rugs from Persia. More than one hundred life-size statues were crafted. The inauguration reception of the hotel in 1936 marked the farewell ceremony for Lady Willingdon as she was called back to England.

The hotel is now owned by the Singh family. Box 6.4 offers a brief history of Hotel Imperial. As the box illustrates, since the beginning the hotel was famous because of its patronage by historical figures such as the Maharaja of Patiala (a town in the State of Punjab, India), Mahatma Gandhi, and other elite members. The Imperial was also signatory to many historical landmark events.

Box 6.4 History of Hotel Imperial

The Imperial was built and managed by Ranjit Singh. Conceptualized in 1934 by Blomfield and inaugurated by Lord Willingdon in 1936, The Imperial is a fine confluence of a rich historical past and a slick international appeal. The 24 king palms that lead up to the porch are an integral part of and witness to the very creation of New Delhi.

The Hotel was designed to be the finest monument in Lutyens' grand vision of the Capital City's original master plan. Blomfield designed the Hotel with a unique blend of Victorian, old colonial and a playful dosage of informal art deco.

During its construction, Lady Willingdon was seen at the Hotel looking after the interior designing. Two Italian marble shops were bought out. Persian rugs and art deco objects d'art were brought in to complement the look. It was Lady Willingdon who gave the name 'The Imperial' to the Hotel. She even conferred the lion insignia upon the Hotel.

The Imperial was placed on the second most important social boulevard of the nation, the prestigious Queensway, now called Janpath, the first being the grand and ceremonious Kingsway, now known as Rajpath. From the time The Imperial opened its doors in the 1930s, when India was beginning to write the last chapters of its saga on independence, there was little space in New Delhi for an Indo-British rubbing of shoulders. The Imperial provided such a space. Pandit Nehru, Mahatma Gandhi, Muhammad Ali Jinnah and Lord Mountbatten would meet at The Imperial under congenial conditions to discuss the partition of India and creation of Pakistan. The Imperial's pillared verandahs, dining rooms, tea lounges, Royal Ballroom and cool and spacious gardens became the venue of many celebrated encounters between the British and Indian aristocracy and gentry. If only walls could speak, here indeed was a repository of fascinating anecdotal material for authors of romantic and detective fiction.

It was here at The Imperial, where you could raise your glasses on the same table as the Viceroys and Indian Royalty, to the war effort or to the Quit India Movement. Replete with tableware from London, Italian marble floors, Burma teak and rosewood furniture, fountains from Florence, original Daniell's and Frazer's on walls and the best of Indian furniture. The Imperial – a unique low-rise structure –creates the aura of the early 19th century English manor.

Extensive restorations over the last five years once again assure The Imperial's place amongst the best. Internationally renowned interior designers have worked on the brief to restore the Hotel to its original character and glory, subtly incorporating technology and modern-day facilities in the rooms. The Imperial still retains its relationship with the era of gracious living and personalized service that is far removed from the slick silicon style of modern hotels. Until the 1970s every important person stayed at The Imperial. Nehru family had a permanent suite here. Thirteen embassies were located in the premises of the Hotel. The tradition continues. No wonder then, that celebrities like James Cameron, Frederick Forsyth, Kate Winslet and more recently the Queen of the Netherlands, King of Morocco and rock star Sting never stay elsewhere when in Delhi.

Source: The Imperial (2009a)

Employee uniforms were created by a designer belonging to a royal family. During the 1950s, The Imperial became the best address in Delhi. Indian tourism promotion during the 1950s and 1960s helped to publicize the hotel. Travelers in search for the bygone splendors of colonial India came to stay at The Imperial rather than choosing a modern hotel. The hotel thus became a hub of economic and social activities.

In 1967, the hotel was badly in need of renovation and heavy investment was required. The owner, Jasdev Singh Akoi, envisioned the idea of merging his hotel

Plate 6.4 Imperial Hotel, New Delhi, India

with a spectacular museum reflecting the colonial era. The contemporary Imperial (see Plates 6.4 and 6.5) has thus become a colonial relic with mural paintings giving life to ancient history.

Plate 6.5 Imperial Hotel, New Delhi, India (entrance)

Today, The Imperial has 230 rooms. The lion face is symbolic of the hotel insignia that was conferred upon The Imperial by Lady Willingdon when it opened. Arts and antiques, collected from various parts of nation, are displayed along the hotel corridors and restaurants. In fact, the hotel is a museum hotel in the right sense of the word. It displays over 4,000 items of art and colonial history at any one point of time. The owners of the hotel searched for old British houseware to decorate some of its restaurants, which capture the cultural ambience of India. As a newspaper quote states:

> the Spice Route gives the feel of a Burmese pagoda, a Thai temple or alternatively of a Kerala fishing village. It just isn't a culinary experience, it's a celebration of the senses, all five of them, and a unique blend of influences from the South and the South-East. It is a visual treat and a general knowledge lesson packed into a dining experience. It never stops creating history. (Hotel Imperial 2009b)

The 'Patiala Peg' was originally called the 'Irish Pub' and was frequented by the Maharaja of Patiala. After his death, it was renamed Patiala Peg to honor his memory.

The hotel has a marketing partnership with Preferred Hotels and Resorts. This happened after the hotel met some 4,000 of the organization's criteria (for instance, the hotel phone is answered within three rings).

Various distribution channels are used by the hotel such as the travel agents, tour operators, meeting and convention planners, consortia, and Internet. Most of the guests to the hotel are business travelers. Promotional strategies include public relations, sales blitz, personal selling, and advertising. Since foreign diplomats frequently patronize the hotel, it receives a fair share of publicity from the media. The long-term heritage health of the product is maintained through renovations. With regard to interpretation material, commonly used tools such as brochures and cultural tours are used to narrate the hotel's history and describe its artwork and artifacts. Tours are regularly provided which describe stories portrayed by the paintings and murals. Visitors are not allowed to photograph the paintings or murals.

As is seen, detailed information on promotional strategies could not be elicited from the hotel staff. Also, answers to most of the questions associated with the sustainable marketing model components such as partnerships and collaboration, environment analysis, research agenda, and local community involvement were stated as 'non-applicable.' It appears that the marketing plan does not consider the aforesaid elements relevant for inclusion in marketing. It is possible that the hotel is pursuing the conventional marketing approach centered solely on the promotional mix.

Hozenji Hotel, Kanazawa City, Japan

Hozenji Hotel is a temple hotel located in Kanazawa city in Japan. The temple was built in the seventeenth century. Today, it offers lodging facilities to visitors. The mission of the temple hotel is to provide a unique experience to visitors. The hotel operates on non-profit principles and the purpose is to break even. Lodging fees are the primary source of livelihood for the monks who run the hotel.

Environment Analysis and Research Plan

The monks keep track of what is going on in the environment to detect strengths and weaknesses for the hotel. Opportunities identified are a unique history and heritage that captures visitors' interests. Because of ongoing demand for the temple accommodation and an increase in the number of international visitors, little emphasis is placed on efforts to identify economic and innovative (technology) factors. The main weakness, however, noted by the management, is the nature of the non-frequent repeat visits. Usually visitors are unlikely to repeat their visits. Most belong to the young generation and they move on. The competitors are Disneyland and Universal Studios.

Random surveys are conducted of visitors who stay to understand their characteristics and preferences. Information is collected using marketing intelligence and observation, and secondary methods. One monk from hotel staff attends city meetings and participates in community drinking so that he can obtain local information.

Distribution and Promotion Strategies

Distribution is mostly done through word of mouth and the local tourism office. Only public relations and publicity are used. The monk lifestyle is sometimes shown on TV, which attracts the interest and attention of the local and national market. Also, Japanese newspapers occasionally provide publicity for the hotel.

Community Involvement and Partnerships

The temple is owned by the public sector. Local community involvement is considered crucial so that the temple does not exist in isolation and suffer a negative image. Hence, locals are encouraged to visit and participate in the temple ceremonies and their suggestions are seriously considered. Events such as fireworks and historical costume festival are hosted to demonstrate support to the local community.

The temple management partners with the Japan Temple association, which is a public sector. Partnerships are also sought with the ministry of tourism which helps bring tours and more visitors. Information is often researched on the demographics of visitors who stay in other temple hotels in Japan. Partnership with the ministry of Japan has given the hotel managers many opportunities to interact with international people who have interest in temples and history.

Conservation and Authenticity

Buddhism preaches originality, and the hotel believes that visitors seek an original experience. Efforts are made to preserve the temple heritage in its original form.

Repair is only done to prevent the risk of complete breakdown. Restoration is also emphasized wherever possible so that the original structure remains intact. Resort represents multiple authenticities. The highest importance in terms of authenticity criteria, however, is given to local representation, real not manufactured, and being true to the original product.

Interpretation and Visitor Mindfulness

The hotel informs visitors of the building's heritage and history. They provide information on what different symbols mean, such as the statues of Lord Buddha, and also the kind and age of the wood used to build the temple. Interpretation tools include pamphlets, guidebooks, and the Internet (website). The monks serve as tour guides and sources of information. The heritage displays and historical accounts are described both in English and in Japanese. Signs are provided to guide visitors and the guests are requested not to touch the artifacts or religious displays.

Summary

The examples used in this chapter aim to provide a global insight into the marketing strategies embraced by heritage hotels/resorts. Based on the information obtained from different properties, it appears that The Imperial and the Culloden House Hotel follow marketing and relationship building philosophies, whereas the Sheraton Wild Horse Pass Resort and the Hozenji Hotel follow a mix of product/manufacturing and social orientations. Evidence of sustainability and local community involvement is also more evident in the Hozenji Hotel and the Sheraton Wild Horse Pass Resort. In fact, the Sheraton Wild Horse Pass Resort can be commended for pursuing a bottom-up partnership approach with regard to community involvement and decision making. Stakeholder collaborations, however, were not the focus of attention in any of the hotels.

Interpretation and visitor mindfulness techniques at the Sheraton Wild Horse Pass Resort appear to be more refined and detailed. It is noted that conservation is given priority by all, although the category and magnitude differs among the properties. Tangible evidence of object authenticity to promote history (colonial or noncolonial), ethnic community heritage, and religious heritage is visible although traces of negotiated authenticity (a compromise between objectivist and constructivist schools of thought) are noted at the Sheraton Wild Horse Pass Resort, Culloden House Hotel and The Imperial. Additionally, all the properties practice sincere authenticity. That is, honest narrations are provided, for instance, the Imperial also informs guests of the fact that several art pieces (displayed on the corridors) were collected later from all over India; and that they are not local, colonial, or an integral part of the original structure. Sincere authenticity is thus embraced.

The use of heritage hotels to promote heritage has received mixed support in academic literature. Several negative claims have been made by previous studies with regard to the commodification of heritage and history advocated by heritage hotels.

For instance, Henderson (2001) expresses concern over the precedence given "to making an historic property pay," and the manner in which the past is manipulated through marketing strategies and the sale of souvenirs. Teo and Huang (1995) argue that hotels specifically based on colonial heritage evoke nostalgia for an elite past often disassociated with the life style of locals. Such properties are patronized by a select marginal portion of the local community as is the case of The Imperial in New Delhi.

Also, many heritage hotels are situated on historic sites such as the Culloden House Hotel in Scotland. Today they present commercial opportunities which are often supported by the public sector for dual reasons: economic imperatives and conservation. As noted by Henderson, such buildings serve as "repositories of a country's or region's heritage" (2001: 24). The Imperial and Culloden House Hotel fall into this bracket. The Hozenji Hotel also provides dual benefits: a religious and learning environment for visitors and economic benefits for the monks.

Other debates on contested and dissonant heritage apply to these heritage attractions-cum-lodging establishments as well. For instance, colonial narrations offer a harmonious view of the colonial era. As pointed out by Peleggi, these narratives and tales run counter to the colonial imperialism imposed on developing countries, thereby providing "historical grounds for the celebration of colonialism's good old days" (2005: 264). Such incongruity is overshadowed by its demand sought by the high-end international market. For instance, The Imperial is frequently patronized by diplomats from various countries. Only a limited section of the local community visits the hotel. This finding concurs with Ang's report on the Raffles Hotel in Singapore. The author states that "despite its prominence in the nation's public image, a recent poll indicated that most respondents did not regard the hotel as a 'national heritage' but a relic of Britain's vanished colonial power" (Ang 2005: 264).

Future marketing strategies should be based on a mixed-orientation approach and embrace local elements to promote both social and cultural capital as well as civic engagement. Also, goals such as preserving buildings intact wherever possible and being sensitive to the local context and individual histories can help resolve dissonant heritage issues associated with the history narrations. Although, "not every one's story can be told," a sincere approach can earn accolades and provide credibility to the entire heritage operation.

Questions

1. What can be some of the uses of heritage hotels as a tourism commodity?
2. Which hotel presents the most adherence to SSHTM?
3. One element remiss in all case studies was local community involvement. Think of ways in which heritage hotels can promote civic engagement and tie in with the community.

7 Heritage Festivals

Cultural events such as festivals have become an indispensable part of a destination's tourism product and their significance lies in their ability to extend the tourist season during slow periods, enhance destination image, attract media attention, improve visitor satisfaction or attract high-yield visitors (Getz 1997). The word 'festival' derives from 'feast' and suggests a distinct moment in time for celebration (Derrett 2004). Hughes (1998) describes festivals as a part of special events which concentrate on a special form of activities over a short period of time. Derrett's description is also worthy of notice: "festivals and events provide authenticity and uniqueness, especially with events based on indigenous values; convenient hospitality and affordability; themes and symbols for participants and spectators" (2004: 32–33).

According to Gilbert and Lizotte, 'transience' is the defining characteristic of a festival (1998: 3). This implies that the same sense of celebration, enthusiasm, and pleasure is not easy to maintain for a more frequent or regular event. It is a unique moment of time, a temporary occurrence that is recognized with ceremony and rituals (Goldplatt 1997). Main goals of festivals include sharing of common interests with each other, celebration of a popular art form, and celebration of local culture (Saayman and Saayman 2006). Festivals can thus bring multiple benefits to the host community, such as:

*   Serving the role of image makers and being catalysts for further development;
*   Helping curtail negative impacts of mass visitation and facilitate better community–visitor relations;
*   Extending the tourist season or introducing a 'new season sparkle' into the local environment;
*   Enhancing the community spirit and pride, facilitating cooperation and leadership, enriching cultural traditions, helping control development, and improving social health and ecological quality;
*   Enhancing destination images to mediate the decline process of a destination life-cycle stage and being more likely to provide destination image improvement benefits. Studies also indicate that places which host community events attract a higher visitor base (Mules and Faulkner 1996; Light 1996).

Festivals can be generated by both the private or corporate sectors and the public sector. Festival events can be mega scaled with national or global outreach. They can be developed and organized by entrepreneurs, companies, the local government, the local community or special interest groups. Festivals delivered by special interest groups often aim to "educate wider audience and showcase cultural practice" (Derrett 2004: 35).

Development of festivals, thus, varies depending on the organizer's goals, which can be social, cultural, and/or economic in nature. Local or state governments often take upon themselves to promote festivals. Their interest can be explained by three reasons: economic benefits, intangible social benefits to the local community (Getz 1991; Ritchie 1984; Boo and Busser 2006), and a potential way of extending the shoulder season and viability of destination (Getz and Frisby 1988).

Manning (1983) is of the view that festival celebrations consist of four core elements: performance through the use and display of cultural icons; entertainment as they are fixed within the play concept; public as they take place within a public environment; and participatory because they connect with spectators and require their participation. Evidently then, festivals are an important form of heritage tourism and contribute substantially to the host economy (Chhabra, Healy *et al.* 2003; Lade and Jackson 2000).

Several festival typologies exist in literature. Numerous studies have classified festivals based on government or non-government sponsorship (Lade and Jackson 2004). O'Sullivan and Jackson (2002) identify three types of festivals. Table 7.1 provides details on the characteristics of each of the following festivals (O'Sullivan and Jackson 2002: 330, 331):

1. Home-grown – a home-grown festival is essentially small scale, bottom-up and run by one or more volunteers for the benefit of the locality.
2. Tourist-tempter – a 'tourist-tempter' festival is aimed specifically at attracting visitors with a purpose of boosting local economic development.

Table 7.1 The Festival Typology

	Festival Type 1 'Home-grown'	Festival Type 2 'Tourist-tempter'	Festival Type 3 'Big-bang'
Size by population	Small	Medium	Large
Spatial geography	Rural/Semi-rural	Urban/Urban fringe	Urban
Major theme	Arts/Culture/ Entertainment	Arts/Culture/ Entertainment	Arts/Culture/ Entertainment
Organizing drivers	Community led/ Public and private sector support	Local authority	Partnership driven
Key management group	Voluntary sector driven	Local authority driven	Partnership driven
Primary purpose for holding a festival	Cultural and/or entertainment benefits for locals and visitors	Economic development via tourism	Economic development for partners/cultural and entertainment benefit for locals and visitors

Source: O'Sullivan and Jackson (2002)

3. Big-bang – a 'big-bang' festival is used essentially as a marketing tool to promote numerous related activities over a specific geographical region.

Next, two different lines of inquiry in festival-related literature can be identified: economic impact (Chhabra *et al.* 2002; Kim *et al.* 1998; Walo, Bull and Green 1996) and motives for attending the festival (Crompton and McKay 1997; Formica and Uysal 1996; Uysal, Gahan and Martin 1993). With regard to the former, supposedly beneficial outcomes in terms of economic benefits are often touted by festival organizers. The later centers on different motive-based theoretical frameworks such as push and pull (Klenosky 2002; Sangpikul 2008), Maslow's (1970) hierarchy of needs, and seeking and escaping dimensions (Iso-Ahola 1989)

Extant marketing-related studies in festival literature have centered on motivation, segmentation, and travel and expenditure behavior. The significance of motivation studies are premised on the notion that this information is important for designing tailor-made offerings for festival attendees, as a way to measure their satisfaction, and as a tool for gaining an insight into their decision-making patterns (Li and Petrick 2006; Crompton and McKay 1997). A majority of the motivation-based studies have been drawn from the frameworks grounded in escape-seeking (Iso Ahola 1982, 1989) and push and pull dichotomies (Crompton 1979; Dann 1981). Table 7.2 captures a summary of recent studies on festival motivation. All the listed studies have made pioneer contributions in 1) developing and replicating a motivational research framework and 2) examining relationships between motivational domains and other important attendee characteristics to identify lucrative and desired market segments.

Market segmentation has received abundant attention in festival literature. As pointed out by Saayman and Saayman (2006), it is difficult to serve the complete market. Therefore, it is necessary for festivals to identify lucrative markets and focus on understanding and satisfying their needs. Several studies have indicated significant relationships between socio-demographic characteristics of attendees and festival travel and spending behavior (Walker, Scott-Melnyk and Sherwood 2002; Jang *et al.* 2004; Cai, Hong and Morrison 1995; Fish and Waggle 1996; Cai 1998).

Attendees/customers are thus the cornerstones of market orientation. For this reason, many studies have focused on identifying lucrative current and potential market segments to improve economic benefits and provide tailor-made product so that superior satisfaction can happen. Thrane (2002) has also argued that successful marketing of festivals depends on information about visitor characteristics, motivations, and satisfaction. More recent studies have identified the following to be promising market segments for festival tourism:

- Short-stay versus long-stay visitors (Davies and Mangan 1992);
- High-income and low-income groups (Leones *et al.* 1998);
- High spenders and low spenders (Chhabra *et al.* 2002);
- Place of residence (international or domestic);
- Motivations, and age groups – for instance, older people have shown a higher propensity to spend at festivals (Oppermann 1993).

Table 7.2 Selected Studies on Festival Motivation

Delineated Factors	Researchers
Stimulus seeking; family togetherness; social contact; meeting or observing new people; learning and discovery; escape from personal and social pressures; nostalgia	Ralston and Crompton (1988)
Escape; excitement/thrills; event novelty; socialization; family togetherness	Uysal *et al*. 1993
Socialization; escape; family togetherness; excitement/uniqueness; event novelty	Mohr *et al*. (1993)
Nature appreciation; event excitement; sociability; family togetherness; curiosity; escape	Scott (1996)
Excitement/thrills; socialization; social leisure; entertainment; event novelty; family togetherness	Formica and Uysal (1996)
Family togethernesss/socialization; social leisure; festival attributes; escape; event excitement	Schneider and Backman (1996)
Cultural exploration; novelty/regression; gregariousness; recover equilibrium; known-group socialization	Crompton and McKay (1997)
Socialization/entertainment; event attraction/excitement; group togetherness; cultural/historical; family togetherness; site novelty	Formica and Uysal (1998); Formica and Murrmann (1998)
External interaction/socialization; novelty/uniqueness; escape; family	Nicholson and Pearce (2000, 2001)
Socialization; novelty/uniqueness; entertainment/excitement; escape; family	Wood (2004)
Novelty/uniqueness; socialization; escape; family	Bowen and Daniels (2005)
Specifics/entertainment; escape; variety; novelty/uniqueness; family; socialization	Faulkner *et al*. (1999)
Event novelty; escape; socialization; family togetherness; excitement/thrills	Dewar, Meyer and Li (2001)
Authenticity	Chhabra, Healy *et al*. (2003); Waitt (2000)

Also, several studies have evaluated the effective management of festivals. A festival product is a complex package of services (Wicks and Fesenmaier 1993) and tangible product elements (Getz 1991). For evaluation purposes, Wicks and Fesenmaier (1993) have used features such as attractiveness of the setting, friendliness and helpfulness of the exhibitors, arts and crafts, organization of the event, quality of art, food, entertainment, and information, fair pricing of arts and crafts, restroom quality, accessible parking, and tolerable crowding. In another study by Jeong (1998), evaluation items comprise of the overall program structure and organization, effectiveness of convenience facilities, festival guidance and quality of public facilities, diversity and uniqueness of exhibitions and spectacles, reasonable food prices and easy parking.

Although there is paucity of research that moves beyond the aforesaid marketing topics, some body of work does exist that offers commendable insight into the marketing orientation pursued by festival organizers, information need perspectives, and environment analyses. Fragmented attention is noted on crucial elements of sustainable marketing such as host community relationships, stakeholder collaborations and partnerships, and authenticity and commodification issues. Sustainable economic impact emphasis of festivals has received meager focus. O'Sullivan and Jackson (2002) examine the potential of three festivals in their ability to contribute to the sustainable economic development of the host region. For the most part, the festivals indicate less evidence of efforts that promote sustainable economic development. Also, strategic sustainable marketing (with a long-term focus) has received scant or fragmented attention. No single festival study has made an effort to embrace a holistic view of marketing.

Of the studies that have discussed the significance of pursuing an orientation, marketing emphasis has received paramount attention. For instance, Crompton and Lamb (1986) define key market orientation in festivals within the context of customers' needs and wants. Lade and Jackson (2000) note that most likely philosophies employed by festival organizers range between the marketing and product ideologies. Three dimensions for strategic marketing (customer-oriented) focus reported by Mayfield and Crompton (1995) are worthy of attention:

1. Visitor orientation – dimensions of visitor orientation include listening to visitor opinions, improving quality based on visitor feedback, visitor needs friendly objectives, ideas drawn from visitor information, improvements based on visitor suggestions, understanding visitor needs, including visitor feedback during the planning and development stages, honoring promises made to visitors, and modifying or creating new products based on visitor needs.
2. Pre-experience assessment – pre-experience assessment dimensions include identification of different market segments based on market research and having a research-friendly market program.
3. Post-experience evaluation – post-experience evaluation dimensions include measurement of visitor satisfaction, addressing visitor complaints, measuring advertising effectiveness based on visitor feedback and measuring service quality.

Slater and Narver (1995) argue that a strong market focus based on the identification of consumer needs and the subsequent response to meet those needs leads to satisfaction and enhanced value of the product. This view of a strong relationship between superior performance and strong market orientation is also confirmed by more recent studies (Getz 2002; Kohli and Jaworski 1990; Mehmetoglu and Ellingsen 2005). What is stressed here is the need for ongoing market research to track consumer feedback and evaluation of festivals.

Several studies have agreed that there is a dire need for strategic planning in community festivals as these events continue to show an unprecedented growth. Three crucial steps are suggested by McDonnell, Allen and O'Toole (1999) and Getz (1997) for strategic planning of events:

1. Set up a mission statement which will help set goals.
2. Stress on stakeholder participation during the vision, mission, and goal-setting process.
3. Scan the internal and external environments influencing the organization in charge of the festival.

Of all the heritage institutions examined in this book, festivals are noted for their pronounced emphasis on community involvement and effective stakeholder collaborations. Community involvement and support is in fact a crucial success factor for festivals. McDonnell *et al.* maintain that "each host organization has responsibility to the host community and other stakeholders for effective management whether they are government agencies, participants and spectators, sponsors, the wider business community, employees and volunteers, suppliers or media" (1999: 35). In fact, a festival emerging from within the community is more likely to receive local support as compared to an opposed festival. There is a growing interest and demand for festivals which provide local sense of place and an insight into the host culture. Success factors identified under community participation and involvement in festivals include (Getz 2002; Goldplatt 1997; Lade and Jackson 2000):

*   Volunteer contribution;
*   Local business support;
*   Development and support of local eateries;
*   Local community sponsorship;
*   Local community workshop;
*   Local contribution of private accommodation;
*   Cooperation of local accommodation establishments;
*   Support of local council and government bodies;
*   Community infrastructure and facilities.

Also, partnerships are considered an important element in heritage festivals. This view is confirmed by Spiropoulos, Gargalianos and Sotiriadou (2006) who state that the successful management of ethnic festivals in multicultural societies often involves strong partnerships between diverse organizations and interest groups belonging to diverse ethnic backgrounds and performing a broad spectrum of functioning roles. According to Getz (1997), stakeholder identification and classification are critical for an effective performance of a festival. These are also crucial in identifying features in the internal and external environments that influence the festival.

Stakeholders can be defined as those groups or people who have a stake in the festival and its outcomes (Getz 1997). Several categorizations of stakeholders are provided in event management literature. For instance, taking a social perspective, Shone and Parry (2001) categorize stakeholders into public, private, and voluntary sectors. McDonnell *et al.* (1999) provide a functional angle and divide stakeholders into the six groupings. See Figure 7.1 for more details. Joint coordination between stakeholders has also been proven to strengthen community cohesion.

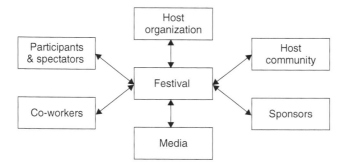

Figure 7.1 The Relation of Stakeholders to Festivals
Adapted from McDonnell *et al.* (1999: 39)

Another significant potential of ethnic festivals has been found to be in its contribution toward the preservation of cultural traditions (Mayfield and Crompton
1995). As reiterated by Spiropoulos *et al.*, ethnic festivals "have an important role
in perpetuating subcultures in the US and offer an opportunity to search out disap-
pearing immigrant customs that people have brought with them in the nature of celebration" (2006: 173). Furthermore, ethnic festivals celebrated away from the
place of origin serve as facilitators of nationhood feeling and patriotism among
immigrants settled in another country. This view is echoed by Bakirathi (2002) in
her study of the South Asian festivals in the United States. She reports that such
events strengthen patriotism among first- and second-generation South Asian
immigrants to the United States.

Nevertheless, the complex role of festivals in representations and narratives of
local culture has received critical examination in academic literature. For instance,
the cultural politics of representation are examined by Labrador (2002). As another
example, Quemuel (1996) uses the Katipunan festival to illustrate the political
functionality of ethnic festivals. Labrador finds representation to have a dual meaning in the context of ethnic festivals. One meaning is associated with the question
of who has the legitimate power to represent whom and the second meaning refers
to a say "in the allocation and redistribution of resources" (Labrador 2002: 300). In
other words, the second meaning refers to the degree of participation and relative
power compared to other groups in the political and the economic allotment
scheme of the festival.

Also, it has been purported that festivals commodify local culture. In fact, this
issue has been the subject of extensive discussion in festival and heritage tourism
literature. Festival commodification in the form of presentation of modified products and traditions to match customer needs is a discursive topic today. This is
attributed to the fact that often an authenticity yardstick is used to measure the
extent of commodification. Authenticity has evolved and today its multiple connotations are debated as stated earlier in this book. One of the postmodern schools of
thought place emphasis on the existentialist form of authenticity: authenticity of the

self and one's state of mind captured in a serendipitous moment. In his noteworthy analysis of festival commodification, Matheson (2005) centers discussion on the tourism commodification process and authenticity within the context of a Celtic festival.

In a nutshell, festivals are about identity, in terms of the nation-state, a sense of place, and the individual and diverse identities of people. Festivities provide a way to decode the inner composition and functions of a society. They are also subject to external pressures that might dictate identity formulations and core representations. Last, as pointed out by Matheson, "festivals can be a battleground where the politics of authenticity are played out" (2005: 151). It has often been contended that commodification poses a barrier to authentic social relations (Selwyn 1996). According to Cohen, "commodification is a process by which things (and activities) come to be evaluated primarily in terms of their exchange value, in a context of trade, thereby becoming goods; developed exchange systems in which exchange value of things (activities) is stated in terms of prices form a market" (1988: 380). This meaning has been extensively debated in literature. Against capitalist notions of commodification, it has been argued that use or symbolic value of a commodity can also be traded in exchange for a counterpart (Kopytoff 1986).

The Commodification Debate

Many commentators have argued that the commodification process has had a devastating impact on the authenticity of a heritage commodity (Greenwood 1977) with "a classic interpretation that host communities commodify culture and traditions for economic gains" (Matheson 2005: 153). Within the context of festivals, it is decreed that commodification "places authenticity of social relations and cultural rituals in jeopardy" (Taylor 2001: 13). According to Greenwood, "commodification of culture in effect robs people of the very meaning by which they organize their lives" (1977: 137). That said, counter arguments also abound in literature. For instance, it is argued that festivals enhance and revive traditions (Halewood and Hannam 2001). The host culture also utilizes commodification to meet its goals such as local comradeship and community identity. Hence, commodification can also prove to be beneficial provided it is initiated from within the local community and not imposed by outsiders, foreign to the host culture. In line with the foregoing view, MacAloon claims that festivals are "occasions where as a culture or society we can reflect upon and define ourselves, dramatize our collective myths and history, present ourselves with alternatives, and eventually change in some ways while remaining the same in others" (1984: 1).

Theory of sociability is one framework which can explain the positive effects of commodification. Festivals are often an alternative form of consumption where social experiences are consumed for "self actualization or authentic self making purposes" (Maffesoli 1996). Identity structures are spontaneously formed in self-enhancement experiences and this explains the construction of a neo-tribalism community. A neo-tribe at its core implies that "an individual embarks on a simplified mode of living, albeit temporarily to satisfy an existential quest for self-making. Within a temporary festival structure, it is a 'time' and 'place' outside of the confines of the everyday, it is a 'space' for the existential self to come into play" (Matheson 2005: 158). In his study of the Celtic festival, Matheson finds that:

> Commodification did affect the festival product and type of musical provision, thereby illustrating the conflicts in tourism-arts relationship. However, this did not negate the authenticity of social relations sought by the attendees. Participation was freely given to attendees and there was little in the way of boundaries within the social space of folk music. In effect, there was no front stage that people attempted to get behind. The accessibility of the backstage region engendered the level of social relations within them, of which there were three dimensions: first through participation in 'real' culture in an intimate environment; second, by playing an instrument or swinging; third through hardening of social networks. Music drew people together into an affective alliance of a neo-tribe and the level of social relations within was neither fiction nor fake, but authentic. Acts of cultural consumption are class bound and celebrants are realizing the existential authentic self through acts of participation in the festival. (2005: 160–161)

Last but not the least, there is also an issue of whether to describe festivals as rituals or spectacles. According to Manning, "a spectacle is a large-scale extravagant cultural production that is replete with striking visual imagery and dramatic action that is watched by a mass audience" (1992: 292). Spectacles are non-participatory in nature and are thus staged. Rituals are described as performances that consist of "invariant sequences of formal acts and utterances not encoded by performers" (Rappaport 1992: 20). Festivals usually consist of both. "The ritual elements are linked to transformation and rites of passage, and are geared toward the transformation of society. The spectacles, on the other hand, are a more passive form of celebration, which hold up a mirror to society" (Manning 1992: 260).

Greenwood (1977) laments that the original ritual function of festivals has moved to increasing spectacularization leading to loss of meaning for local communities and less interest in the cultural rituals and more emphasis on commoditization. Some festivals provide a more nuanced view of contemporary relationships between modernity, tradition, and cultural festivals while others do not follow a strong dichotomy between modernity and traditions and advocate 'festive sociability' (Greenwood 1977: 262). As noted by Richards, "one of the underpinnings of the commoditization argument is that cultural events have increasingly become oriented toward the needs of visitors or tourists rather than local residents. However, the extent to which this is true depends on the type of event being considered" (1996: 265). The 'socialization' function of festivals cannot be ignored. For instance, in a Spanish festival contest, the "reclamation of tradition and cultural celebrations became part of a civic project to build social cohesion and to forge Catalan identity" (Richards 1996: 272). In such cases, a socialization approach to cultural events can prove to be far more effective in enhancing the community development portfolio. Festivals and short-term events can thus help to build social capital.

In this chapter, three popular festivals are examined using the proposed sustainable marketing portfolio: Grandfather Mountain Highland Games, North Carolina, USA; Kumbh Mela, Allahabad, India; and Day of the Dead festival in Mexico. All three include characteristics of both home-grown and tourist-tempter categories. A vast range of stakeholders are more evident in the case of Grandfather Mountain Highland Games and the Kumbh Mela while the Day of the Dead festival is more of a public sector phenomenon (that is, created and promoted mostly by the government).

Grandfather Mountain Highland Games, North Carolina, USA

Grandfather Mountain Highland Games in Linville, North Carolina, are one of the oldest and most visited games in the United States. They host annual meetings of many nationwide clan societies. Grandfather Mountain Highland Games (GMHG) are held annually on MacRae Meadows on the slopes of Grandfather Mountain. This setting closely resembles the Highland landscape of Scotland. The GMHG office reported 15,000 visitors in 1996 while a further increase in visitation to 30,000 visitors was reported in 1998, and 1999 witnessed 40,000 visitors (GMHG office, 1999). The number of visitors has grown since 1999. The key target markets at the GMHG have been mostly families and baby boomers. In the recent years, the GMHG has diversified its programs to attract Generation X. Also, a diverse range of children activities are now offered to invest into the future adults of the United States.

The mission statement of GMHG is: to carry on and promote the annual Grandfather Mountain Highland Games and Gathering of Scottish Clans, to foster and restore interest in traditional dancing, piping, drumming, athletic achievement, music and Gaelic culture, and to establish scholarship funds to assist students from Avery County High School to study at American colleges and universities. The guiding principles are (GMHG 2009):

- We will continually strive to improve our Scottish games and relationship to those involved, the safety of our events and good fiscal stewardship.
- We will pursue excellence in all we do and remain focused on those we serve and to more fully meet the cultural and educational expectations of all who attend and are involved in our event.
- We will work as a team for our ultimate mission and to achieve mutual and agreed upon goals through trust and respect in our team approach.
- We will continue our tradition of excellence through activities that demonstrate that we care for the environment around us and for the people who attend our events.
- We will maintain a strong and frugal financial policy in order to better serve and to help achieve our cultural and educational goals.
- We will never compromise our integrity. Our decisions and actions will show all that we have the highest ethical and moral standards.

Environment Analysis and Research Plan

Although environment analysis does not feature formally in the festival management portfolio, there are economic, political, natural, and technological factors that inform several events and marketing strategies employed by the GMHG. For instance, refinement of the GMHG website helps inform visitors of the purpose and festival schedule every year. Weather factors are taken into consideration when planning events. In regard to research, the Highland Games office supports student research projects to elicit information on GMHG visitors. Secondary research is also used to compute visitor statistics based on onsite ticket sales, volunteer observations, member information, etc. (Chhabra, Sills *et al.* 2003)

Distribution and Promotion Strategies

The GMHG has used both direct and indirect channels to distribute its annual festival information. These have included other Highland games in the United States, clan newsletters, the Grandfather Mountain, the State Tourism office, and the Boone Convention and Visitors Bureau. The GMHG has used personal selling, public relations, and publicity. Word of mouth is also a strong promotional tool. The GMHG considers word-of-mouth publicity to be an important promotional tool and this is facilitated by providing consistent service quality every year. Sporadically, other promotional strategies are used (such as advertisement in the local newspapers and Highland Games magazines). Websites have proved to be an important tool for promotion.

Local Community Involvement

The GMHG uses volunteers from the local community to help to successfully manage the festival and the local and tourist traffic. However, with regard to local community involvement in planning and designing the festival, a tokenism approach is employed. The festival has a board which makes all important decisions regarding the core elements of the GMHG.

Partnerships and Coordination

The GMHG scores high on this element. It has a variety of non-profit and for profit partners who help to accomplish sustainable success. A variety of services by local agencies such as Crossnore Volunteer Fire Department (shuttle bus service), Linville Central Rescue Squad (parking, concessions, first aid tent), Newland Volunteer Fire Department (concessions, first responder), Hospice of Avery (concessions, handicap helpers), Avery Citizens Against Domestic Abuse (ticket sales, checkers and greeters), and Kiwanis of Banner Elk (souvenir program sales). Other examples of coordination are with the Boone Convention and Visitors Bureau, the Grandfather Mountain management, and the local schools.

Conservation and Authenticity

Chhabra, Sills *et al*. (2003) had noted that the GMHG are staged authenticity since they are reconstructed to instill nostalgic memories of the Scottish Highland past. Nevertheless, the authenticity of the games is consistently maintained by carefully selecting activities and events and involving pioneers from Scotland. Their non-nprofit nature also ensures that guidelines, relevant to the core values advocated by the festival, are followed. These games offer an opportunity to Scottish Americans to investigate their genealogy. Several events offered at the GMHG endorse its authenticity such as Highland dancing and the parade of the tartans. Also, interaction with fellow clan members is considered an authentic activity because it can be traced back to Scottish history when interaction with fellow clan members was the most important aspect of the Highland gatherings. Festivals such as the GMHG are held to promote nostalgia for the past and strengthen their cultural ties. What is staged is then not all pseudo and contrived because it includes essential ingredients of the original tradition (Chhabra, Sills *et al*. 2003).

Interpretation and Visitor Mindfulness

Interpretation techniques include signs, brochures, narrations and one-on-one con-servations with various clan members. Visitor engagement with Scottish culture is also evident in music and dance lessons offered to interested the audience at the introductory level. Hands-on activities are also offered to kinds. Additionally, sev-eral events display Scottish rituals. Visitor mindfulness is enhanced by the overall ambience, the traditional Scottish dress worn by patrons and many in the audience, and the topography provided by the festival site.

Kumbh Mela, Allahabad, India

The Kumbha Mela (festival) is one of the largest religious gatherings in the world. Its mission is to represent religious beliefs and practices of Indian tradition. It is held every twelve years in Allahabad, located in the State of Uttar Pradesh (UP). Allahabad is considered a holy site because of the confluence of the three holy rivers of India: the Ganges, Yumuna, and Saraswati. Kumbha Mela is revered as a sacred religious pilgrimage of the Hindus. The period during which it takes place is blessed with an auspicious planetary alignment (in the same position) that is believed to medicate the Ganges waters and change the river into nectar. It is based on planetary alignment that happens every twelve years. More than 10 million people visit this festival. According to the UP Tourism Office, more than 30 million pilgrims visited Allahabad to take a dip in the Ganges in 2001 and approximately one million of these were foreigners. The key activity is a ritual bath in the river. Other activities include religious discussions, singing by devotees, and religious gatherings where doctrines are argued and harmonized (standardized).

It is believed that a person obtains liberation if he/she takes a bath at the Sangam (confluence) of the Ganges, Yamuna and underground Saraswati on one of the

Plate 7.1 Kumbh Mela Bathing

main recommended main bathing days (see Plate 7.1). One's sins are washed away and the bathing is believed to benefit eighty-eight ancestral generations. During the festival, a huge temporary city is built to host millions of pilgrims that come for the most auspicious bathing days. Kumbha Mela resembles Yogi congregation, where yogis, devotees, preachers, priests, sadhus (saints), holy people, and pilgrims descend from all over India. Many sadhus arrive from different holy places, the most secluded forests, and mountain caves from the Himalayas. The most famous are the sadhus seen dressed in saffron sheets and their skin is covered with ashes and powder as per the ancient traditions (see Plate 7.2).

In sum, the festival is a blend of religious and culture traits created by an atmosphere of chiming bells, incense and flower fragrance, Vedic chants, colorful costumes, beating of drums, etc. Kumbh Mela can be of two types: Maha Kumbh that is held every twelve years and Ardh Kumbh every six years. Allahabad is famous for the Maha Kumbh Mela which runs for over a month. It is considered a once in a lifetime event and is one of the largest gathering in the world. Prayag in Allahabad is the place where the three holy rivers meet. It is considered a holy place by the devotees.

Environment Analysis and Research

Efforts are being made by the festival management to accommodate contemporary macro environment factors such as demographic changes and preferences, economic situation, politics and technology. According to a recent report (Kumbh Mela Report 2009):

Plate 7.2 Sadhus in Kumbh Mela

The older generation of the present society is very keen in this regard but the younger generation does not seem interested or does not have enough time to look into these affairs. Due to advancement of modern technologies and in the age of high materialistic culture, our ideas and sentiments are sometimes bound to shrink. So this is very important that a fruitful creative dialogue should be established between the older and younger generation to save our rich cultural heritage.

Distribution and Promotion Strategies

The festival is a popular international event. The indirect distribution channels include the Uttar Pradesh Tourism Office, travel agents and tour operators, and many international organizations such as the UNESCO. The festival receives heavy publicity because of its religious, spiritual, astronomical, and historical significance, from the local, national, and international press. Public relation activities include close contact with the various publics involved and others interested in the festival.

Community Involvement, Partnerships and Collaboration

The Department of Culture, Government of Uttar Pradesh is the main agency in Uttar Pradesh which promotes cultural events. The department acts as a facilitator to ensure coordination between various stakeholders, other concerned departments in the government, NGOs, religious associations, and the Hindu community of India, both rural and urban.

Authenticity and Conservation

The festival relies on object and negotiated versions of authenticity to project itself. Object elements are guided by the fundamental religious tenets which have been carried over many centuries. Hence old principles are used to authenticate the festival. This view is confirmed by the description and narration of activities provided in Box 7.1.

Traces of negotiated authenticity are also evident in the narratives adapted to various types of visiting audience. Additionally, continued adherence to the traditional activities confirms support for objective authenticity such as:

Box 7.1 Authentic Elements of Kumbh Mela

- Mahakumbh is a religious congregation in which millions of people assemble for bathing in Sangam on the five auspicious days of Magh (January–February). People from all over world come to Prayag in this holy month to attain spiritual power and meditation.
- This festival combines many aspects of the society. In Indian society, theories of Varna, Ashram and Purushartha are well known. Four Purusharthas – Dharma, Arth, Kama and Moksha – are defined as a base of life in which Dharma and Moksha are closely inter-related.
- According to Hindu philosophy of life, everybody should follow the doctrine of Dharma and try to achieve Moksha in his life. The assemblage in such holy places like Prayagraj is considered the most authentic way to accomplish these goals. Procession of Nagas and Sadhus at Sangam symolizes a special religious significance. This place reverberates with vedic hymns, mantras, chiming bells, fragrance of incense and followers. It depicts the rich Indian culture in all its grandeur and magnificent manner to the visitors.
- This mega event is full of devotion and ritualistic performances, religious preachings, Rasa-leela and Ram-leela, Naga processions, Hathyogies and other folk forms of any Mela. During the icy cold season in the month of Magh (January–February) naked nagas and sadhus proceed in a procession for a holy dip in Sangam.
- Ordinary people Kalpavasis, and other piligrims also take baths daily during Kumbh Mela. Ritual performances of Kalpavasis, Bhajans and Aarti are the main attraction of this Mela. Many Hathyogies are easly seen in their typical Sadhana.

Source: Kumbh Mela Report (2009)

- The main bathing ceremony;
- Shahi Procession of Nagas/Sadhus for a holy dip at the Sangam;
- Month-long rigorous Kalpavasa by Kalpavasis, residing in the camps of Magh Mela;
- Traditional prayer rituals such as Pooja, Bhajan, Arti at least twice a day;
- Religious performances such as Ram-leela, Rasa-leela, Pravachan, etc.;
- Craft fair;
- Cultural programs based on religion.

With regard to conservation strategies, several recent and current efforts to safeguard the element include:

- The District Administration of Allahabad, with the help of Department of Urban Development, Government of Uttar Pradesh and Magh Mela Samiti, Allahabad organizes this Mega Religious Event.
- Shahi procession (carnival) of Nagas and Sadhus proceeding for a holy dip in Sangam is the main attraction. Rural people, such as the Kalpavasis, perform month-long daily rituals in their camps and on the confluence of Sangam; this forms another remarkable feature of the Mahakumbh festival. The devotees, Kalpavasis and pilgrims are engaged in several religious activities as participants or viewers. Examples include: Pooja-archana, Bhajan, Aarti, Pravachan, Raas-leela and Ram-leela, etc.They ensure all possible measures are in place to provide an authentic experience. Other safeguarding measures include the following instructions (Kumbh Mela Report 2009):

  - Seminars and symposia, to safeguard the element Awareness Programs regarding Mahakumbh, should be organized;
  - Special awareness programs need to be conducted to ensure the maximum participation of the younger generation;
  - Multimedia presentations, audio-video CDs and documentary films should be prepared;
  - Books, posters, handbills, brochures, etc. should be published and distributed;
  - Programs – plastic arts and visual arts should be organized.

Day of the Dead Festival, Huaquechula, Mexico

Day of the Dead is a popular festival in Mexico and refers to the period between October 31 and November 2. It celebrates and honors the dead ones in the family. The underlying belief is that during the selected period, the spirits of the loved ones return to the Earth to be with their families. The celebration centers around building home altars and decorating the tombs of the dead. The spirits are greeted with food and other favorite offerings of the deceased. This ritual is celebrated in diverse ways in various regions of Mexico. Nutini describes the Day of the Dead as a ritual that represents "a time of homecoming, remembering, and propitiating the dead, cementing and intensifying one's kinship and compadarazgo (ritual kinship) relationships, and sacralizing albeit temporarily, interpersonal relationships on a community wide basis" (1988: 57).

In the south of Mexico, the festival is more colorful, whereas in rural areas it is more sober. Regardless of the region, all Mexicans visit the graves of their loved ones, decorate them, and spend time there. It is, in fact, the most famous holiday in Mexico and has become a popular tourist attraction. During this time, many foreign visitors go to the country to enjoy the spectacular display of ritual performances and artistic decorations. This ritual, however, continues to change due to mixing of cultures and customs. Nevertheless, it is ardently supported and promoted by the Mexican government. Huaquechula is a small Mixtec Indian village located in the south-central part of the Puebla State. This town is known for its designer skills. For instance, some altars include a mirror which symbolizes 'a projection into nothingness.'

Although it was not possible to elicit most of the marketing-related information from the festival organizers, a review of multiple sources offers useful insights. Day of the Dead at Huaquechula is attended by both heritage and recreationist tourists. Some are driven by the quest to witness pre-Hispanic authenticity. This event is promoted through public relations and publicity. The government attends and supports the event for promotional reasons. Challenges to conservation include lack of funding and the spectacular nature of the event. However, monetary contributions of tourists are meager. Infrastructure issues continue. According to Cano and Mysyk (2004), this event is not originally pre-Hispanic in a primitive sense. Its ideology and beliefs are drawn from the pre-Hispanic era, while from a structural perspective it is more or less a combination of pre-Hispanic and Spanish Catholic elements. However, today is being promoted by the Mexican government as a pre-Hispanic festival.

Summary and Conclusions

It appears that the GMHG and the Kumbh Mela are more inclined toward pursuing a mix of marketing, social marketing, and product/manufacturing philosophies. Educating the audience is also a pronounced priority here. Additionally, relationship building is the focus of GMHG as 50 percent of the visitors are repeat and the organizers are keen to secure long-term connections with the visiting audience. Traces of tribal marketing emphasis are evident in the Kumbh festival as efforts exist to promote a 'communitas' feeling among the visiting audience. The Day of the Dead festival is more of a personal family event, although it has been spectacularized and commodified to attract tourists and promote community cohesion. Hence this festival appears to place more emphasis on the marketing philosophy.

All three festivals discussed in this chapter are geared toward both the local community and the tourists. Of the three, Kumbh Mela is unique because it is held every twelve years and promotes both pilgrimage tourism and heritage tourism. Economic numerations appear to motivate the public sector support for the Day of the Dead festival and this motive also finds partial support in the objectives of the

GMHG, although the later is a non-profit event. As far as the Kumbh festival is concerned, it contains a strong religious element in it and the pilgrims form a part of the spectacle for the heritage tourists. In the recent years, the UP government has also reflected keen interest to make this festival an important component of the heritage tourism portfolio in the state.

It can also be noted that object authenticity is a distinctive feature of all three festivals. The focus here is on ancient traditions. This is not to say that traces of negotiated versions are not visible. For instance, the GMHG also desires to attract a broad spectrum of tourists and has diversified its product to capture the interest of emerging markets. Festivals such as the Scottish Highland Games and the Kumbh Mela provide an excellent case study to serve as a guide for future festival promotions. Such festivals enhance the tourist appeal of their host regions and encourage repeat visitation and loyalty. Both strive to offer consistency in the quality of service to encourage repeat patronage. Preservation and restoration goals are pursued by the GMHG and the Kumbh. The Day of the Dead festival is more of reconstruction of spectacle in publicly visible areas.

Short-term events such as festivals are important elements of heritage tourism. Such forms of heritage tourism provide economic benefits and cultural sustainability to local communities. Demand for such cultural and heritage travel offerings is likely to continue (Bowen and Daniels 2005).

Questions

1. What is the most popular type of festival classification reported by documented literature?
2. Briefly describe the authenticity ideology pursued by Grandfather Mountain Highland Games.
3. What are the three popular dimensions of strategic planning pursued by festivals?

8 Heritage Tourism Merchandise

For today's travelers, tourism and shopping are inseparable activities. In fact, shopping is considered the most preferred activity and an extremely important aspect of tourism (Law and Au 2000). From a heritage tourism perspective, it serves as a motivating factor for heritage travel (Timothy 2005). Many researchers claim that without shopping activity, a heritage tour cannot be a complete traveling experience (Cohen 2000; Kent, Shock and Snow 1983; Keowin 1989; Hitchcock and Teague 2000). As noted by Swanson, it is human nature to return from travel with a souvenir to serve as a "reminder of special moments or events" (2004: 363). Graburn states that "few tourists come home from vacation without something to show ... as proof that they really did make the journey (1987: 395). The Travel Industry Association of America (2008a) reports that tourists spend one-third of their tourism expenditures on shopping, thereby demonstrating a high propensity to spend while on vacation. It is also an established fact that most heritage tourists have high disposable incomes and are inclined to make more purchases than their counterparts (Silberberg 1995; Chhabra *et al.* 2002; Chhabra 2005). Shopping of heritage merchandise serves many functions:

- Providing economic numerations in the area of production, distribution, and retailing (Timothy and Boyd 2003).
- Building a favorable image of the visited destination (Chhabra, Healy *et al.* 2003; Hitchcock and Teague 2000).
- Serving as a cultural marker and a medium through which economic, social, and cultural values of a destination or community are conveyed (Cohen 2000; Halewood and Hannam 2001).
- Providing a distinctive competitive advantage to a tourism destination (Cohen 1993a; Revilla and Dodd 2003; Esperanza 2008).

Earlier research on heritage tourism merchandise has mainly centered on souvenirs. In fact, the notion of sacredness illustrates the souvenir phenomena (Gordon 1986). The sacredness theory implies that tourism allows individuals to move temporarily from their routine life to experience something exotic, extraordinary, and be in a sacred state. Because the tourist cannot stay in this state forever, they need a tangible piece of the extraordinary in the form of a souvenir to remind themselves of their unique experience. Souvenirs are thus universally related with tourism as a commercially produced and purchased object and have always been an important part of the tourism experience (Jansen-Verbeke 1998). It is of no surprise then that much of the literature on heritage tourism merchandise has sought to explore souvenirs.

This chapter commences by nesting heritage buying within the broader context of the tourism shopping phenomenon. It is argued that the broad picture can assist in drawing specific inferences to the heritage tourism merchandising process. Next, an overview of research studies on souvenirs and other categories of heritage merchandise is provided. This is followed by an insight into the marketing strategies pursued by suppliers of three unique and most popular kinds of heritage merchandise: Kashmiri shawls, Canadian totems, and Scottish tartans.

Heritage Shopping

Before embarking into the intricacies and complexities associated with the heritage tourism merchandise process, it is important first to gain an insight into the overall shopping phenomenon associated with tourism in general. As stated earlier, shopping has become the most preferred consumptive activity among tourists, both domestic and international, in most countries across the globe. For instance, Tourism Research Australia (2006) reports that shopping is the second most preferred activity among international visitors to Australia. Almost 82 percent of the international tourists to Australia shop for pleasure. Shopping is also one of the top motivators for travel in Great Britain (VisitBritain 2009). Similar activity trends are reported by the Travel Industry Association of America (2009).

Scholarly views have extended shopping beyond the conventional utilitarian perspective and it has become known that it is also driven by intrinsic motivations and desire for hedonic experiences (Bloch, Ridgway and Nelson 1991; Baker 2000). The status of shopping as a serious leisure activity is reiterated by Timothy (2005) and Chhabra (2005). Timothy is of the view that the following intrinsic and extrinsic attributes make shopping leisurely (2005: 12):

- Intrinsic – among the intrinsic variables, the following exert a significant influence: demographic and psychographic characteristics, personal needs, cultural background and perceived and expected outcomes of consumers.
- Extrinsic – under this category, primary influences consist of retail venue features, the destination and its characteristics, customer service and retail management, price and product related attributes.

Shopping behavior is thus motivated by both utilitarian and leisure needs. Carr (1990) presents a functional-leisure shopping spectrum which shows that the shopping behavior may be described by different levels of functionality and leisure. Four key points exist along Carr's continuum: quartermastering, technical, expressive, and recreational. Quartermastering represents the routine buying of necessary items and technical refers to the purchase of mechanical items that perform a utilitarian function such as cars, bicycles, refrigerators, etc. Expressive shopping refers to a more leisured state as progress is made toward the leisure end of the spectrum; it consists of purchasing those goods that can help portray a desired image.

Examples include designer clothing, jewelry, sports cars, etc. Finally, recreational shopping occurs when the activity is solely pursued for leisure motivations. In combination with leisure time, a tripartite typology of environments associated with leisure shopping was proposed by Johnson and Howard (1990):

- Ambient leisure – this environment aims to provide a pleasant and enhanced leisure experience with an objective to draw visitors from other competing shopping venues. Also, efforts are made to make them shop for an extended length of time.
- Magnet leisure – this form constitutes the new leisure shopping mall where dual activities are provided: recreation and leisure.
- Heritage-destination leisure – in this environment, historic settings form the main attraction and "nearby shops and eating establishments feast off the traffic" (Timothy 2005: 25). Examples include historic cities where shopping venues or opportunities are provided/located adjacent to cathedrals, temples, museums, and historic houses.

The magnet shopping concept can be further extended to embrace impulse shopping. Impulse shopping is an important source of income for retailers. It is not planned and happens when a decision to purchase something is made after the shopper has entered, for instance, a souvenir store (Bellenger, Robertson and Hirschman 1978). Several forms of impulsive purchasing are reported by literature such as pure impulse buying, reminder impulse purchasing, suggestion impulse buying, and planned impulse purchases. Pure impulse purchases occur when shoppers are inside the store and spurred by the in-store stimuli. Reminder form of buying happens when memory of a need is evoked on seeing a product at the store. Suggestion type refers to a need arousal upon seeing a product and planned impulse purchases occur when a tourist enters a store with a specific aim in mind but is not sure of the brand. As Figure 8.1 demonstrates, numerous factors facilitate impulsive buying.

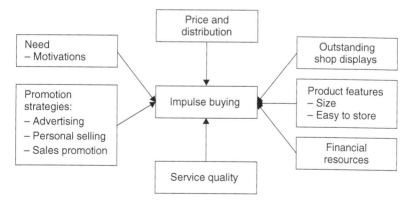

Figure 8.1 Factors Contributing to Impulse Shopping
Source: After Stern (1962)

Heritage tourism merchandise shopping destinations include shopping malls, festivals and events, museums and historic houses, rural and urban villages, hotels and resorts, conference centers, airport shops, bus station shops, cruise ships, railway stations, the Internet, and cross-border venues. Cross-border shopping has, in fact, received considerable attention in the recent decades and refers to shopping in border areas of different towns, provinces, counties, states, and countries. It is premised on the notion of outshopping which denotes domestic cross-border shopping outside the shopper's home environment (Timothy 2005). International cross-border shopping is a popular phenomenon and is commonly referred to as a tourism activity and people who indulge in it are called international arrivals (Jansen-Verbeke 1990; Timothy 2002). Door to cross-frontier consumption can be accessed if the environment across the border is unique to the shopper and has comparably lower exchange rates and taxes, a wide range of merchandise exists, extended hours of regulation, relaxed entry regulations, and an enjoyable environment (Timothy 2005). Most popular international cross-border shopping destinations include Switzerland–Italy, Switzerland–France, Germany–Austria, Canada–USA, Mexico–USA, and England–France (Timothy 2005).

Extant literature claims that numerous motivations entice heritage tourists to shop. These include prestige, nostalgia, vanity, and lower prices (Butler 1991). Travel Industry Association of America (2001) reports the following motivations in order of importance: something to do, to buy something for others, the event or holiday required buying, desire to buy a souvenir, and like to shop. Adding to this list, the following factors are also reported by documented literature: quest for authenticity, functional needs, altruism, culture, and nationality. Altruism is driven by the desire to support a specific cause such as a charitable foundation, conservation movement, or a religious association. Also, Timothy (2005) notes that certain nationalities are devoted to shopping and have earned the status of being ardent and consistent tourist shoppers.

Souvenirs as Heritage Tourism Merchandise

As noted earlier, souvenirs are the most commonly purchased heritage category of items across the world and are a dominant element of the tourism system. They can be described as mementos, popular keepsakes, etc. They offer a range from primitive handicrafts to mass-manufactured items. The commonly used classification of souvenirs is the one suggested by Gordon (1986). He presents five types of souvenirs: pictorial, piece of rock, symbolic shorthand, markers, and local products. Examples under each category are given below:

- Pictorial – postcards, books, and photographs.
- Piece-of-rock – rocks, shells, plants, wood, fossils, bones, and pinecones.
- Symbolic shorthand – replicas of famous attractions, miniature images, and manufactured items that represent images of the place where they are purchased.
- Markers – these are not representative of the place but marked with words and logos such as coffee mugs, coasters, shot glasses, and spoons.

- Local products – these are indicative of local merchandise such as food, drinks, cooking utensils, clothing, and handicrafts.
- Non-local products – to the above list can be added the non-local handicrafts and craftwork category. These are imported from countries which form the ancestral home of immigrants settled in another nation. That is, these products are brought from the place of origin.

It is posited that pictorial, symbolic shorthand, and local and non-local product types of souvenirs such as handicrafts and other pieces of ancient art serve as important icons of the past as they are a symbolic representation of socio-cultural assets of different communities across the globe. In fact, handicrafts and art form the most common types of souvenirs (Timothy 2005). Handicrafts can be defined as merchandise that is made by hand with a special focus on design and raw material. Popular examples include textiles, pottery, baskets, figurines, wood carvings, and jewelry. In fact, handicrafts have become the largest source of income in the developing world after agriculture. Historically, handicrafts were produced to fulfill functional and ceremonial needs within a specific community (Popelka and Littrell 1991). Economic necessity forced craft producers to seek tourism markets and satisfy a heritage tourism need. Art in the Americas has been broadly classified into four categories based on its meaning, utility, artist perceptions, and the relationship the artist has with the consumer (Feest 1992):

- Tribal art – this form serves functional utility for the tribal groups. The core purpose of its production is its usefulness.
- Ethnic art – this kind of artwork is created for use by other ethnic groups. It has become a source of revenue and also a symbol of the artisan's ethnic identity.
- Pan-Indian art – this form is the outcome of demand external to the local region. It is made to meet that demand and is modified to match consumer needs.
- Indian mainstream art – Timothy explains that this "work is created by artists who just happen to be Indians. Each artist has his/her own expressions and the theme of their work may be based in part at least on their ethnic heritage." (2005: 107)

Previous literature has also examined factors that have led to transformation in handicrafts and art forms. It is noted that multiple factors, both internal and external, have changed the form and functionality of traditional handicrafts and arts and lead to their commercialization and commodification (Cohen 2000). Airport art or tourist art is the outcome of this commodification process (Graburn 1976). Cohen conducted an extensive examination of folk crafts in Thailand and identified multiple factors that led to changes in their development and production. Two paths stand out in souvenir research explorations: producer and vendor strategies, and consumer preferences and behavior. Along the first path, researchers have examined producers and retailer environments and issues (Cohen 1992; Chhabra 2005). The second path centers on the tourist consumers of souvenirs. Explorations within the second context delineate into meanings that tourists attach to souvenirs (Bentor 1993; Gordon 1986; Littrell 1990; Wallendorf and Arnould 1988); motivations (Bansal and Eiselt 2004; Crompton 1979; Josiam, Mattson and Sullivan 2004; Swanson 2004; Swanson and Horridge 2006); influence of product preferences on travel behavior (Graburn 1989; Littrell *et al.* 1994; Moscardo and Pearce 1999); debates on souvenir authenticity (Cohen 1988; Cohen 2000; Littrell *et al.* 1993; Chhabra 2005; Hitchcock and Teague 2000); and influence of socio-economic characteristics on souvenir purchase intention and behavior (Anderson and Littrell 1995, 1996). Many of the aforesaid studies have direct or direct implications on the heritage tourism merchandise marketing process.

With regard to consumer characteristics, several typologies of shoppers are documented. One of the earliest typologies was presented by Stone (1954). Stone suggested four types of consumers: economic shoppers, personalizing shoppers, ethical shoppers, and apathetic shoppers. Lesser and Hughes (1986) reported seven categories of shoppers: active, service, traditional, dedicated fringe, price, transitional, convenience and unclassified. Other classifications include Finn, McQuilty and Rigby's (1994) five categories of mall-based shoppers: light consumers, multiple consumers, leisure users, social users, and combined purpose consumers. Light consumers shop with a specific goal in mind, multiple consumers tend to purchase multiple items from different stores or one store, leisure users are driven by recreation and entertainment, social users head to the mall or a shopping venue to be with someone or show someone around, and combined purpose consumers are motivated by several needs such as buying a particular item, window shopping, entertainment, consuming a meal, or socializing. Bloch, Ridgeway and Dawson (1994) present a four-fold classification: mall enthusiasts, traditionalists, grazers, and minimalists. Last, product purchase types and retail locations such as in town, out of town, urban, rural, suburban, etc. have also served as a basis for segmenting the shopping market (Marjanen 1995).

It is also contended that shoppers' characteristics influence tourist shopping. These include personal factors such as motivations and personality, psychographic attributes, and behaviors. Based on spending behavior, a tripartite taxonomy is presented by Mok and Iverson (2000): light spenders, medium spenders, and heavy spenders. In the context of textile souvenirs, five clusters of consumers were identified by Littrell (1990):

- Shopping-oriented tourists – this cluster seeks shops, craftspeople, good bargains, and has a foreign dialect. Their shopping experience is enhanced by meeting with the artisans. In fact, they are keen on seeking interactions and engaging experiences with the sellers and or crafters. This to them creates a memorable and nostalgic visit.
- Authenticity-seeking tourists – many tourists travel to seek the authentic. This category of tourists desires textile souvenirs that fulfill one or more of the following authenticity criteria: genuineness, indigenous, traditional, and representing a piece of the local heritage. Thus, they mostly demand objectivist versions of authenticity.

- Special-trip tourists – this cluster is keen to endorse their trip memories with a souvenir. They are not concerned about the association between the souvenir and the culture visited. These types place emphasis on memories of special moments experienced with other people and bonds formed and strengthened during the trip. They also enjoy making friends during their visit.
- Textiles for enjoyment tourists – this kind of tourist is bonded by the intricacy and intrinsic beauty in textile design, workmanship, and enjoy distinct colors. They purchase items to proudly display in their homes.
- Apparel-oriented tourists – this category has flamboyant lifestyles and purchase apparel to wear at home. Their clothing preferences stem from the desire to be fashionable and showy.

Few studies have also appeared that examine the relationship between souvenir purchase intentions and travel motivations. For instance, another study by Anderson and Littrell (1996) report five profiles of women shoppers based on buying behavior and liking:

- Low involvement travelers – this group is the least likely to buy souvenirs when traveling. They are also not keen on seeking engaged and interactive experiences.
- Laid back travelers – they travel extensively and plan their travel and shopping activity more diligently.
- Centrist travelers – this group indulges in traveling more often in comparison with the other two and plan their travel in advance. They are known to make incidental souvenir purchases.
- Goal-attainment tourists – this category belongs to organized trip planners and they indulge in both planned and impulsive buying behavior. They prefer to set goals and organize their travel activity meticulously.
- Eclectic tourists – this group is known for making pre-planned trips and demonstrate a tendency to go for both planned and unplanned purchases.

Vendors and Producers

Numerous studies on souvenirs and handicrafts have also pursued a two-fold path to seek the perspectives of both vendors and producers, know their characteristics, and understand their dynamism within the context of management, production, and retailing policies. Middlemen such as the distributors have also been the subject of focus. Sometimes retailers are also referred as middlemen between producers and consumers.

As noted by Esperanza (2008), middlemen have a long existence in the history of commodified handicrafts and artwork. They inject significant interventions in the production and sale process by introducing novel and innovative production techniques, offering new materials to artisans, favoring certain styles over others, and selecting objects to be distributed outside the region to the outside world. A seminal work by Cohen (2000) is worthy of attention in this aspect. He is of the view that local crafts change or get commodified due to social, political, and economic interventions such as war, hybridization of styles from other cultures, etc.

Cohen argues against the claims that the commercialization of arts and crafts because of external demand causes decline and debasement of "authentic, vital, and unchanging traditions of the past" and the commodified products thereby become "meaningless to the locals and even to their producers" (2000: 4). The argument is premised on the contention that since early times, the indigenous and tribal people of the developing world were subject to external influences and their arts and crafts have undergone processes of transformation because of interaction with other cultures, political regulations, etc. Cohen is of the view that "commercialization and other processes brought by modern global forces do not constitute a unique gradient in the history of the third and fourth world handicrafts, but are only another stage in their historical process of change" (Cohen 2000: 4). The complexity of these processes of change is explained by using four principal dichotomous variables (Cohen 2000):

* Perpetuation vs. innovation – these relate to the extent to which the art or craft changes that it loses its original elements. That is, the degree to which reproduction is tended or new elements change the nature of the original structure.
* Orthogenesis vs. heterogenesis – this dichotomy refers to the nature of the 'stylistic innovations' whether inherent traditional styles continue to be used by artisans or new radical style elements are introduced which are not related to the base-line style or to the general cultural norms of the artisan.
* Internal vs. external audience – this variable refers to two types of audience. The first type of audience shares similar cultural values with those of the artisans while the other audience is foreign to the local cultural values.
* Spontaneous vs. sponsored production – this attribute is associated with self-initiative toward commercialization versus being driven by an external source such as a government or non-government agency or a private entrepreneur.

In fact, many scholars agree with Cohen and maintain that tourism is not the only culprit for commercialization of handicrafts and artwork (Chibnik 2003; Causey 2003; Errington 1998; Phillips and Steiner 1999). They claim that ethnic art production has always been changing and has been influenced by external sources and factors since earlier times. But these transformations are more visible today. Esperanza explains this phenomenon by stating that "it is only today within the recent era of later global capitalism that cultural borrowing has become more transparent, more quickly recognizable" (2008: 76).

Esperanza refers to middlemen as cultural and economic gatekeepers and is of the view that these mediators not only control the flow of these commodities, but also control their cultural values and meanings in multiple ways. The author uses the phrase "Outsourcing of Otherness" to describe how local artisans in Bali are contracted to continue the work of imagining Otherness; to continue the simulacrum of subaltern culture imagined by those who hold economic and political influence (Esperanza 2008: 74). External buyers place value on stories about the producers and/or cultural traditions which create the objects. Corpus of heritage knowledge is useful for distributors as they are able to attach a myth or folk tale with the product thereby making it more marketable and saleable.

Authenticity of Heritage Merchandise

A perusal of literature indicates that authenticity perceptions have mostly centered on the views of either consumers (tourists) or suppliers. Regardless of audience, products belonging to the place of origin are perceived to contain the highest degree of authenticity. Tourists are known to be motivated by the quest to experience the 'other' culture (Cohen 1993b; Asplet and Cooper 2000). "Made by local hands" and in the "place of origin" are commonly claimed to be crucial features of authenticity (Asplet and Cooper 2000: 308).

It is known that authenticity is often staged and commodified to satisfy the tourist quest. Tourists are shown contrived backstages made to look as genuine. As explained in Chapter 2, taking the essentialist view, MacCannell (1992) claims that the 'authentic' is understood to be an objectively defined entity that is seldom shown to the tourist in a real sense. Supporting the objectivist version of authenticity, Cohen (1988) suggests an ethnographic notion, which embraces an artifact's tangible properties such as being handmade by members of an ethnic group, made of natural materials, and not manufactured in the market.

Furthermore, Cohen (1988) also posits that the authenticity levels sought depend on the tourist profile. What he means here is that authenticity is a "socially constructed notion" (1988: 374). In line with this contention, Littrell *et al.* (1993) indicate that different tourists have different criteria which are influenced by their travel behavior and travel frequency. These criteria include uniqueness and originality, workmanship, aesthetics, cultural and historic integrity, craftsperson and materials, shopping experience, and genuineness. Littrell *et al.* (1993) also highlight the significance of the craftsperson characteristics, the tourist-producer/retailer interaction, and the shopping experience itself.

In a second perspective, Cohen refers to authenticity as a subjective notion and argues that "authenticity in the objects we buy and study is seen as a sign of our own alienation. Or as a means of preserving their own historicity" (1993a: 142). According to him, its social connotations are negotiable. Hollinshead (1996) holds that the authenticity of historical markers and heritage symbols has been revised, recast, and reinvigorated under the postmodernity influences. To this, Hollinshead (1996) points out that the exaggerations and ornamentations of the past are not solely a postmodern phenomenon; history and heritage have always been blemished by the present. In other words, authenticity has always been a fluid and contrived phenomenon.

In a lighter perspective, some of the recent research on merchandise has indicated that authenticity is not a tangible asset but a judgment or value conferred on the setting or product by the visiting audience (Stebbins 1996; Walle 1997; Moscardo and Pearce 1999; Xie and Wall 2002). Modernists have thus referred to authenticity as a negotiation process. It has been claimed that it is a "personally constructed, contextual, and changing concept" (DeLyser 1999; Littrell *et al.* 1993:

199). The underpinnings of this argument is that tourists are active creators of authenticity and the degree and type of authenticity portrayed and promoted is dictated by consumer demand.

From an opposite perspective, however, it has also been posited that heritage suppliers are architects of authenticity. Taylor (2001) maintains that suppliers often use the past as a exemplar of the original. For instance, the Aotearoa Maori Tourism Federation in New Zealand embraces the following measure for authenticity: from the mind of a Maori, by the hand of a Maori, and with a genealogical and spiritual connection to a tupuna Maori (Asplet and Cooper 2000: 308). In a similar manner, authenticity of artifacts in museums is often paralleled with the notion that they are not influenced by commercialization (Price 1999). Most of the research on suppliers of heritage merchandise has centered on devising techniques of packaging authenticity for sale in the market. For instance, Graburn (1982) states that several factors are needed for continuous production of authentic products such as persistent demand, availability of traditional materials, existence of workforce, knowledge, and the continuous utility of the product in the daily life of the community. Producers use various methods to convince the tourists about the authenticity of crafts.

Revilla and Dodd (2003) report that producers sometimes make an object exclusive and hard to find to confer on it an authentic status. Some use the market skimming pricing strategy to highlight its authentic qualities. Also, there is a contemporary trend toward the production of new kinds of functional objects which are modified as per the needs and lifestyles of the audience (Cohen 1993). Thus authenticity discourses on heritage merchandise resonate with the mainstream versions derived from general heritage tourism literature (See Chapter 2).

Beyond tourism, a recent surge of interest in authenticity can be noted in the general marketing discipline. According to Beverland, Lindgreen and Vink (2008), authenticity has become the keystone of contemporary marketing. It has taken an altogether different meaning in brand-related advertising. Beverland (2005) points out that modern usage of this term has gone beyond the genuine claims and has permeated the product with a set of values that make it distinct from other commercial brands. Examples of producers who are extensively using authenticity as a positioning tool in their advertising campaigns include Wrangler Jeans and fine wine and beer producers. It has been claimed that because advertising is a mass media tool, using it as a platform is antithetical of the core values of authenticity. Beverland *et al.* (2008) examine consumer assessment of the authenticity messages portrayed by two well-known beer brands: Trappist and Abbey. The key question that authors aimed to answer was how advertising can successfully create or reinforce authenticity. How authenticity images are received by the consumers is crucial to know. Based on interpretations of consumers, marketers, and business buyer/industry associations of images which included pictures of production plants, historic buildings, new and old objects, and social situations, Beverland *et al.* (2008: 7–12) identified four forms of authenticity:

- *Pure (Literal) Authenticity* – defined in terms of unbroken commitments to tradition and place of origin. In this case, the informants draw on historic cues to make a judgment that the product has remained completely unchanged from the original. This indexical form of authenticity – absolute fealty to historic traditions (as demonstrated by the exemplar cues in Table 8.1) – was critical to consumers seeking to make quick in situ judgments about the genuineness of a product class.

- *Approximate Authenticity* – in this case, the informants focused on symbolic or abstract impressions of tradition created by the advertisements. Here, although authenticity was referred to in terms of traditions, an absolute fealty was not considered crucial. This is an iconic version of authenticity whereby products or objects are authentic if they approximate historical referents. Informants define authenticity as a 'feeling' that creates an 'aura' or 'mystique.' They are open to changes in the practices associated with the Trappist brands, as long as such changes did not undermine the brand's essence. The cues in form are not necessarily factual links to time and place but are based on the overall impression created by the blend of historic and modern cues. Informants in this case prefer a sincere impression. That is, the informants openly acknowledge that such cues are used for commercial purposes but are appreciative of the fact that the producers retain important traditional ingredients and do not hide their contemporary strategies. Therefore, consumers did not have a problem considering objects in this category authentic.
- *Moral Authenticity* – this form is related to moral judgments accorded to the traditional craft process per se, thereby respecting iconic authenticity. The age or origin of the brand is not of meaning to this type of informants. From their perspective, authenticity refers to the way a passionate creator is involved in making products, and is motivated mainly by their love of craft rather than the likelihood of obtaining a monetary reward. Akin to approximate authenticity, this form is a self-authentication act in that it is related to the preferred consumption of the informant rather than to the object-based historical criteria. That is, consumers seeking moral authenticity are less interested in history or connection to time and place; rather they choose brands based on the genuine intention of the makers or the producers. As Table 8.1 illustrates, this intent can be driven by commitment to social programs or by the genuine regard for the craft itself. In sum then, Beverland's study demonstrates that advertising performs an important role in fortifying images of authenticity and different versions of authenticity provoke different responses.

The aforementioned forms of authenticity are comparable to the ones identified in heritage tourism literature. For instance, pure or literal form is similar to the objectivist, essentialist form and the approximate form can be equated to the negotiated version identified by Chhabra (2008) in her study on museums. The moral form is a unique finding and can be extended (see Table 8.1) to the sincere type of authenticity mentioned by tourism scholars (Taylor 2001). Taylor (2001) introduced the notion of sincere authenticity within the context of Maori presentations during touristic encounters in New Zealand. Sincere authenticity "implies an interactive sharing of experience between participants within a given touristic encounter"

Table 8.1 Authenticity and its Cues

Authenticity	Purpose of Cues	Exemplar Cues

Pure (Literal) Authenticity	Provide consumer with in situ guarantee of the genuine article	Indexical cues involving the brand:
		1. Pictures of craftspeople actively engaged in the production process.
		2. Cues that show that active use of traditional practices including:
		  a. Pictures of beer being produced with traditional apparatus.
		  b. Images of beer being stocked in cellars.
		  c. Pictures of service staff in traditional costumes serving beer.
		  d. Historically precise colors, font, and typesetting.

Approximate Authenticity	Provide consumer with a feeling that this brand will help achieve self-authentication through connecting with place and time	Iconic cues that build an impression that the brand is connected to "the past."
		For example:
		1. Stylized links to place of production (religious abbeys).
		2. Stylized link between creators and the product (monks).
		3. Use of traditional product identifiers ('Triple,' 'Double,' etc.).
		4. Cues that clearly delineate the brand from 'gaudy' and complex mass-market alternatives via:
		  a. Simple color plot.
		  b. Simple typeface.
		  c. Simple labeling and packaging.

Moral Authenticity	Provide consumer with a feeling that this brand will help accomplish self-authentication by establishing a connection with personal moral values	Indexical or iconic images of: 1. Involvement of individual creators in the production process. 2. Small batch or craft production techniques and procedure. 3. Love of the craft process.
Sincere Authenticity	Provide consumer with a sincere account of how object authenticity is modified to accommodate the firm's mission and product parameters	Iconic images of: 1. Adaptations and rationale thereof. 2. Efforts to retain original character.

Source: After Beverland *et al.* (2008: 8)

(Taylor 2001: 16). It has been argued that sincerity allows for better and realistic communication of localized images. Within the context of marketing, a sincere attempt or message by a heritage firm should not be undermined in its intent to promote 'moments of truth' or 'cautious' treatment of heritage. That is, a sincere account of how object authenticity is modified to accommodate the firm's mission and product parameters can earn respect and attention of the intended audience.

Traces of existentialist stance within the context of being in a genuine state of mind and being true to oneself are visible in approximate and moral forms of authenticity. Important inferences from Beverland *et al.*'s study can be drawn for the marketing managers of heritage merchandise or heritage tourism in general. To date, no study in heritage tourism has branded authenticity in advertising or tested the preferences or perceptions of multiple publics simultaneously by producing a set of authentic advertising images. A preliminary application of this technique can jump start the bandwagon and help test audience reaction before formal promotional strategies can be designed or launched.

Management Tools

Marketing management of authenticity is but one aspect of the heritage shopping phenomenon. Timothy (2005) points out that heritage tourism shopping management is also subject to certain guidelines as in general retailing. Creating an appealing environment so that tourists are provoked to buy depends on the elements such as location, design, pricing, branding, merchandising, etc. Retail location selection should be based on knowledge of the trade area and the store type that will carry the souvenirs such as a community store, a destination store or store in a convenience center. The managers should also understand the spatial tendencies of consumption. For instance, other elements include shopping venue design (its exterior such as size, windows, lighting, signage, doorways, parking, physical accessibility, and interior such as the displays and the layout), selection and exhibition of merchandise, decisions regarding variety and depth of merchandise, pricing, branding, quality and exclusivity, availability, and producer/supplier selection.

Community-level issues should also form an important field of concern for shopping management. As suggested by Timothy (2005), communities in rural and agricultural regions can be re-oriented into flourishing tourist shopping venues. Three ways of re-orientation are identified by Getz (1993: 24–26):

• Natural evolution – tourism-oriented services evolve in a natural manner while responding to the growing demand for natural and heritage attractions.
• Entrepreneur-driven development – in this case, an individual or corporation takes the development initiative. An intentional effort is made to involve the local community members so that they are able to benefit.
• Purpose-planned development – this kind of development is planned in areas which do not have shopping villages or in areas which already have tourist traffic because of their heritage and natural attractions.

Community participation at all levels of planning is suggested. Opportunities need to be offered to learn about tourism and its impacts, both positive and negative. Informing the local community can foster a higher level of cooperation (Getz 1993). These views echo the core purpose of the participation rung of Arnstein's ladder (see Chapter 3), which advocates healthy partnerships, delegated power, and citizen control. Other elements which require management focus are related to the spatial planning principle in urban shopping: clustering (Mok and Iverson 2000), people management such as managing human resources (selection, recruitment, training, and retention of employees), and visitors (such as carrying capacity management).

Although an in-depth exploration of the aforesaid issues is beyond the scope of this chapter, it is hoped that a brief overview will assist in providing a bigger picture to assist in the marketing of heritage merchandise. It is an established fact that heritage and tourism make good partners as they complement each other and enhance the leisure/tourism environment.

Having obtained an insight into the different aspects of shopping and heritage merchandise and their management, attention is now turned to the three unique handicrafts selected for this chapter. The management (with special focus on marketing) strategies of Kashmiri shawls made in India, Scottish tartans sold in the USA, and totems made in Canada are examined to ascertain the extent to which sustainable efforts are employed.

Kashmir Shawls, Jammu and Kashmir, India

The Kashmiri shawls have increasingly gained the attention of tourists, both domestic and international, interested in Kashmir heritage. The fineness of embroidery and raw material in the shawl represent a way of life of Kashmir which is to a large extent dictated by the harsh winter. The Kashmir shawls are mainly of three types: wool, pashmina, and shahtoosh. These differ on the basis of the fabric. The woolen shawls are affordable where as the shahtoosh shawls are the most expensive and mostly form a one-in-a-lifetime purchase. The pashmina ones are priced in the middle. A brief description of each category shows how the local heritage is entwined in the making process of these shawls:

• *Woolen shawls* –these shawls have beautiful embroidery work on them. They are priced based on the type and quality (such as fineness) of wool used and the intricacy of the embroidery (see Plate 8.1). Raffel is one example of Kashmiri wool which is 100 percent pure and its unique embroidery is reflective of the Kashmir valley culture.

Plate 8.1 Woolen Shawls with Embroidery

Plate 8.2 Pashmina Shawl

- *Pashmina shawls* – pashmina shawls from Kashmir are one of the most popular shopping items of the state (see Plate 8.2). The shawls are adorned with delicate and beautiful embroidery and are exceptionally soft. Three types of embroidery is mostly done on these shawls: sozni, papier-mache and aari. Sozni consists of needlework in a panel on the sides of the shawl; it uses abstract designs or stylized paisleys and flowers as motifs. Papier-mache consists of needlework either in broad panels on either side along the breadth of a shawl or covering the entire surface of a shawl. Motifs are based on flowers and leaves sketched in black. Aari is hook embroidery that also uses flower design motifs.
- *Shahtoosh shawls* – shahtoosh shawls are made from the hair of an indigenous goat, the Tibetan antelope, found in the higher plateau of Tibet and the eastern part of Ladakh (at an altitude of above 5,000 meters). These shawls are soft, warm, and expensive because of sparse raw material. They are made from shahtoosh yarn alone or are mixed with pashmina. Pure shahtoosh shawls are rarely dyed and contain little embroidery.

Political factors have played a dominant role in shaping the tradition and demand for Kashmiri shawls. The present design elements can be traced to the political history of Kashmir since shawls were an important feature of royalty. Unique shawl designs and textures are the product of craftsmanship which flourished under the imperial patronage of the Mughal rulers. The Kashmiris, however, suffered a severe blow under the Afghan kings who were not keen to promote the shawl culture. But later regimes under the Sikhs, the Dogras, the French, and the British not only promoted this handicraft but also helped Kashmiri vendors to enhance shawls designs and use indigenous colors.

Kashmir Shawl Vendors, Delhi, India

Fifteen Kashmiri shawl vendors in India situated either in popular hotels/resorts or popular marketing centers were intercepted in 2006 to elicit a sense of marketing strategies pursued by these retailers. An aggregate account of the survey results is given in this section. The mission statements of all the selected vendors focused on two core elements: profitability and promotion of the Kashmiri shawl heritage.

With regard to the market breakdown of consumers who visit Kashmiri vendors, it is found that 21 percent of the demand is from the non-resident Indian market (that is, Indians settled abroad), 32 percent from the local market, and 52 percent from foreigners. The foreigners mostly belong to Italy, Great Britain, and North America (mainly Canada and the United States). The local market comprises residents with both Kashmiri and non-Kashmiri heritage. Embroidered shawls in the form of pashmina shawls (followed by shahtoosh) top the list of the Kashmiri handicraft items in demand followed by carpets.

Environment Analysis and Research Plan

Several factors have affected the contemporary design and supply of Kashmiri shawls. The 9/11 attacks in the United States and terrorism in the Kashmir valley resulted in the virtual absence of tourists in the valley. However, these did not deter shawl production but rather encouraged local vendors to find new pastures outside of the State of Jammu and Kashmir. This movement was facilitated by improved means of communication, the secular and non-discriminating nature of the government in India, and education that offered ideas to pursue alternative opportunities. Instead of waiting on the marginal tourists or giving up their traditional occupation, the Kashmiri vendors moved away from Kashmir; many thus established their outlets in the Indian capital, New Delhi.

Community Involvement

An interesting point to note is that almost all the vendors surveyed were Kashmiris. The sales men employed were also of the same heritage. The vendors mostly had their own production house or center in Kashmir, which was overseen by relatives. This illustrates that shawl making is very much a part of the family tradition. The ongoing strong ties with Kashmir is an important part of the authentic production and retailing process. Two criteria were identified by vendors to hire Kashmiri salesperson: partnerships and collaboration with the Kashmiri community.

Distribution and Promotion Strategies

Both direct and indirect distribution channels are used to promote the awareness and sale of Kashmiri shawls, including websites, producer-owned retail outlets, other retailers, and cooperative agencies.

Authenticity and Conservation

As far as authenticity is concerned, the Kashmiri vendor today has a mixed story to tell. Even though genuine Kashmir shawls are still available and some of them still maintain the traditional values, paucity of both labor and genuine material, development of education, and easier accessibility of wider markets have encouraged many of them to sell spurious items in the name of genuine products to the ignorant and unsuspecting visitors. The days of royalty being over, the sale of unique shawls has not been easy. Not many consumers today can afford to buy the authentic.

Analysis of promotional texts such as brochures used by Kashmiri vendors and producers reveal information with regard to authenticity. For instance, Ghulam Ahmed and Sons is a company with its head office in Kashmir. It produces, distributes, and sells shawls. They feel it is their family duty to keep alive aesthetic Kashmiri traditions and art forms. According to their brochure, "Making the best carpets and shawls is how we pay homage to the rich heritage that has been left behind by our noble ancestors" (Citizen Arts Emporium). They insist that they keep ancient traditions in mind when they design shawls and carpets. They believe their eyes seek perfection all the time and know how to achieve it because their minds have known it for six hundred years. They have a family collection that includes hundreds of years of priceless shawls. Natural dyes found in the Himalayas are used. These shawls are woven and embroidered by traditional weavers who have been in this occupation from early times, and it has been their family tradition since the time of the Mughals. These weavers proudly narrate stories of their forefathers who served the Mughals. Even today their fine art exists, and some shawls take months to be completed. However, demand for such shawls has declined.

The most important criteria for authenticity are identified by vendors as quality of the material. According to the majority of them, high-value end products have to represent the finest grade wool. Authenticity of pashmina is determined by the wool collected from the fleece of the wild mountain goat generic to the region. It is sold as an item prized by the elite. Most of the producers agree that this shawl epitomizes the glorious history of Himalayan craftsmanship. The promotional brochures claim the connection of pashmina products to princes and rulers of ancient times, even nicknamed as the "fiber of Kings" (Ames 1999). In the eighteenth century, the legacy of the Great Mughals spread to Europe and they introduced shawl culture wherever they went. A Citizen Arts Emporium brochure states that:

> It is said that in 1796 Abdullah Khan, the Afghan Governor of Kashmir, gifted an exquisite pashmina shawl to Sayyid Yahaya, a visitor of Baghdad. Yahya presented the shawl to the Khedive in Egypt who in turn, presented it to Napolean Bonaparte. Napoleon found the shawl fit to adorn the shoulders of the future Empress, Josephine.

Asli-tus (i.e., genuine tus shawl) is the highest quality of tus, famously identified with the fine 'ring shawls' of Mughal fame – shawls that can be drawn through a thumb ring. Pashmina is thus sold in the name of tradition and authenticity. Fifty percent of the vendors accord the highest degree of authenticity to traditionally fashioned 'jamawars' and state that it takes sixteen months to produce a real 'jamawar.' 'Jamawars' are shawls that were originally crafted gown-pieces for the royalty. They are as famous as antiques and embody the aesthetics of an ancient art which were made popular by Mughal patronage. According to one vendor who was surveyed in 2006 "as a tribute to our heritage, we have revived the art, painstakingly recreating the highest form of shawls." However, today fake 'jamawars' are being produced that take less than sixteen minutes to produce. Another 20 percent of the vendors stated that authenticity is represented by pashmina shawls that have embroidery in them not hook work (they state that anybody can do hook work).

According to 25 percent of the vendors, authenticity is depicted through design, quality, and material. This segment believes that authenticity does not exist any more. They assert that so much has changed over the past few years, and almost 70 percent of the market is fake. One vendor in this category stated that it is a dying art, especially fine embroidery. An antique jamawar is no more easily available for paucity of karigars (workers) who are hardworking craftsmen. However, according to the remaining 25 percent, Kashmiri shawls have retained 100 percent originality. With regard to threats to authenticity and Kashmiri merchants, fake jamawars produced from Amritsar (outside of the Jammu and Kashmir State) constituted the biggest threat followed by shawls imported from Nepal (neighboring country), which are produced with cheap raw materials. Several vendors stated that producers today have no patience for jamawar shawls since they take a long time to make and are expensive. The export of the Nepal slip pashmina has overshadowed the original pashmina.

Approximately 20 percent of the vendors are of the view that needlework in pashmina and jamawar depicts Kashmiri culture. According to 25 percent, Kashmiri Kani shawls depict Kashmiri culture and to some extent the Chinar and Khanikar shawl. However, according to the other half, very little Kashmiri culture is portrayed in the shawls today.

It is interesting to note that where Kashmir shawls are concerned, different versions of authenticity exist between the vendors and the artisans, the local community, and the government. The report by Jayakar asserts that this handicraft does not represent Kashmiri culture and is the result of trade (1973). The Kashmiris sell it in the name of heritage to lure tourists to visit Kashmir. The local community associates with shawls as a part of their textile heritage.

Scottish Tartans, Franklin, USA

The focus here is on the gift shop inside the Tartans Museum in Franklin, North Carolina, USA. This shop is known all over the United States for its authentic Scottish merchandise such as the tartans. Before providing an insight into the marketing strategies employed by the gift shop, a brief description of tartan and its history (The Tartans of Scotland 2009) warrant attention.

The term 'tartan' is synonymous with Scotland and Scottish clans in particular.

Originally, the word 'tartan' described the way the thread was woven to make the cloth: each thread passed over two threads then under two threads, and so on. The oldest known piece of tartan is said to be 1,700 years old. It was found buried in a pot filled with over 1,900 silver Roman coins in the ground near Falkirk, Scotland. Originally, tartans were intended to be decorative. However, their patterns were representative of districts that manufactured them. This eventually introduced the idea of district tartans, which implied original association between the land, the community, and its cloth. Strong clans started being recognized based on their tartan. When tartan was banned, only the government (the Black Watch pattern) was allowed. The Tartans of Scotland trace the history of tartans and their commodification as described in Box 8.1.

Box 8.1 History of Tartans

- By the early 1800s, it was realized that the knowledge of tartans before 1745 was being lost and, simultaneously, there was a romantic movement concerning Scotland's past. This lead to institutional and individual efforts to preserve tartan designs. Tartans were reconstructed from a variety of authentic sources such as portraits, collected on pilgrimages, demanded from clan chiefs and recovered from weaver's notes.
- Tartans became a backdrop. The weaving and tailoring industries received a boost by George IV's visit to Edinburgh in 1822 and by Sir Walter Scott's statement, as the visit's manager, "Let every man wear his tartan". Queen Victoria gave considerable encouragement thereafter, although this encouraged both fantasy and fact in the study of tartan.
- The significance of tartan as national dress, worn under different circumstances, created clan tartans for every 'name', even those that previously had none.
- Further variety was added by fashion, fancy or trade tartans to fill any niche, including various colors of a single pattern. Dancing tartans originate from the ARISAID or dress tartans. Some mourning tartans were also developed.
- In recent years, the corporate tartans have become popular. In this case, an institution or company adopts a tartan design for livery and use in merchandising. Where no clan tartan existed, families have developed new family tartans. Generally which tartan is worn is controlled by convention there not being a statute for its government.
- Disputed as to the use and production, tartans rely on the civil law of the Copyright, Design Act. Manufacturers often offer a given tartan design in a variety of color effects called 'Modern, Reproduction, Ancient,' etc.

Source: The Tartans of Scotland (2009)

Marketing Strategy of the Scottish Gift Shop

The mission of the gift shop is twofold: to provide a source of funding for the museum and to continue the ongoing tradition of the Highland dress by providing a venue of quality products, authentic tartan clothing and accessories so that people can participate in the tartan tradition themselves. The shop not only sells tartans to those who physically visit the museum in Franklin, North Carolina, but also their website has attracted clients from across the globe. In the United States, their customers are mostly US residents of Scottish heritage who participate at the various Highland Games and other Scottish–American cultural activities. The shop also receives frequent orders for tartan from Canada, France, Australia, the UK, and sometimes other countries.

The shop staff occasionally participate in online discussion forums for those who wear the kilt to stay abreast of what people are looking for how they like to shop for their tartan goods. They also remain in touch with the manufacturers of tartan and tartan clothing items through the Scottish Tartans Authority. No formal environment analysis procedure is used. However, frequent efforts are made simply to remain aware of what other Scottish-import retail shops are doing.

Distribution and Promotion Strategies

The shop management makes efforts to keep their gift shop website updated and user friendly. They promote their shop heavily through the use of online discussion forums for kilt wearers, so they reach their target base directly. Promotional tools include advertising in local tourist papers in western North Carolina to reach the tourist base. They also set up information tents at Highland games held on the east coast of the United States in states such as North Carolina, South Carolina, Georgia, Florida, and Tennessee. At the games, the purpose is to promote the museum and give away brochures and flyers. The management also try to make people aware of the fact that by purchasing tartan items from their gift shop, they are helping to support the museum, and hence contribute to the preservation of their heritage.

Local Community Involvement, Partnerships, Authenticity and Conservation

With regard to local or Scottish community involvement, the museum management does not directly solicit opinions from the community when making marketing decisions for the gift shop. But they do try to be aware of the wants and needs of their clients and gear decisions toward that aspect. No partnership schemes are included in the marketing plan. Important criteria used to ensure authenticity of Scottish merchandise made either in Scotland, the USA, or Canada is to ensure consistent standards. Merchandise is made in a manner that reflects the integrity of the Scottish heritage that is trying to be preserved. From recent times, conscious efforts have been being made to feature more hand-crafted goods in the gift shop to showcase local artists of Scottish–American descent. On conservation, the most important category considered for the long-term health of the Scottish tartans is preservation.

Interpretation and Visitor Mindfulness

Several forms of interpretation techniques are used. The interpreters are mostly local. In the museum gallery, the story of the tartan tradition in Scotland is told and through the gift shop visitors are offered an opportunity to take a bit of that tradition home with them. Tartan has always been an industry in Scotland, as well as a fashion, and the gift shop wants people to participate in that fashion and keep that industry alive through the products it sells. Visitor mindfulness is facilitated through interpretive signage as well as a video display in the museum. The staff also deal directly one-on-one with visitors and answer any questions they might have.

Canadian Totems

Totem poles are one of the dominant cultural symbols of Canada. They present wonderful examples of aboriginal art. This ancient practice of totem carving has been passed down for several generations. It is a way of preserving the history of local native heritage as well as honoring tribal rituals and sacred spirits of people. These poles earlier consisted of numerous Northwest Native figures carved on tall, western cedar poles and each figure was intended to portray a traditional meaning. Totem poles performed many symbolic functions in the past. Tribes such as the Kwakwak'wakw and Nuu-cha-nulth built large totem poles to serve as human welcome symbols. Memorial poles represented the ancestors and were often positioned at the house entrance in honor of the departed chiefs. Later mortuary poles were also built in the nineteenth century and these were placed at the top of the house. Also, there were free-standing type of poles which served as doorways at the house entrance. Some poles were made to support roof beams (please note information Canadian Totems is derived from multiple websites).

In the early part of the nineteenth century, totems became a part of the West Coast art. Tribes who spearheaded this transformation were the Northwest Coast Native tribes such as the Haida, Tlingit and Tsimshian in BC and southeast Alaska. Other tribes in the Northwest soon followed suit. Totem poles were always raised in a ceremonial manner known as 'potlaches.' In the later nineteenth century, these ceremonies were banned and, as a result, the Northwest Native tribes stopped making totem poles. However, they continued to carve small models of poles as artwork and souvenirs for tourists. It was in 1951 that the ban was lifted and today totem poles continue to be carved for traditional and religious purposes.

Totem poles have thus become one of the cultural icons of Canada and have been installed in some of the Canadian embassies in foreign countries such as Japan and Germany. The pole carving art has been embraced by artists from other Native tribes who have gained knowledge of the West Coast totem pole modus operandi. Marketing strategies planned for the sale of totem poles today by numerous kinds of suppliers form an interesting case study. This chapter focuses on the totems made by the craftspeople of the Cowichan tribe, which is the largest tribe in British Columbia, and the totems created by them. Seven tribes make up the Quw'utsun' people and approximately 3,900 Quw'utsun' people reside in the Cowichan Valley today.

The Quw'utsun' culture is based on oral history and its elders have the responsibility of sharing ancestral stories with today's tribal generation. They serve as the history custodians. Because the Quw'utsun' people are keenly aware of the risk of losing their storytelling culture, they video and audio-tape the storytelling gatherings. Like many other British Columbia First Nations, the Cowichan tribes are also in the process of treaty negotiations with the government of British Columbia and Canada.

Quw'utsun Totems

The focus is the gift shop inside the Quw'utsun Cultural and Conference Center in the town of Duncan in British Columbia, Canada. The purpose of the center is to provide recognition and a selling outlet for the tribal artisans such as the Quw'utsun' knitters, carvers, and jewelry makers, while also serving to communicate the Quw'utsun' culture and history to the world. The center is owned by the Cowichan Tribes and was opened in 1990. The center strives to generate economic viability for the tribal people. The goal is also to foster and promote pride in their culture, to offer a high-quality experience to all visitors and to provide a professional conference facility. The vision statement for the center also applies to the gift shop:

> To share and build the pride of we, the First People, through education, art and entertainment of our Guests and ourselves by reflecting the past, striving in the present, to enhance the future of our Native cultures. Our mission shall require Great Deeds of we the First People and our Friends.

The gift shop consumers are mostly guests who frequent the Cultural and Conference Center. Approximately, 20 percent of the guests are above sixty years of age and 71 percent are between 20 and 59 years old. Sixty-seven percent of the visitors are foreigners (from outside of Canada). Totem pole souvenirs are becoming very popular with young boys who lure their parents to buy these for them.

There is no specific research plan to guide the marketing efforts. Much information on the visitors is obtained through visitor–staff interactions, with the tour guides also providing an important source. Technological, political, and demographic factors influence marketing strategies at the shop. There is evidence of distinct and strong local community involvement. Since the center is owned by the native tribe, a bottom-up participatory partnership approach, which advocates local community empowerment and ownership, is employed. Also, the center believes in maintaining effective partnerships and collaboration with the other sectors of the travel and tourism industry and other tribes in the region.

The main source of direct distribution is the website. Indirect distribution channels include travel agents, tour operators, the local tourism office, and other handicraft stores in town. Promotional strategies include advertising, personal selling and sales promotion. Coupons are sometimes offered at the gift shop. Promotional collateral includes brochures, pamphlets, and video. Interpretation techniques include cultural tours, signs, and text next to exhibits.

Summary and Conclusions

This chapter has provided an overview of the heritage merchandise nomenclature within the broader tourism and leisure shopping environments, while at the same time offering a brushstroke of the areas linked to the marketing of heritage goods such as the functions, attributes of shopping, typology of shopping environments, shopping destinations, contemporary research focus, a discussion of marketing-related studies on heritage merchandise/souvenirs, souvenir research explorations taking the vendor and producer views, numerous shopper market segments, authenticity discourse using the heritage merchandise perspective, handicrafts and artwork characteristics, and management areas and issues associated with the heritage merchandise shopping venues.

Several selected topics are furthered in this chapter such as the handicraft evolution process, the producer and vendor influences on handicraft, and the authenticity dilemma associated with heritage merchandise. With respect to the handicraft evolution, what emerges is that multiple factors are responsible for its commercialization. The heritage tourist is only one element in the equation. Social relationships which the producers and vendors construct along the way during the design and making process, before the handicraft reaches the consumer, often define the merchandise and influence its narrations. Also, an important part of heritage merchandise management is authenticity. As is pointed out by many scholars, authenticity has today become a fluid notion. Nevertheless, the objective version of authenticity receives paramount attention from the perspective of devoted and traditional suppliers and serious heritage tourists. Another element of authenticity that is appreciated by tourists is sincerity. An honest depiction and narration of authenticity can earn the regard and interest of the heritage market. Important themes emerge from each of the aforesaid topics.

The case study analysis using the sustainability portfolio reveals interesting insights into the marketing process employed by the shawl, tartan, and totem vendors. Both intrinsic and extrinsic motivations influence buying behavior. For instance, tartans, shawls, and totems are considered a fashionable souvenir in addition to their traditional value for visitors associated with the place of origin or the handicraft/souvenir culture. For instance, Kashmiri Indians settled abroad will purchase shawls during their visit to India to feel connected with their traditions. Also, expressive and recreational shopping mostly define the shopping behavior of the handicrafts. With regard to the leisure environment category, tartan and totems are mostly sold in heritage-destination environments, while all shawls are mostly made available through ambient and magnet leisure environments. For instance, the ambient leisure environment relates to urban or rural shopping villages in India such as the Janpath (New Delhi), where shawl vendors compete with vendors selling handicrafts from other states in India. Shawl vendors also have shops in Indian malls in addition to being visible in the shopping arcades of luxurious hotels in the big cities of India. With regard to buyer market segments, it is evident that there is a strong international demand for all three handicrafts. All three are sought by international visitors, although the tartan shop and the shawl vendors also focus/rely on the domestic market. The tartan shop always makes an effort to have a booth at Scottish festivals and remain visible at the Highland games in the United States.

A few similarities emerge such as significance given to local community involvement and place of handicraft origin emphasis in the case of shawls and totems. Tartan production also follows the essentialist authenticity guidelines but in a different manner. It places more weight on ingredients and method than bringing it from its place of origin. With regard to conservation, preservation and restoration occupy the main emphasis in all three cases.

Shawls and totems fall into the partnership category of Arnstein's model because of the production and distribution empowerment enjoyed by the locals. The tartan shop relies more on the tartan society. A previous study of Scottish merchandise had also indicated trade society and the influence of other non-government organizations on the tartan authenticity. Here the level of community involvement occupies a lower level in the ladder, probably positioned somewhere between the non-participation and tokenism categories.

The Internet is heavily used by the sellers of totems and tartans, while Indian vendors are in the process of utilizing online sources to market their products. Elaborate interpretation techniques are more evident in the case of totems and tartans because both shops are situated in a heritage environment. A variety of visitor mindfulness techniques are evident. The shawls provide authentic interpretation to some extent because the local community from its place of origin is engaged in selling the product. However, visitor mindfulness strategies are not embraced in this case. For some, the core purpose is profit not promotion of Kashmiri heritage. Also, elements of commodification are visible in all three cases. Shawls and tartans use non-traditional raw material to make cheap and affordable souvenirs because traditional material is expensive. In this case, some modifications are introduced to accommodate the lower income visitors. This is not to say that high-end authentic products are not available or not in demand. However, the mass-market need has to be accommodated. In both cases, a sincere account of the modifications is offered. Therefore, a sincere version of authenticity is employed.

Sustainable marketing of heritage merchandise and souvenirs is not an easy task, for their notations are often juxtaposed within in multidimensional and complex environments. Such products are also driven by multiple and often polarized objectives: making profit and preservation and restoration of old traditions. One of the primary aims of marketing managers of handicrafts should be to provide an accurate historical account of the merchandise to the heritage tourist. With regard to location, proximity to places of connected historical significance can enhance sale and promotion of the merchandise heritage. If modifications are necessary to meet the needs of the mass market, sincere narrations can maintain credibility. Strategic planning is missing in all three cases. The next chapter provides suggestions on how to address some of the issues raised by this chapter.

Questions

1. Describe shopper typologies briefly.
2. What are some of the factors that contribute to impulse shopping?
3. What kind of needs trigger shopping behavior?
4. Compare and contrast the marketing strategies pursued by the vendors of shawls, tartans, and totems as described in this chapter.

9   Future of Sustainable Marketing
Contemplation and Challenges

Sustainable marketing in heritage tourism is emerging as an important management function and area of scholarly inquiry. The sustainable praxis in the industry is in fact driven by both the custodians and the contemporary consumers of heritage. This book is about sustainable marketing of heritage tourism; it has been written with the primary aim of testing the theoretical underpinnings of sustainability among the management strategies of heritage and cultural suppliers. It is unique in this perspective because no single extended body of work exists currently in heritage tourism literature that marries heritage with tourism using a sustainable marketing base. The approach is both broad and holistic in an attempt to converge multiple constituencies of sustainability. A wide range of heritage suppliers are examined using a case-study approach to test the practical applicability of the proposed sustainable marketing model and demonstrate the marketing function embraced by the heritage institutions. This concluding chapter aims to first present an overall synopsis of the findings penned down in the foregoing chapters. Next, it presents an outline of opportunities and pitfalls associated with making sustainable marketing real in heritage tourism. It concludes with a discursive note on the future of sustainable marketing within the realm of heritage institutions and scholarly research.

Sustainable Marketing of Heritage Tourism

A reflection across the diverse spectrum of heritage custodians reveals both commonalities and some peculiarities unique to a heritage institution. On commonalities, worthy of note is the highest importance accorded to objectivist/essentialist authenticity. Also, confirmed is the need to negotiate authenticity so that the contemporary markets are engaged. Civic engagement (partnership category of Arnstein's ladder – Figure 3.2) is more evident in the heritage institutions based in the United States than in other countries. Partnership-driven community involvement is an inherent feature of the Sheraton Wild Horse Pass Resort on the Tribal Reservation and this approach is embraced to some extent by the Heard Museum in the United States. Maison Tavel in Switzerland also recognizes the significance of local community perspectives when designing relevant programs and events. The museums in India, on the other hand, shows marginal emphasis on this important aspect of sustainable marketing.

With regard to the festivals, civic engagement forms a core characteristic of the Highland games whereas the Day of the Dead festival is supported by the government for economic benefits. The Kumbh Mela also shows civic engagement at the national level as the event is popularly patronized by the domestic pilgrims who also partake in spectacularized rituals. The government support is more driven by the need for regulation, infrastructure needs, and security. With regard to heritage merchandise, elements of commodification are visible across all three unique handicrafts: shawls, tartan, and totems. Shawl heritage in India is maintained and promoted by the grass-roots level engagement of the handicraft-producing community. Canadian totems also follow a similar approach.

A perusal of heritage literature in another part of the world reveals that active civic engagement offered by the heritage institutions is at its infancy stage in Australia. Sites in competitive markets are more prone to embrace elements of the marketing philosophy such as those in the UK, USA, and Switzerland. Examples from these countries also show inclusion of the social marketing philosophy in their marketing missions.

A strategic marketing approach is to some extent followed by the museums and historic houses situated in the UK, USA, and Switzerland, although SWOT (strengths, weaknesses, opportunities, and threats) analysis is not a priority in the UK and Switzerland-based case studies. The main reason appears to be lack of manpower and shortage of funds. Indian examples show traces of strategic planning for the Kumbh festival to some extent, but shawls and the museums' efforts for a long-term plan are not evident. One reason can be the fact that the museums under focus are stand-alone museums. They are less threatened by competition and are more driven by product orientation and national status. That said, a quick online review of the mission statements of other museums in India show a similar orientation. In retrospect to all foregoing discussion then, all heritage institutions use some components of sustainable marketing but differ in their approach and emphases. Several lessons can be learnt from the case studies provided in this book:

- There is global support for objective/essentialist version authenticity of heritage. However, carefully negotiated versions are deemed necessary to maintain the attention and engagement of the contemporary audience.
- There is also global advocacy for preservation and restoration of heritage.
- Marketing is still in its infancy stage at the heritage institutions in developing countries such as India while its commercial purpose is actively embraced in developed countries. A review of other developing countries indicate an active role of consumer-oriented marketing in the near future, whereas the developed countries are now showing a slant toward societal and tribal marketing.
- Sustainable marketing of heritage is followed in different degrees across the globe. However, its education is crucial and needs to be advocated and facilitated by the public sector all over the world.
- Strategic planning for civic engagement and long-term economic viability needs to be actively embraced in all marketing plans.

- Broader level cross-sector collaborations are remiss across all heritage institutions and this view is supported by the contemporary literature.

It is suggested that all heritage institutions pursue a tripartite-orientation approach at the base level: product, marketing with further efforts to promote tribal relationship building, and social marketing. Regardless of the geographical location and developed or developing status of a country, a review of literature presents ongoing debates in some areas that are of relevance to all:

- Politics of heritage;
- Identification of relevant stakeholders and effective collaborations between them;
- Opportunities presented by the emerging middle class across the world;
- Authenticity as an emerging marketing brand;
- Technological opportunities and pitfalls;
- Effectiveness of alternative marketing paradigms such as tribal marketing, de-marketing, select marketing, and educational marketing are needed;
- Ethics of marketing.

Politics of Heritage

As explained by Timothy and Boyd (2003), it is common for officiating governments to use heritage to structure public views, to foster nationalist sentiments, and to build images that portray their political ideologies. Nations are often called imagined communities whose boundaries are endorsed by maps and advocacy of shared heritage. In line with this, several countries have introduced new versions of heritage to redefine nationalist ideals.

Heritage dissonance also exists at the community level. They may disagree with "what heritage to preserve, value, and incorporate into their identity" (Frost 2006: 6). Howard holds that "heritage always benefits someone ... [It also] disadvantages someone else" (2003: 4). Examples of heritage exclusions exist all across the world. For instance, the 1988 bicentenary organizers in Australia had made efforts to exclude indigenous groups. Heritage dissonance will continue being a contentious issue. Marketing managers should make attempts to understand the history behind these conflicts and narrate an honest and sincere story by illustrating multiple views, to their audience.

Stakeholder Collaborations

As pointed out by Timur and Getz (2009), it is crucial to engage and manage stakeholders so that successful sustainable policies may be developed. International conventions and charters are more than simple tools for the protection of heritage, they are mechanisms for the sustainable management of cultural heritage. They can create the enabling environment needed for partnerships between countries to grow, thereby allowing all to operate equitably and share a similar vision. It is thus important to recognize that all strategies for sustainable development of cultural heritage should include adherence to such principles.

Cross-frontier initiatives between different regions and states can help share marketing costs and facilitate advocacy for sustainable development. For instance, 'mutual heritage' agreements between states can facilitate cross-frontier initiatives in cultural heritage, as all parties can evaluate their costs and benefits. Numerous examples of this are found in Mauritius. Other countries which offer financial assistance to mutual cross-country heritage projects include India, France, and The Netherlands. This can facilitate dialogue and strengthen relations between the peoples of the countries.

The Emerging New Middle Class

As has been noted earlier, the emerging middle class in the developed countries is becoming increasingly interested in ethical consumption and meaningful experiences, and is willing to spend more on responsible and society-friendly activities. It is also actively supporting tourism codes of ethics. The rising middle-class culture in developing countries such as China, India, and Nepal has also been a subject of much discussion. In her study of Nepal, Liechty (2002) notes that the middle class in Nepal is linked to global patterns of capitalist promotion, distribution, and labor relations. Theses members are keen to mold ancient, local cultural narratives (such as notions of propriety, orthodoxy, and honor) with a 'modern' sense of value and truth associated with achievement, progress, and development; their aim is to build a novel socio-cultural space and profess legitimacy for their own middle-class values. Another example can be drawn from India. India's new relationship with the global economy in both cultural and economic terms has defined a new cultural standard for its rising middle-class population. According to Fernandes, "the rising middle class has left behind its dependence on austerity and state protection and has embraced an open India that is at ease with broader processes of globalization" (2000: 89). It has also been noted that this population cohort has become the driving force for the modified imaging of the Indian nation in the context of globalization. Marketing managers in developed countries should use sustainable themes to attract this potential market segment, whereas the same in developing countries should make efforts to educate and generate awareness for ethical consumption and code of ethics within the middle-class citizens.

Authenticity as the Emerging Marketing Brand

Although the consumer desire to seek a genuine product is nothing new, it is only recently that heritage institutions feel the need to integrate authenticity into their promotion strategies, thereby using it as a bait to attract a wide range of audience. However, despite being highly valued as a conservation tool, use of authenticity in marketing has also been condemned for being modified to meet visitor motivations and deviating from the essentialist emphasis.

This dual support suggests that heritage institutions will continue to craft adaptive strategies to satisfy constructivist and existentialist needs of the consumers. Parallel to this, efforts will continue to develop pure/objectivist forms of authenticity and this version will remain at one end of the demand and supply spectrums. Developing countries, currently more centered on essentialist/objectivist ideologies, are likely to shift their focus in this direction. The developed countries, on the other hand, are likely to reverse their steps and move more toward essentialist concepts as the emerging middle class demands more educative, object-oriented and ethical experiences. Additionally, moral and sincere versions of adapted authenticity will become the fashion.

It is worthwhile to note here that the authenticity concept has gained wide acceptance in the non-heritage commercial industry where brands are seeking "their aura of distinction and pedigree through allusions of time and space" (Alexander 2009: 551). Numerous signifiers of history such as patent date, an associated historical event, etc. are being used to proffer heritage ambience on the product. Hence, this trend is likely to continue in the foreseeable future. Authenticity will be increasingly used to endorse the brand aura while framing marketing strategies (Hede and Tryne 2007). Important inferences from the non-heritage tourism marketing literature can offer useful insights for marketing managers of heritage institutions.

In sum, based on the combined review of heritage and non-heritage literature, it can be concluded that six forms of authenticity exist: objectivist/essentialist, negotiationist/approximate, constructivist, existentialist, moral, and sincere. Alexander in his study of the Brewer Brain and Co. (sponsoring organization of Welsh Rugby Union) reports five techniques of engagement and negotiation to present the brand as a pertinent and authentic cultural reserve (2009: 558):

- Iconic and reflexive brand persona – the objective of this image creation is to distance the brand from much hyped and homogenizing conceits of traditional advertising;
- Coat-tailing on cultural epicenters – here the aim is to be a part of the community rather than try to be 'parasites on it';
- Life world emplacement – the objective of this technique is to use a real-life framework;
- Stealth branding – the purpose in this case is to use indirect net-based viral communication channels to place the brand within a real-life structure and consumer space.

The strategy is thus based on an understanding of socio-cultural roots and dynamics and efforts to engage the community on objective, constructive, and existentialist levels. By establishing a co-branding relationship with the sponsored community, Brewer Brains is able to rearticulate its identity and the "brand's relationship to place and the downplaying of commercial motives as seen as fundamental to the brand message and creation of the brand aura" (Alexander 2009: 558).

Hede and Thyne undertook a study to provide insights into how authenticity can be used to enhance the efficacy of branding and the brand for organizational survival. The authors conclude that the form of authenticity that is the most closely associated with building brands in heritage tourism is existential or activity/experience-related rather than objectivist or constructivist. The authors further state that absence of objective authenticity in a literary heritage attraction does not necessarily detract from visitors' experience; what appears to be more important in ensuring the literary heritage attraction's sustainability is the need for "brand managers to empower visitors to construct their own experience either with the personal assistance of the guides or independently" (2007: 426, 427).

Branding authenticity in heritage tourism is a complex task. It is known that branding is integral to an organization's success in the marketing environment. Aaker (2004) notes that brands endorse credibility and are the product's foundation in spirit and substance. The notion of brand is a complicated one because multiple attributes define a brand such as real versus illusionary, rational versus emotional, and tangible versus intangible (Ambler and Styles 1996). Use of authenticity in branding presents several challenges. For instance, Keller (2003) points out that looking to a brand's history to communicate authenticity, while juxtaposing the historical information with other brand messages more contemporary in nature, runs the risk of compromising the brand value.

Also, with growing proliferation of authenticity in the marketing arena, there has emerged an overwhelming need to strategize the use of authenticity. As pointed out by Pine II and Gilmore, "business executives must learn to understand, manage, and excel at delivering authenticity" (2008: 35). The authors highlight the significance of the 'execution zone' which offers a boundary within which decisions and actions should be made by a company or an organization while remaining moral and true to themselves. Pine II and Gilmore offer eight principles to guide a company or organization in setting delineations of their own execution zone (2008: 35–39):

1. Study your heritage – innovation and marketing opportunities need to be embraced in the light of an organization's unique origin and history. The marketing plan should be apposite to the past otherwise the organization will be labeled as inauthentic and fake.
2. Ascertain market and industry positioning – an analysis of the immediate environment can provide an important setting for designing a compelling, do-able, strategic direction for the enterprise. It is crucial to comprehend the contemporary innovations and trends.
3. Gauge your trajectory – after gaining a full understanding of the company or organization's history, should a marketing manager decide the direction and speed of marketing. It is easy to fall into the pitfall of misconstruing the immediate environment and create a misleading strategic position.
4. Know your limits – it is important to determine the boundaries and limits of the execution zone. Phony positions that lie outside the execution zone should be eliminated. It is best to set the limits and thresholds of the execution zone by defining the set of actions the organization will not follow. Ethics and compliance to the mission statement is crucial. A company should keep in mind its body of values in determining the appropriate boundaries.

5. Stretch your execution capabilities – seek a set of desirable goals that stretch the organization's potential toward success. Increase speed of execution and flexibility and make obtainable strategic positions at the far edges of your execution zone increasingly over time. Whatever best defines the company, follow it into new possibilities for creating value.

6. Scan the periphery – it is also crucial to know your current and future competitors. In fact, an enterprise should keep an eye on new competitors who are innovating along three dimensions of competitive reality: offerings, capabilities, and customers.

7. Formulate your strategic intention – an incremental innovation approach should be used. That is, regardless of the competition emerging from the periphery or the traditional industry, an organization should not try to beat the competitors by watching what they do and trying to surpass them. The best way is to craft out a future position after due consideration to all opportunities. Thus position should be in line with the mission statement and within the limits of the execution zone.

8. Execute well – if the company/organization or enterprise is able to apply the previous seven principles in a proficient manner, then what is left to do is successful execution of it, year after year.

Economic Viability of Heritage Tourism

Economic enumerations are a prerequisite to develop heritage tourism in an area. Despite the pronounced economic emphasis, heritage institutions across the world should aim to develop strategies that maximize local economic benefits and reduce leakages (Coetze, Niekerk and Saayman 2008). Also, they should ensure local community benefits through increased income, employment, and tax contributions from tourists (Chhabra, Healy *et al.* 2003). Marketing managers of these institutions have an important role to perform. They can develop a local community-friendly marketing mix so that more benefits are reaped locally. High-end products made by local artisans can fetch revenue for both the producers and the retailers. Cross-selling other services of the local community to on-site visitors can also facilitate local earnings through purchase of ancillary products. For example, offering coupons for or information on a local restaurant or entertainment complex or lodging facility can strengthen liaison with the other travel and tourism industry partners in the region.

Leveraging Technology

Heritage institutions also need to be stay updated on technological innovations. By embracing innovative tools for marketing, heritage tourism organizations can gain a leverage on their competitors and obtain a distinct edge in cost reduction, revenue growth, marketing research, and customer retention (Buhalis and Law 2008). As pointed out by Gretzel, Yuan and Fesenmaier (2000), the Internet offers multi-promotion and distribution opportunities. Internet Communication Technologies

(ICT) has revolutionized the tradition distribution function in tourism which was dominated by intermediaries such as the travel agents and tour operators during the pre-Internet era. Organizations are now able to distribute their products directly. The 'disintermediating' trend also implies that tour operators can sell direct to suppliers and eliminate travel agents, and travel agents are bundling their own packages and excluding tour operators in the process (Buhalis and Law 2008). Also, a new class of electronic intermediaries is emerging who are challenging the traditional intermediaries. For example:

> Expedia and Lastminute.com are challenging the business models of Thomson and Thomas Cook, forcing them to rethink their operations and strategies. Auction sites such as eBay.com, price comparison sites such as Kelkoo and Kayak.com; price reversing strategies such as Priceline.com also provide a great challenge for pricing of both suppliers and intermediaries. In addition, Web 2.0 or Travel 2.0 providers such as Tripadvisor.com, IGOUGO.com, and Wayn.com also enable consumers to interact and to offer peer to peer advice. (Buhalis and Law 2008: 618)

Another significant impact of the Internet has occurred on the pricing component of the marketing mix. Pricing has become transparent today, thereby enforcing the need to guarantee price parity, both online and offline. This has compelled organizations to revisit their brand and positioning strategies. Another innovation is associated with eLearning, which comprises of all technology-assisted learning. This tool is extensively used for training, education, and research. Virtual Learning Environments (VLEs) have become popular among tourism educators. ICTs aim to develop info-structure for the entire industry. Also, eTourism is becoming more and more focused on consumer-based technology innovations to enable organizations/agencies to facilitate interactions with their consumers (Buhalis and Law 2008).

Within the heritage tourism turf, Mitsche *et al.* (2008) have explored the application of eTourism in interpretation. Heritage institutions today recognize that ICT can ease the distribution of information from inaccessible locations, thereby offering an opportunity to heritage operators to take control of the information available to visitors prior to visiting the attraction as well post-visit explorations. Although e-Services have been used by museums for heritage interpretation, limited research exists in regard to widening application of the Internet to interpretation techniques. Mitsche *et al.* (2008) point out that the heritage industry has the potential to apply e-Services in support of online heritage interpretation. Technology thus offers unique opportunities for heritage institutions such as the museums to touch "peoples' minds and spirits" (Var, Chon and Doh 2002). Var *et al.* (2002) echo the view of Buhalis and Law (2008) when they reiterate that the effects of ICT on cultural tourism are profound and there is a need for the heritage institutions to seek updated technological innovations. It is an established fact that the Internet has led to unprecedented growth and development in promotional endeavors.

Ethics of Marketing

Marketing ethics are an ongoing subject of intense discourse in marketing literature although their discussions have received limited attention in heritage tourism studies. Marketing ethics are a "systematic study of how moral standards are applied to marketing decisions, behaviors, and institutions" (Murphy *et al.* 2005: xviii). The applied scope of marketing ethics is broad as Table 9.1 demonstrates.

Table 9.1 Applied Scope of Marketing Ethics

	Issues Related to
Functional areas	Product
	Price
	Distribution
	Promotion
Sub-disciplines of marketing	Sales
	Consumers/Consumption
	International marketing
	Marketing ethics education
	Marketing research
	Social marketing
	Sustainable marketing
	Responsible marketing
	Internet marketing
	Law and ethics
Specific ethics related topics	Ethics and society
	Ethical decision-making models
	Ethical responsibility toward stakeholders
	Ethical values
	Norm generations and definition
	Marketing ethics and implementation
	Relationship between ethics and religion
	Discrimination and harassment
	Green marketing
	Ethical consumption
	Vulnerable consumers
	Inexperienced consumers

Source: After Nill and Schibrowsky (2007: 258)

It has been envisaged that the premises of ethical issues lie in deontological and teleological frameworks. The deontological approach relates to behavior and actions as the basis of judgment. A set of rules determine ethical behavior and actions in this case. Teleological theories, on the other hand, stress on perceived outcomes rather than behavior. That is, possible outcomes of an individual's actions serve to guide the individual. However, as explained by Parson and Maclaran (2009), teleological perspectives differ based on whether the emphasis is on individual interests or collective interests of the society as a whole.

Moving forward, regardless of the approach, ethical issues are mostly tackled using two perspectives: normative and positive. The normative perspective focuses on provision of a set of recommendations on how to practice marketing (Laczniak and Murphy 2006) such as required action by organizations or individuals and ideal marketing systems in the society to promote ethical behavior (Hunt 1976). Parson and Maclaran (2009) point out that a key challenge in the normative perspective is lack of awareness on the part of the managers that knowledge on marketing ethics can be gained. To address this dilemma, Laczniak and Murphy have developed a set of seven fundamental perspectives to guide marketing managers (2006: 157):

- BP1: Giving first priority to people;
- BP2: Achieving a behavioral standard beyond what regulations permit;
- BP3: Taking full responsibility of their marketing action;
- BP4: Organizations cultivating high moral awareness among managers and employees;
- BP5: Articulating and embracing a set of ethical principles;
- BP6: Adopting a stakeholder orientation as this is crucial for guiding ethical marketing decisions;
- BP7: Delineating an ethical decision-making protocol.

Although normative perspectives have dominated the debate on marketing ethics, positive approaches are increasingly gaining attention. A series of paradigms have been developed by researchers over the past few decades to assist in the ethical decision-making process. The most popular framework is the 'General Theory of Marketing Ethics' Model by Hunt and Vitell (2006):

> In this model, marketers draw on both teleological and deontological evaluations and build both of these elements in the model. It is recognized that the cultural, industry, and organizational environments, as well as past personal experiences, impact upon the person's perception of the ethical problem. These factors also impact on the perceived alternatives available to them. Hence, both deontological and teleological evaluation of the alternatives is taken into consideration. The deontological evaluation is based on the understanding that an individual evaluates alternatives against a set of norms including personal values and beliefs. Four constructs are considered for teleological evaluation: 1) the perceived consequences of each alternative for various stakeholder groups, 2) the probability that each consequence will occur to each stakeholder group, 3) the desirability or undesirability of each consequence and 4) the importance of each stakeholder group. (Hunt and Vitell cited and quoted in Parson and Maclaran (2009: 127, 128))

Finally, Parson and Maclaran (2009) provide examples of marketing functions which are under frequent ethical criticisms. These include marketing research, advertising, and product and brand management. The ethics of data collection and presentation pose ethical challenges which need to be addressed. With regard to advertising, one paramount criticism levied against the possible manipulation of the consumer is the practice of designing deceptive messages and depicting myths and stereotypes instead of realities (Sirakaya and Sonmez 2000). Positioning of the product and brand also demonstrate pitfalls concerned with social responsibility and sincere disclosures. The heritage tourism marketing managers need to educate themselves on ethical marketing practices. This will help to ensure brand sincerity and earn long-term loyalty of potential target markets.

Alternative Forms of Sustainable Marketing

Demarketing

Kotler and Levy define demarketing as "discouraging in general or a certain class of customers in particular on either a temporary or a permanent basis" (1969b: 75). Scenarios which demand or need such an approach are where demand exceeds supply and suppliers are not either motivated or able to meet the demand (Medway and Warnaby 2008). In such cases then, efforts can be made to modify demand such as using differential pricing strategies, reducing promotional reach, and service expediency (Baker 1998).

Although demarketing is commonly described as the "reverse of marketing" (Koschnick 1995: 148), it is argued in contemporary marketing literature that it is an "intrinsic aspect within marketing management" (Beeton and Benfield 2002: 499). As stated by Kotler and Levy:

> The tasks of coping with shrinking demand or deliberately discouraging segments of the market call for the use of all major marketing tools. As such, marketing thinking is just as relevant to the problem of reducing demand as it is to the problem of increasing demand. (1969b: 75)

Examples of demarketing have mostly centered on crises situations such as health-related crisis. In such cases, precautionary measures include demarketing of the affected place such as the outbreaks of the contagious H5N1 influenza in Southeast Asia, the foot and mouth disease in UK, and the Bird flu (Medway and Warnaby 2008). Heritage is a finite resource; hence, it is important for heritage institutions dealing with tangible, intangible, and built heritage to pursue demarketing strategies occasionally so that cultural and heritage sustainability is maintained. Demarketing can be in the form of general passive demarketing. In this case:

> demarketing occurs by default, rather than specific intention in effort or emphasis. It invariably incorporates a low marketing effort, typically as a measure for managing demand and ensuring place sustainability in the face of over-popularity, where places do not have to overtly market their positive attributes. (Medway and Warnaby 2008: 649)

Tribal Marketing Applications

While more conceptual underpinnings are required to explore the opportunities that can be tapped associated with demarketing, another form of marketing that is advocated as promoting sustainable behavior among consumers is tribal marketing. Postmodern tribes are ephemeral and a person can belong to several postmodern tribes at any one point of time. The boundaries of a postmodern tribe are conceptual and members are related by shared feelings or emotions. The fragmented society, triggered by the developments and innovations produced by industry and commerce are the distinct features of postmodernism. Maffesoli (2000) maintains that postmodernity is a synergy between archaism and technological development. There is re-rooting need as individuals consistently get uprooted through fragmentations. They rally people around locality, kinship, emotion, and passion. Tribal marketing can help promote and gain acceptance of sustainable behavior because of interactive engagement within the audience. Demand trends can change if an audience is convinced of intrinsic benefits by embracing sustainable behavior.

Furthering Social Marketing

Andreasen (2002) maintains that social marketers can reach their maximum potential if they are able to determine the following:

- An irreducible essence of social marketing that enables the careful observer to recognize it when he or she sees it;
- Appropriate knowledge and awareness exists in the marketer claiming to be a social marketer;
- Ability of social marketing to highlight an aspect of a social or cultural problem;
- Making an appropriate use of social marketing.

A social marketing approach should move beyond theory and distinct set of techniques to development of processes aiming to implement social change programs akin to the ones used to implement commercial marketing techniques. Andreasen suggests the fundamental tenets of social marketing as: 1) holding behavior change as its 'bottom line'; 2) being consumer-driven; 3) planning creative and attractive exchanges that encourage behavior. In sum, the following are six benchmarks for implementing social marketing orientation (Andreasen 2002: 7):

- Behavior-change is the benchmark to design and evaluate alternatives.
- Projects consistently use audience research to a) understand target audiences at the outset of interventions, b) routinely pretest intervention elements before they are implemented, and c) monitor interventions as they are rolled out.
- There is careful segmentation of target audiences to ensure maximum efficiency and effectiveness in the use of scarce resources.
- The central element of any influence strategy is creating attractive and motivational exchanges with target audiences.

- The strategy attempts to use all four Ps of the traditional marketing mix; for example, it is not just advertising or communications. That is, it creates attractive packages (products) while minimizing costs (price) wherever possible, making the exchange convenient and easy (place) and communicating powerful messages through media to – and preferred by – target audiences (promotion).
- Careful attention is paid to the competition faced by the desired behavior.

Widespread behavior change using social marketing orientation is also a basic tenet of sustainability. It is suggested that programs promoting sustainable behavior use a "hybrid combination of psychology and social marketing" (Geller 1989). McKenzie-Mohr (2000) refers to this hybrid form as community-based social marketing. It is been increasing reported that this form of marketing is successful in fostering sustainable behavior. Its effectiveness is due to its pragmatic approach, which involves the following steps: carefully selecting an activity to be promoted; identifying barriers when possible; piloting the strategy with a small segment of a community; and finally, evaluating the impact of the program once it has been implemented across the community (McKenzie-Mohr 2000: 532). Examples of behavior-change tools include commitment, prompts, piloting, and evaluation.

Opportunities and Pitfalls in Promoting Sustainability

Moscardo's (2008) work challenging the basic assumptions of sustainable tourism is commendable. He presents a lens through which progress accomplished so far in sustainable tourism can be examined. Moscardo argues that there is no such thing as sustainable tourism and states that "if we begin with the assumption that tourism cannot be sustainable in its own right but may contribute to the sustainable development of some regions under some circumstance, then a number of new approaches to tourism development strategy emerge" (2008: 4). According to the author, the basic concept of sustainable development is laden with questionable contemplations. One limitation is associated with the obsession on continuity of tourism rather than the contribution of tourism to sustainable outcomes (Coccossis 1996), another concern is about tourism posing a barrier to rather than a contributor of sustainable development. A further impediment is that it is often considered in isolation from other sectors and activities (Butler 1999b; Keitumetse 2001). Another barrier is posed by the involvement of external agents in the tourism development process (Johnson and Wilson 2000). Another criticism raised against the conventional sustainable approach is regarding host community only as a resource for tourism development (Hall 2000). Connected to this is the negative outcome caused by the "disempowerment of local residents and other local stakeholders in the tourism development and management process" (Moscardo 2008: 7).

Moscardo claims that limited research has emphasized ascertaining tourism as a resource for regional communities. For instance, some alternative forms of tourism such as ecotourism and volunteer tourism are introduced in indigenous regions solely for the purpose of providing viable income (Keitumetse 2001). In line with this view, three types of synergies are identified by Holmefjord (2000) that can help local communities use tourism to their advantage:

- Product synergies – these suggest finding a tourism type that fits into the existing infrastructure and blends in with other non-tourism activities and businesses.
- Market synergies – this category suggests utilizing the existing customer base to buy tourism products and services. As explained by Moscardo, "the critical element here is to determine the needs of the non-tourism activity and then seek to attract the appropriate type of tourism to support that" (2008: 8). Within this scenario, tourists can be seen to play a broader role than being mere customers; they can be considered a human resource as in the case of volunteer tourism where tourists pay to assist and participate in community projects (Wearing 2001).
- Marketing synergies – these suggest ways to use tourism to produce a broader consciousness of other features of the region. For instance, "joint use of marketing distribution systems, the use of tourists themselves as a promotion tool for regional products and the joint development of regional brands" (Moscardo 2008: 8). An example is efforts to develop regional brands by collaborating with other stakeholders belonging to broader business portfolio.

Against the conventional tourism planning methods, Moscardo (2008) comes up with a list of questions that center on general sustainable development of combined products and services (see Box 9.1). The objective is to gear energies toward an all-inclusive tourism development.

Box 9.1 All-inclusive Tourism Development

1. Are the tourists likely to be attracted to this tourism development also likely to purchase other products?
2. Are the tourists likely to be attracted to this tourism development likely to promote other products or services to others in their work and home environments?
3. Does this form of tourism provide support for the development of infrastructure for non-tourism economic development activities?
4. Will this form of tourism create pressures that will limit the expansion of other activities in the region?
5. Does the destination brand proposed for this form of tourism match or enhance the brands for other products and services?

Source: Moscardo (2008: 9)

Although important lessons can be learnt from the foregoing discussion, it can be argued that Moscardo's basket theory of inclusion and homogeneity does not take into account the complex nature of tourism itself. Also, it assumes that local products can be easily synergized regardless of their distinct characteristics or fragility. While it can be argued that standardization can work for some tourism products, not all can be hybridized. The 'basket' marketing approach suggests undifferentiated positioning strategies. For instance, heritage tourism encompasses fragile objects and environments that have to stay exclusive because of their uniqueness. Their brand is their exclusiveness and elusiveness. Mixing heritage products such as artifacts and historic house museums with other enterprises in one basket departs from some of the core principles of sustainability such as conservation and objectivist/essentialist authenticity. Nevertheless, this strategy serves a useful purpose and can apply to some heritage tourism-related products such as community festivals and heritage hotels. Numerous community festivals seek to represent all that is unique to a destination, both tourism and non-tourism based, and many heritage hotels focus on existing customers who utilize their facility for multi-purpose usage such as conferences and conventions. In such cases, since customers happen to be there, cross-selling can be facilitated; for instance, they can be lured to purchase souvenirs or local food or participate in a cultural tour or activity.

One important lesson to learn from the above discourse is that 'one size does not fit all.' Both homogeneous and heterogeneous product strategies are required. Appropriate scenarios have to be explored to bridge the gap between heritage tourism and not only non-tourism sectors and enterprises, but also heritage tourism and other forms of tourism. In some cases, exploration of opportunities beyond the realm of heritage tourism can make heritage operations more successful and viable. Meaningful collaborations can enhance mutual benefits. For instance, Keitumetse (2009) suggests an eco-cultural tourism approach, that is, an eco-tourism of cultural heritage tourism (CHT). He posits that integration of cultural resources in natural resources management tactics presents an opportunity to resurrect and support community conservation of biodiversity as well as curtail resource use conflicts by cultivating and strengthening communities' sense of place and feelings of civic identity. In other words, natural resource management strategies should not be planned in isolation with the CHT management. Embracing extends resources.

Edwards, Martinac and Miller (2008) suggest a research agenda which includes multiple themes to assist in implementing synergistic efforts between alternative forms of tourism and also between tourism and non-tourism enterprises. Five broad areas were identified to guide the research agenda. As is visible from the description provided below, designing innovation strategies to translate sustainable concepts into practice is not an easy task. It requires a systematic and holistic approach (Edwards *et al.* 2008: 57–59):

- Private sector and small business owners – these are strategies specific to the private sector such as their sustainable priorities, barriers to innovation, business culture, influence of innovation on competitive advantage, motivations for innovation, and attitudes and value of top management levels. Tasks include efforts to examine links between innovations and new product/service development plans, key motivators on innovation, identify mechanisms of risk management in innovation and cost of conversion to sustainable products, identify best practices that contribute the most to environmental sustainability, and examine the importance of corporate culture to successful innovation. With regard to small business enterprises, identify motivations and barriers toward acceptance of sustainable innovative practices, understand factors that help capture their long-term interest, identify stakeholders that can strengthen the innovative capacities of small and medium enterprises (SMEs).

- Knowledge creation and diffusion – understand the meaning of innovation and sustainability, effective use of technology to assist firms, identify mechanisms for distribution of innovative ideas, aggregation, and sharing of sustainable innovations and best practices between sectors and across regions, and understand innovation training needs in the tourism industry.
- Socio-cultural – issues in this category include awareness of different viewpoints of tourism managers, stakeholders etc., impact of macro environment factors such as changing demographics on firms, examine challenges associated with balancing the needs of different stakeholders, examine the role of ethics and corporate governance related to moral issues that can effect innovative initiatives to accomplish sustainable development, and learn to use social marketing to influence social trends.
- Consumer – the consumer perspective includes tasks such as acquiring information on consumer willingness to pay, consumer role in facilitating innovative strategies, understanding consumer perceptions, needs versus wants and guiding them toward sustainable advocacy and behavior, and design methods on how to involve the consumers in the innovative process.
- Government – examine political issues or laws that are likely to affect the private sector success, and identify the role of government in facilitating, supporting or hindering sustainable innovations in the private sector. Other tasks include identifying the role of government in accessing and supporting innovation and sustainability of SMEs, policy and legislation at all governmental levels that facilitate or hinder innovative efforts, political processes required to promote sustainable innovation, develop tools to assist SMEs in the monitoring and regulation of the implementation of sustainable practices and understand perceived value of sustainable practices in developing and emerging tourism destinations.

Contemporary Marketing

Today, the marketing emphasis is more on intangibles as is evident from the mission statements of most of the heritage organizations. Marketing has become the purveyor of signs, symbols, and images. Brown presents seven characteristics of postmodernism that are likely to have a profound influence on sustainable marketing strategies in heritage tourism (1995: 106):

- Fragmentation – political instability and mass-market economy have given rise to feelings of disconnectedness. This is particularly heighted by the incoherent images portrayed through mass advertising and the media. Consequently, mass-marketing approaches are collapsing and markets are being fragmented into small market segments.

- De-differentiation – conventional hierarchies of high/low culture, global/local marketplaces etc. are becoming blurred. For instance, pictures of football heroes appear next to royalty in leading UK newspapers. Thus traditional social class delineations are being collapsed and overridden into the celebrity culture category.
- Hyperreality – simulations are becoming real. Trends are slanted toward consumer fantasy. This characteristic is evident in virtual reality and themed environments provided in pubs, hotels, etc.
- Chronology – postmodernism seeks solace in the past rather than developing progressive orientation toward an unknown future. It has nostalgic connections with the past and seeks aesthetic consumptions of by gone periods. This view reinforces consumer demand for objectivist and sincere authenticity. In fact, it is the baby-boom generation that has spearheaded this era of nostalgic consumption.
- Pastiche – postmodernity also implies preference for collage effects and hybridity by mixing style, past and present. This view is reinforced by the demand for negotiated versions of authenticity by a certain section of today's population.
- Anti-foundationalism – this era is known for deconstructing what is orthodox. Excessive or conventional lifestyles produced by consumerism practices are a product of the bygone era. Demand today is for green and sustainable marketing. In fact, today the time is ripe to pursue these themes because of the increasing recognition proffered on them.
- Pluralism – this implies relativism and advocates shunning of absolute truth. Diversity is valued. Multiculturalism is in fact a byproduct of this phenomenon. Supporters of existentialist authenticity fall within this bracket for they also believe reality is socially constructed and a state of mind.

Thus a variety of trends define the postmodernist era today. Evidenced from the foregoing description, some contradict each other. From a positive standpoint, there is something for everyone today. The aforementioned information provides useful insight into the dynamism behind the contemporary market preferences and needs. Hence the sustainable marketing should be able to relate to these trends.

In closing, a furthering view of the sustainable marketing paradigm is offered to guide sustainable marketing of heritage tourism for both the present and the future generations, in addition to promoting viable social, cultural, and economic environments. Sustainable marketing should seek effective partnerships by engaging with other enterprises in addition to retaining its exclusivity and uniqueness. The themes presented in Figure 9.1 add to the proposed portfolio (see Figure 2.2). One can safely conclude that civic engagement to foster beneficial relationship with the local community and promotion of ethical consumption among tourists are both crucial for the successful application of sustainable marketing. Additionally,

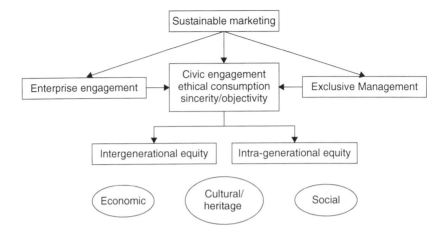

Figure 9.1 Furthering the Sustainable Marketing Paradigm

objectivist and sincere versions of authenticity are needed to promote and provide engaging and satisfying heritage experiences. Marketing strategies should ensure the heritage products signify these ideologies. Also, continued emphasis on conservation through visitor mindfulness can help maintain the long-term health of the heritage offering. These should be the ultimate objective while striving to promote social, economic, and cultural benefits for the local community.

Bibliography

Aaker, D. (2004). *Brand Portfolio Strategy: Creating Relevance, Differentiation, Energy, Leverage, and Clarity*. New York: Simon and Schuster.

AAM (1996). *American Association of Museums Code of Ethics for Museums*. Retrieved April 2008 from www.aam.us.org/museumresources/ethics/coe.cfm.

AAM (2009). *Museum Resources and Museum Facts*. Retrieved August 2008 from www.speakupformuseums.org/museum_facts.htm.

Aas, C., Ladkin, S., and Fletcher, J. (2005). Stakeholder Collaboration and Heritage Management. *Annals of Tourism Research*, 32(1): 28–48.

Adams, V. (1996). *Tigers of the Snow and Other Virtual Sherpas: An Ethnography of Himalayan Encounters*. Princeton: Princeton University Press.

Alexander, E. (1996). *Museums in Motion*. Lanham, MD: Rowman and Littlefield.

Alexander, N. (2009). Brand Authentication: Creating and Maintaining Brand Auras. *European Journal of Marketing*, 43(3/4): 551–562.

Alzua, A., O'Leary, J.T., and Morrison, A.M. (1998). Cultural and Heritage Tourism: Identifying Niches for International Travelers. *Journal of Tourism Studies*, 9(2): 2–13.

AMA (2007). *Definition of Marketing*. Retrieved November 2007 from: http://www.marketingpower.com/AboutAMA/Pages/DefinitionofMarketing.aspx.

Ambler, T. and Styles, C. (1996). Brand Development versus New Product Development: Towards a Process Model of Extension Decisions. *Marketing Management Intelligence and Planning*, 14(7): 10–19.

Ames, F. (1999). *The Kashmir Shawl and its Indo-French Influence*. Woodridge, Suffolk: Antique Collectors' Club Ltd.

Ames, P. (1988). A Challenge to Modern Museum Management: Meshing Mission and Market. *International Journal of Museum Management and Curatorship*, 7(2): 151–7.

Anderson, L. and Littrell, M. (1995). Souvenir-purchase Behavior of Women Tourists. *Annals of Tourism Research*, 22(2): 328–48.

Anderson, L. and Littrell, M. (1996). Group Profiles of Women as Tourists and Purchasers of Souvenirs. *Family and Consumer Sciences Research Journal*, 25(1): 28–56.

Andreasen, A. (2002). Marketing Social Marketing in the Social Change Marketplace. *Journal of Public Policy & Marketing*, 21(1): 3–13.

Ang, H. (2005). *Historic Hotels and Modern Tourism in Singapore and Vietnam*. Honours thesis, Southeast Asian Studies Programme, National University of Singapore.

Apostolakis, A. (2003). The Convergence Process in Heritage Tourism. *Annals of Tourism Research*, 30(4): 795–812.

Arizona Office of Tourism (2009). *Native American Resources*. Retrieved May 15, 2009 from http://www.azot.gov/page.aspx?pid=219.

Arnold, D. (2005). Virtual Tourism – A Niche in Cultural Heritage. In Novelli, M. (ed.) *Niche Tourism: Contemporary Issues, Trends and Cases.* Burlington, MA: Elsevier.

Arnould, E. and Thompson, C. (2005). Consumer Culture Theory (CCT): Twenty Years of Research. *Journal of Consumer Research*, 31(4): 868–862.

Arnstein, S. (1969). A Ladder of Citizen Participation. *Journal of American Institute of Planners,* 35, 216–224.

Ashworth, G. (1992). Whose History? Whose Heritage? Management Means Choice. *Managing Tourism in Historic Cities.* Proceedings of Seminar. International Cultural Center, Krakow, 57–66.

Ashworth, G. (2003). *Heritage: Management, Interpretation, Identity.* London: Continuum Books

Ashworth, G. and Larkham, P. (eds.) (1994). *Marketing in the Tourism Industry.* London: Routledge.

Ashworth, G. and Tunbridge, J. (2000). *The Tourist-historic City.* Amsterdam: Pergamon.

Asplet, M. and Cooper, M. (2000). Cultural Designs in New Zealand Souvenir Clothing: the Question of Authenticity. *Tourism Management*, 21, 307–312.

Augustyn, M. and Knowles, T. (2000). Performance of Tourism Partnerships: A Focus on York. *Tourism Management*, 21, 341–351.

Austin, J. (1982). Their Face to the Rising Sun: Trends in the Development of Black Museums. *Museum News*, 60(3): 28–32.

Bagnall, G. (1996). Consuming the Past. In Edgell S., Hetherington K., Warde, A. (eds) *Consumption Matters: The Production and Experience of Consumptions* (pp. 227–247). Cambridge, MA: Blackwell.

Baker, A. (2000). *Serious Shopping: Psychotherapy and Consumerism.* London: Free Association Books.

Baker, M. (1987). *One More Time: What is Marketing?* London: Heinemann.

Baker, M. (1998). *MacMillan Dictionary of Marketing and Advertising.* Basingstoke: Macmillan Business.

Bakirathi, M. (2002). *The Imagination of South Asian America: Cultural Politics in the Making of Diaspora.* Ph.D. Dissertation: Stanford University.

Bankston, III, C. and Henry, J. (2000). Spectacles of Ethnicity: Festivals and the Commodification of Ethnic Culture among Louisiana Cajuns. *Sociological Spectrum*, 20, 377–407.

Bansal, H. and Eiselt, H. (2004). Exploratory Research of Tourist Motivations and Planning. *Tourism Management*, 25, 387–396.

Beeton, S. and Benfield, R. (2002). Demand Control: The Case for Demarketing as a Visitor and Environment Management Tool. *Journal of Sustainable Tourism*, 10(6): 497–513.

Bellenger, D., Robertson, D., and Hirschman, E. (1978). Impulse Buying Varies by Product. *Journal of Advertising Research*, 18(6): 15–18.

Bennett, T. (1995). *The Birth of the Museums: History, Theory, Politics.* Routledge: London.

Bentor, Y. (1993). Tibetan Tourist Thangkas in the Kathmandu Valley. *Annals of Tourism Research*, 20(1): 107–37.

Bernard, B. and Lane, B. (1993). Sustainable Tourism: An Evolving Global Approach. *Journal of Sustainable Tourism*, 1(1): 1–5.

Berry, S. and Ladkin, A. (1997). Sustainable Tourism: A Regional Perspective. *Tourism Management*, 18(7): 433–440.

Besculides, A., Lee, M., and McCormick, P. (2002). Residents' Perceptions of the Cultural Benefits of Tourism. *Annals of Tourism Research*, 29(2): 303–319.

Beverland, M. (2005). Crafting Brand Authenticity: The Case of Luxury Wine. *Journal of Management Studies*, 42, 1003–1030.

Beverland, M., Lindgreen, A., and Vink, M. (2008). Projecting Authenticity Through Advertising. *Journal of Advertising*, 37(1): 5–15.

Bloch, P., Ridgway, N., and Nelson, J. (1991). Leisure and the Shopping Mall. *Advances in Consumer Research*, 18, 445–452.

Bloch, P., Ridgway, N., and Dawson, S. (1994). The Shopping Mall as a Consumer Habit. *Journal of Retailing*, 70(1): 23–42.

Boniface, P. and Fowler, P. (1993). *Heritage and Tourism in the Global Village*. London: Routledge.

Boo, S. and Busser, J. (2006). Impact Analysis of a Tourism Festival on Tourists Destination Images. *Event Management*, 9, 223–237.

Boorstin, J. (1964). *The Image: A Guide to Pseudo-Events in America*. New York: Harper and Row.

Bowen, H. and Daniels, M. (2005). Does the Music Matter? Motivations for Attending a Music Festival. Event Management, 9(3): 155–164.

Boyd, S. (2002). Cultural and Heritage Tourism in Canada: Opportunities, Principles, and Challenges. *International Journal of Tourism and Hospitality Research*, 3(3): 211–33.

Bramwell, B. and Lane, B. (1993). Interpretation and Sustainable Tourism: The Potential and the Pitfalls. *Journal of Sustainable Tourism*, 1(2): 71–80.

Bramwell, B. and Lane, B. (eds.) (2000). *Tourism Collaboration and Partnerships: Politics, Practice and Sustainability*. Clevedon: Channel View.

Brandes, S. (1997). Sugar, Colonialism, and Death: On the Origins of Mexico's Day of the Dead. *Comparative Studies in Society and History*, 39(2): 270–299.

Brandes, S. (1998). The Day of the Dead, Halloween, and the Quest for Mexican National Identity. *The Journal of American Folklore*, 111(442): 359–380.

Brown, B. (2005). Travelling with a Purpose: Understanding the Motives and Benefits of Volunteer Vacationers. *Current Issues in Tourism*, 8(6): 479–496

Brown, G. (2004). Corporate Social Responsibility. A Government Update. DTI. www.csr.gov.uk.

Brown, S. (1995). *Postmodern Marketing*. London: Routledge.

Bruner, E. (1994). Abraham Lincoln as Authentic Reproduction: A Critique of Postmodernism. *American Anthropologist*, 96(2): 397–415.

Buhalis, D. and Law, R. (2008). Progress in Information Technology and Tourism Management: 20 Years on and 10 Years after the Internet – The State of eTourism Research. *Tourism Management*, 29, 609–623.

Burgers, J. (2000). Urban landscapes on Public Space in the Post-industrial City. *Journal of Housing and Built Environment*, 15(7): 145–164.

Burgers, M. (1992). Edutainment. In Blackall, S. and J. Meek (eds.) *Marketing the Arts*. (pp. 189–196). Lanham, MD: International Council of Museums.

Burns, L. (1993). *Busy Bodies: Why Our Time Obsessed Society Keeps Us Running in Place*. New York: WW Norton & Co. Ltd.

Butcher-Younghans, S. (1993). *A Practical Handbook for Their Care, Preservation and Management*. Oxford: Oxford University Press.

Butler, D. (2001). Whitewashing Plantations: The Commodification of a Slave-free Antebellum South. *International Journal of Hospitality and Tourism Administration*, 2, 163–175.

Butler, J. (1980). *The Economics of Historic Country Houses*. Oxford: Bocardo Press.

Butler, R. (1998). Sustainable Tourism: Looking Backwards in order to Progress? In C.M. Hall and A.A. Lew (eds.) *Sustainable Tourism: A Geographical Perspective* (pp. 25–34). Harlow: Addison-Wesley Longman.

Butler, R. (1991). West Edmonton Mall as a Tourist Attraction. *Canadian Geographer*, 35(3): 287–295.

Butler, R. (1999a). Sustainable Tourism: A State-of-the-Art Review. *Tourism Geographies*, 1(1): 7–25.

Butler, R. (1999b). Problems and Issues of Integrating Tourism Development. In Pearce, D. and Butler, R. (eds.) *Contemporary Issues in Tourism Development* (pp. 65–80). London: Routledge.

Butler, P. (2002). Past, Present, Future: The Place of the House Museum in the Museum Community. In J.F. Donnelly (ed.) *Interpreting Historic House Museums*. Lanham, MD: Alta Mira Press.

Cai, L. (1998). Analyzing Household Food Expenditure Patterns on Trips and Vacations: A Tobit Model. *Journal of Hospitality and Tourism Research*, 22(4): 338–358.

Cai, L., Hong, G., and Morrison, A. (1995). Household Expenditure Patterns for Tourism Products and Services. *Journal of Travel and Tourism Marketing*, 4(4): 15–40.

Caldwell, L. (1996). Heritage tourism: A tool for economic development. In P. Atkinson-Wells (ed.) *Keys to the marketplace: Problems and issues in cultural and heritage tourism* (pp. 125–131). Middlesex, UK: Hisarlik Press.

Callicott, J. and Mumford, K. (1997). Ecological Sustainability as a Conservation Concept. *Conservation Biology*, 11(1): 32–40.

Cameron, C. and Gatewood, J. (2000). Excursions into the Un-Remembered Past: What People Want from Visits to Historical Sites. *The Public Historian*, 22(3): 107–127.

Cano, L. and Mysyk, A. (2004). Cultural Tourism, The State, and The Day of the Dead. *Annals of Tourism Research*, 31(4): 879–898.

Carr, J. (1990). The Social Aspects of Shopping: Pleasure or Core? *The Consumer Perspective. Royal Society of Arts Journal*, 138, 189.

Carter, E. (1993). Ecotourism in the Third World: Problems for Sustainable Tourism Development. *Tourism Management*, 14(2): 85–90.

Caserta, S. and Russo, A. (2002). More Means Worse: Asymmetric Information, Spatial Displacement and Sustainable Heritage Tourism. *Journal of Cultural Economics*, 26, 245–260.

Causey, A. (2003). *Hard Bargaining in Sumatra: Western Travelers and Toba Bataks in the Marketplace of Souvenirs*. Honolulu: University of Hawaii Press.

Chang, T. (1997). Heritage as a Tourism Commodity: Traversing the Tourist-Local Divide. *Singapore Journal of Tropical Geography*, 18(1): 46–68.

Chen, J. and Hsu, C. (2000). Measurement of Korean Tourists' Perceived Images of Overseas Destinations. *Journal of Travel Research*, 38(4): 411–416.

Cheong, S. and Miller, S. (2000). Power and Tourism: A Foucauldian Observation. *Annals of Tourism Research*, 27, 371–390.

Chernish, W. (1998). Literary Lodgings: Historic Hotels in Britain Where Famous Writers Lived. *Journal of Hospitality and Tourism Research*, 21(3): 117–120.

Chhabra, D. (2005). Defining Authenticity and Its Determinants: Toward an Authenticity Flow Model. *Journal of Travel Research*, 44(1): 64–73.

Chhabra, D. (2008). Positioning Museums on an Authenticity Continuum. *Annals of Tourism Research*, 35(2): 427–447.

Chhabra, D. (2009). Proposing a Sustainable Marketing Framework for Heritage Tourism. *Journal of Sustainable Tourism*, 17(3): 313–320.

Chhabra, D., Healy, R., and Sills, E., (2003). Staged Authenticity and Heritage Tourism. *Annals of Tourism Research*, 30, 702–719.

Chhabra, D., Sills, E., and Rea, P. (2002). Tourist Expenditures at Heritage Festivals. *Event Management,* 7(4): 221–230.

Chhabra, D., Sills, E., and Cubbage, F. (2003). Significance of Festivals to Rural Economies: Estimating the Economic Impacts of Scottish Highland Games in North Carolina. *Journal of Travel Research*, 41(4): 421–436.

Chibnik, M. (2003). *Crafting Tradition: The Making and Marketing of Oaxacan Wood Carvings.* Austin: The University of Texas Press.

Chogull. M. (1996). A Ladder of Community Participation for Underdeveloped Countries. *Habitat International*, 20(3): 431–444.

Chronis, A. and Hampton, R. (2008). Consuming the Authentic Gettysburg: How a Tourist Landscape Becomes an Authentic Experience. *Journal of Consumer Research*, 7(2): 111–126.

Clarke, J. (1997). A Framework of Approaches to Sustainable Tourism. *Journal of Sustainable Tourism*, 5(3): 224–33

Coccossis, H. (1996). Tourism and Sustainability: Perspectives and Implications, In G.K. Priestley, A. Edwards and H. Coccossis (eds.) *Sustainable Tourism? European Experiences*. Wallingford, UK: CAB International, pp. 1–21.

Coccossis, H. (2008). Cultural Heritage, Local Resources, and Sustainable Tourism. *International Journal of Services, Technology and Management*, 10(1): 54–60.

Coetze, W., Nierkerk, M., and Saayman, M. (2008). Applying Economic Guidelines for Responsible Tourism in a World Heritage Site. *KOEDOE African Protected Area Conservation and Science*, 50(1): 54–60.

Cogswell, L. (1996). Grassroots Issues in Cultural Tourism. In P. Wells (ed.) *Keys to Marketplace: Problems and Issues in Cultural and Heritage Tourism*. Middlesex, UK: Hisarlik Press.

Cohen, E. (1988). Authenticity and Commodification in Tourism. *Annals of Tourism Research*, 15, 371–386.

Cohen, E. (1992). Tourists Arts. *Progress in Tourism, Recreation, and Hospitality Management*, 4, 3–32.

Cohen, E. (1993a). Introduction: Investigating Tourist Art. *Annals of Tourism Research*, 20(1): 1–8.

Cohen, E. (1993b). The Heterogeneization of Tourist Art. *Annals of Tourism Research*, 20(1): 138–63.

Cohen, E. (2000). *The Commercialized Crafts of Thailand.* Honolulu: University of Hawaii Press.

Cohen, E. (2007). Authenticity in Tourism Studies. *Tourism Recreation Research*, 32(2): 75–82.

Cole, D. (1985). *Captured Heritage.* Seattle and London: University of Washington Press.

Cony, S. (2002). Give Your Staff the Marketing Edge. *Camping Magazine*, 75(2): 42–43.

Cooper, L. and Inoue, A. (1996). Building Structures from Consumer Preferences. *Journal of Marketing Research,* 33(3): 293–306.

Cossons, N. (1989). Heritage Tourism- Trends and Tribulations. *Tourism Management*, 10(3): 192–194.

Cova, B. (1997). Community and Consumption and Consumption: Towards a Definition of the Linking Value of Product or Services. *European Journal of Marketing*, 31(3/4): 297–316.

Cova, B. and Cova, V. (2002). Tribal Market: The Tribalization of Society and its Impact on the Conduct of Marketing. *European Journal of Marketing*, 36(5/6): 595–620.

Cracolici, M., Cuffaro, M., and Nijkamp, P. (2008). Sustainable Tourist Development in Italian Holiday Destinations. *International Journal of Services Technology and Management*, 10(1): 39–47.

Creswell, J. and Clark, V. (2007). *Designing and Conducting Mixed Methods Research.* Newbury Park, CA: Sage Publications.

Croall, J. (1995). *Preserve or Destroy: Tourism and the Environment.* London: Calouste Gulbenkian Foundation.

Crompton, J. (1979). Motivations for Pleasure Vacation. *Annals of Tourism Research*, 6(4): 408–424.

Crompton, J. (2006). Economic Impact Studies: Instruments for Political Shenanigans. *Journal of Travel Research,* 45(1): 67–82

Crompton, J. and Lamb, C. (1986). *Marketing Government and Social Services.* New York: John Wiley & Sons, Inc.

Crompton, J. and McKay, S. (1997). Motivations for Pleasure Vacation. *Annals of Tourism Research*, 6(4): 408–424.

Crompton, J. and McKay, S. (2006). Adapting Herzberg: A Conceptualization of the Effects of Hygiene and Motivator Attributes in Perceptions of Event Quality. *Journal of Travel Research*, 24(2): 425–439.

Crompton, J., Lee, S., and Shuster, T. (2001). A Guide for Undertaking Economic Impact Studies: The Springfest Example. *Journal of Travel Research*, 40(1): 79–87.

Cronis, A. and Hampton, R. (2008). Consuming the Authentic Gettysburg: How a Tourist Landscape Becomes an Authentic Experience. *Journal of Consumer Behavior*, 7, 111–126.

Csikszentmihalyi, M. (1996). *Creativity: Flow and the Psychology of Discovery and Invention.* New York: HarperCollins.

Culloden House (2009). *Culloden House History.* Inverness, Scotland: Culloden House Hotel.

Daniel, Y. (1996). Tourism Dance Performances Authenticity and Creativity. *Annals of Tourism Research*, 23(4): 780–797.

Dann, G. (1981). Tourist Motivation an Appraisal: *Annals of Tourism Re*search, 8(2): 187–219.

Davies, B. and Mangan, J. (1992). Family Expenditures on Hotels and Holidays. *Annals of Tourism Research*, 19, 691–600.

DeLyser, D. (1999). Authenticity on the Ground: Engaging the Past in a California Ghost Town. *Annals of the Association of American Geographers*, 89(4): 602–632.

Derrett, R. (2004). Festivals, Events, and the Destination. In Yeoman, I., Robertson, M., Ali-Knight, J., Drummond, S. and McMahon-Beattie (eds.) *Festival and Events Management: An International Arts and Culture Perspective* (pp. 32–52). New York: Elsevier.

Dewar, K., Meyer, D., and Li, W. (2001). Harbin, Lanterns of Ice, Sculptures of Snow. *Tourism Management*, 22: 523–532.

Dibb, S. and Simkin, L. (1996). *The Market Segmentation Workbook: Target Marketing for Marketing Managers.* Thomson: London.

Dinan, C. and Sargeant, A. (2000). Social Marketing and Sustainability: Is there a Match? *International Journal of Tourism Research*, 2(1): 1–14.

Dincer, F. (2003). Economic Impact of Heritage Tourism Hotels in Istanbul. *The Journal of Tourism Studies,* 14(2): 23–34.

Dodds, W., Monroe, K., and Grewal, D. (1991). Effects of Price, Brand, and Store Information on Buyer's Product Evaluations. *Journal of Marketing Research*, 28(3): 307–319.

du Cros, H. (2001). A New Model to Assist in Planning for Sustainable Cultural Heritage Tourism. *International Journal of Tourism Research*, 3(2): 165–170.

du Cros, H. (2007). Too Much of a Good Thing? Visitor Congestion Management Issues for Popular World Heritage Tourist Attractions. *Journal of Heritage Tourism*, 2(3): 225–237.

du Cros, H. (2009). Emerging Issues for Cultural Tourism in Macau. *Journal of Current Chinese Affairs,* 38(1): 73–99.

Dutton, S. and Busby, G. (2002). Antiques-based Tourism: Our Common Heritage? *Acta Turistica*, 14(2): 97–119.

East Sussex County Council (1994). *Tourism in East Sussex*. Lewes: East Sussex County Council.

Edwards, D., Martinac, I., and Miller, G. (2008). Research Agenda for Innovation in Sustainable Tourism. *Tourism and Hospitality* Research, 8(1): 56–61.

Ehrlich, P. and Ehrlich, A. (1990). *The Population Explosion*. New York: Simon and Schuster.

Eichstedt, J. and Small, S. (2002). *Representation of Slavery: Race and Ideology in Southern Plantation Museum*. Washington DC: Smithsonian Institute Press.

English Heritage (2009). *Research and Conservation*. Retrieved April 15, 2009 from http://www.english-heritage.org.uk/.

Errington, S. (1998). *The Death of Authentic Primitive Art and Other Tales of Progress*. Berkeley: University of California Press.

Esperanza, J. (2008). Outsourcing Otherness: Crafting and Marketing Culture in the Global Handicrafts Market. *Research in Economic Anthropology*, 28, 71–95.

Faulkner, B. and Moscardo, G. (eds.) *Embracing and Managing Change in Tourism: International Case Studies*. Routledge: London.

Faulkner, B., Fredline, E., Larson, M., and Tomljenovac, R. (1999). A Marketing Analysis of Sweden's Storsjoyran Music Festival. *Tourism Analysis*, 4, 157–171.

Fayissa, B., Nsiah, C., and Tadasse, B. (2007). *The Impact of Tourism on Econimic Growth and Development in Africa*. Department of Economic and Finance Development Series. Retrieved July 18, 2008 from http://frank.mtsu.edu/~berc/working/TourismAfricawp.pdf.

Feest, C. (1992). *Native Arts of North America*. London: Thames and Hudson.

Fernandes, L. (2000). Nationalizing 'Global': Media Images, Cultural Politics and the Middle Class in India. *Media Culture Society*, 22, 611–628.

Finn, A., McQuilty, S., and Rigby, J. (1994). Residents' Acceptance and Use of a Mega-multi-mall: West Edmonton Mall Evidence. *International Journal of Research and Marketing*, 11, 127–44.

Fish, M. and Waggle, D. (1996). Current Income versus Total Expenditure Measures in Regression Models of Vacation and Pleasure Travel. *Journal of Travel Research*, 35(2): 70–74.

Formica, S. (1998). The Development of Festivals and Special Events Studies. *Festival Management and Event Tourism*, 5, 131–137.

Formica, S. and Murrmann, S. (1998). The Effects of Group Membership and Motivation on Attendance: An International Festival Case. *Tourism Analysis*, 3, 197–207.

Formica, D. and Uysal, M. (1996). A Market Segmentation of Festival Visitors: Umbria Jazz Festival in Italy. *Festival Management and Event Tourism*, 3(4): 175–182.

Formica, S. and Uysal, M. (1998). Market Segmentation of an International Cultural-historical Event in Italy. *Journal of Travel Research*, 36(4): 16–24.

France, L. (1998). Local Participation in Tourism in the West Indian Islands. In E. Laws, B. Faulkner, and G. Moscardo (eds.) *Embracing and Managing Change in Tourism* (pp. 222–234). London: Routledge.

French, Y. (2001). *Forces.* Leisure Management, 21(3): 30–31.

Freud, S. (1961). *The Ego and The Id.* London: Hogarth Press.

Freud Museum (2009a). *Exhibits.* Retrieved on June 21, 2009 from http://www.freud.org.uk/indexdream.html

Freud Museum (2009b). *The Interpretation of Dreams.* Retrieved May 10, 2009 from http://www.freud.org.uk/daughter.html

Frey, A. (1961). *Advertising*, 3rd edn. New York: The Ronald Press.

Frochot, I. (2005). A Benefit Segmentation of Tourists in Rural Areas: A Scottish Perspective. *Tourism Management,* 26, 335–346.

Frochot, I. and Morrison, A. (2000). Benefit Segmentation: A Review of its Application to Travel and Tourism Research. *Journal of Travel and Tourism Marketing,* 9(4): 21–45.

Frost, W. (2006). *Cultural Heritage and Tourism in Australia: Concepts and Issues.* Department of Management Working Paper Series: Monash University.

Fuller, N. (1992). The Museum as a Vehicle for Community Empowerment: The Ak-Chin Indian Community Ecomuseum Project. In Karp, I., Mullen, C. and Lavine, S. (eds.) *Museums and Communities: The Politics of Public Culture* (pp. 327–365). Washington DC: Smithsonian Institution Press.

Fyall, A. and Garrod, B. (1998). Heritage Tourism: At What Price. *Managing Leisure*, 3: 213–228.

Gandhi Memorial Museum (2009). *History.* Retrieved June 20, 2009 from http://www.gandhimuseum.org/aboutus.htm

Garrod, B. and Fyall, A. (2001). Managing Heritage Tourism: A Question of Definition. *Annals of Tourism Research*, 28, 1049–52.

Garrod, B. and Fyall, A. (1998). Beyond the Rhetoric of Sustainable Tourism. *Tourism Management*, 19(3): 199–212.

Gartner, W. (1993). Image Formation Process: Communicating Tourism Supplier Services; Building Repeat Visitor Relationships. *Journal of Travel and Tourism Marketing,* 2(2/3): 191–216.

Geissler, G. (2006). Understanding the Role of Service Convenience in Art Museum Marketing: An Exploratory Study. *Journal of Hospitality and Leisure Marketing*, 14(4): 69–87.

Geller, E.S. (1989). Applied Behavior Analysis and Social Marketing: An Integration for Environmental Preservation. *Journal of Social Issues,* 45(1): 17–36.

Getz, D. (1991). *Festivals, Special Events, and Tourism.* New York: Van Nostrand Reinhold.

Getz, D. (1993). Tourist Shopping Villages: Development and Planning Strategies. *Tourism Management*, 14(1): 15–26.

Getz, D. (1997). *Event Management and Event Tourism.* New York: Cognizant Communication Corporation.

Getz, D. (2002). Why Festivals Fail? *Event Management*, 7, 209–219.

Getz, D. and Frisby, W. (1988). Evaluating Management Effectiveness in Community-run Festivals. *Journal of Travel Research*, 27, 22–27.

Gilbert, D. (1996). Relationship Marketing and Airline Loyalty Schemes. *Tourism Management*, 17(8): 575–582.

Gilbert, D. and Lizotte, M. (1998). Tourism and the Performing Arts. *Travel and Tourism Analyst*, 1, 82–96.

Goldplatt, J. (1997). *Special Events: Best Practices in Event Management*, 2nd edn. New York: VNR.

Goodwin, H. and Francis, J. (2003). Ethical and Responsible Tourism: Consumer Trends in the UK. *Journal of Vacation Marketing*, 9(3): 271–285.

Gordon, N. (1986). The Souvenir: Messenger of the Extraordinary. *Journal of Popular Culture*, 20(3): 135–46.

Gorgas, M. (2001). Reality as Illusion, the Historic Houses that Become Museums. *Museum International*, 53(2): 10–15.

Goss, J. (1993). The Magic of the Mall: An Analysis of Form, Function and Meaning in the Contemporary Retail Built Environment. *Annals of the Association of American Geographers,* 83(1): 18–47.

Goulding, C. (2000). The Museum Environment and the Visitor Experience. European *Journal of Marketing*, 34 (3 and 4): 261–278.

Graburn, N. (1976). Introduction: Arts of the Fourth World. In N. Graburn (ed.) *Ethnic Arts and Tourist Arts: Cultural Expressions from the Fourth World* (pp. 1–32). Berkeley: University of California Press.

Graburn, N. (1982). The Dynamics of Change in Tourist Arts. *Cultural Survival Quarterly*, 6(4): 7–11.

Graburn, N. (1987). The Evolution of Tourist Arts. *Annals of Tourism Research*, 11(3): 393–420.

Graburn, N. (1989). The Sacred Journey. In V. Smith and M. Brent (eds.) *Hosts and Guests Revisited: Issues in the 21ˢᵗ Century* (pp. 21–36). New York: Cognizant.

Graham, B., Ashworth, G., and Tunbridge, J. (2000). *A Geography of Heritage: Power, Culture and Economy*. Arnold: London.

Grandfather Mountain Highland Games (GMHG) Office (1999). *Information*. Linville, NC: Grandfather Mountain Highland Games Inc.

Gray, B. (1985). Conditions Facilitating Interorganizational Collaboration. *Human Relations,* 38(10): 911–936.

Gray, N. and Campbell, L. (2007). A Decommodified Experience: Exploring Aesthetic, Economic and Ethical Values for Volunteer Ecotourism in Costa Rica. *Journal of Sustainable Tourism*, 15(5): 463–482.

Grayson, K. and Martinec, R. (2004). Consumer Perceptions of Iconicity and Indexicality and Their Influence on Assessments of Authentic Market Offerings. *Journal of Consumer Research*, 31, 296–312.

Greenwood, D. (1977). Culture by the Pound: An Anthropological Perspective on Tourism as Cultural Commodification. In V.L. Smith (ed.) *Hosts and Guests: The Anthropology of Tourism* (pp. 129–139). Philadelphia: Philadelphia University Press.

Gretzel, U., Yuan, Y., and Fesenmaier, D. (2000). Preparing for the New Economy: Advertising Strategies and Changes in Destination Marketing Organization. *Journal of Travel Research*, 39(2): 146–156.

Gronroos, C. (1990). Relationship Approach to the Marketing Function in Service Contexts: the Marketing and Organization Behavior Interface. *Journal of Business Interface*, 20(1): 3–12.

Gronroos, C. (1994). From Marketing Mix to Relationship Marketing: Towards a Paradigm Shift in Marketing. *Management Decision*, 35(4): 322–329.

Gummesson, E. (1999). *Total Relationship Marketing: Rethinking Marketing from 4 Ps to 30 Rs*. Oxford: Butterworth Heinemann.

Gunn, C. (1994). *Tourism Planning: Basics, Concepts, Cases*. 3rd edn. Washington, DC: Taylor and Francis.

Gursoy, D., Jurowski, C., and Uysal, M. (2002). Resident Attitudes: A Structural Modeling Approach. *Annals of Tourism Research*, 29(1): 79–105.

Halewood, C. and Hannam, K. (2001). Viking heritage tourism: Authenticity and Commodification. *Annals of Tourism Research*, 28(3): 565–580.

Hall, C. (1994). *Tourism and Politics: Policy, Power and Place*. Chichester: Wiley.

Hall, C. (2000). *Tourism: Rethinking the Social Science of Mobility*. Harlow: Prentice Hall.

Hall, C. (2005). *Rethinking the Social Science of Mobility*. Harlow: Person Education.

Hanquin, Z. and Lam, T. (1999). An Analysis of Mainland Chinese Visitors' Motivations to Visit Hong Kong. *Tourism Management*, 20, 587–594.

Harris, R. and Leiper, N. (eds.) (1995). *Sustainable Tourism: An Australian Perspective*. Oxford: Butterworth-Heinemann.

Harris, R., Jago, L., Allen, J., and Huyskens, M. (2001). Towards an Australian Research Agenda: First Steps. *Event Management*, 6, 213–221.

Harrison, R. (1994). London's Tower Bridge. In R. Harrison (ed.) *Manual of Heritage Management* (pp. 315–319). Oxford: Butterworth Heinemann.

Hart, W. (1994). Elegant Survivors: Historic Hotel Renovation in Oregon. *Cornell Hotel and Restaurant Administration Quarterly*, 35(4): 39–56.

Harvey, C. (1996). The Heritage Embroglio: Quagmires of Politics. In P.A. Wells (ed.) *Keys to the Marketplace: Problems and Issues in Cultural and Heritage Tourism*, (pp. 43–63). London: Hisarlik Press.

Hassan, S. (2000). Determinants of Market Competitiveness in an Environmentally Sustainable Tourism Industry. *Journal of Travel Research*, 38, 239–245.

Heard Museum (2009). *About the Heard*. Retrieved, May 15, 2009 from http://www.heard.org/

Hede, A. (2007). World Heritage Listing and the Evolving Issues Related to Tourism and Heritage: Cases from Australia and New Zealand. *Journal of Heritage Tourism*, 2(3): 133–144.

Hede, A. and Thyne, M. (2007). *Authenticity and Branding for Literary Heritage Attractions*. ANZMA Papers: University of Otago.

Henderson, J. (2001). Conserving Colonial Heritage: Raffles Hotel in Singapore. *International Journal of Heritage Studies*, 7(1): 7–24.

Henderson, J. (2005). Exhibiting Cultures: Singapore's Asian Civilisations Museum. *International Journal of Heritage Studies*, 11(3): 183–195.

Herbert, D. (1989). Leisure Trends and the Heritage Market. In Herbert D., Prentice, R. and Thomas, C. (eds.) *Heritage Sites: Strategies for Marketing and Development* (pp.10–14). Avesbury: Aldershot.

Herbert, D. (ed.) (1995). Heritage, Tourism, and Society. London: Mansell.

Hinsley, C. (1982). *Savages and Scientists*. Washington DC: Smithsonian Press.

Historic Houses Association (2009). *Annual Report*. Retrieved June 5, 2009 from http://www.hha.org.uk/metadot/index.pl?id=24156&isa=Category&op=show

Hitchcock, M. and Teague, K. (eds.) (2000). *Souvenirs: The Material Culture of Tourism*. Sydney: Ashgate.

Hollinshead, K. (1996). Disney and Commodity Aesthetics: A Critique of Fjellman's Analysis of "Distory" and "Historicide" of the Past. *Current Issues in Tourism*, 1(1): 58–97.

Hollinshead, K. (1999). Tourism as Public Culture: Horne's Ideological Commentary on the Legerdomain of Tourism. *International Journal of Tourism Research*, 1(4): 267–292.

Holloway, C. (2004). *Marketing for Tourism*. Harlow, UK: Prentice Hall.

Holmefjord, K. (2000). Synergies in Linking Product, Industries and Place? Is Co-operation Between Tourism and Food Industries a Local Coping Strategy in Lofoten and Hardanger? Paper presented at the MOST CCPPP Workshop: Whether, How and Why Regional Policies are Working in Concert with Coping Strategies Locally, Joensuu, Finland.

Howard, P. (2003). *Heritage: Management, Monuments, and Museums: The Past in the Present*. Melbourne: Melbourne University Press.

Hsieh, S. and O'Leary, J. (1993). Communication Channels to Segment Pleasure Travelers. Communicating Tourism Supplier Services: Building Repeat Visitor Relationships. *Journal of Travel and Tourism Marketing,* 2(2/3): 57–76.

Hughes, G. (1995). Authenticity in Tourism. *Annals of Tourism Research,* 22(4): 781–803.

Hughes, H. (1998). Theater in London and the Inter-relationship with Tourism. *Tourism Management,* 19(5) 445–452.

Hughes, H. (2000). *Arts, Entertainment, and Tourism*. Oxford: Butterworth.

Hunt, S. (1976). The Nature and Scope of Marketing. *Journal of Marketing,* 40, 17–28.

Hunt, S. and Vitell, S. (2006). The General Theory of Marketing Ethics: A Revision and Three Questions. *Journal of Macromarketing,* 12(26): 143–153.

Hunter, C. (1997). Sustainable Tourism as an Adaptive Paradigm. *Annals of Tourism Research,* 24(4): 850–867.

ICOM (1987). *Definition of a 'Museum.'* Incorporated on the Statures of the International Council of Museums and adopted at the 11th General Assembly of ICOM in Copenhagen. Retrieved from http://icom.museum/statutes.html#2

ICOMOS (2004). *ICOMOS Charter*. Retrieved, June 10, 2008 from www.international.icomos.org/charters.htm

Innskeep, E. (1991). *Tourism Planning: An Integrated and Sustainable Development Approach.* New York: Van Nostrand Reinhold.

Innskeep, E. (1994). *National and Regional Tourism Planning.* A World Tourism Organization (WTO) Publication. London: Routledge.

Iso-Ahola, S. (1982). Toward a Social Psychological Theory of Tourism Motivation. *Annals of Tourism Research,* 9, 256–262.

Iso-Ahola, S. (1989). Motivation for Leisure. In E.L. Jackson and T.L. Burton (eds.), *Understanding Leisure and Recreation: Mapping the Past Charting the Future* (pp. 247–279). State College, PA: Venture Publishing.

Jamieson, W. (ed.) (1997). *Sustainable Tourism.* Workbook prepared by the Centre for Environmental Design Research and Outreach. The Faculty of Environmental Design: The University of Calgary.

Jamieson, W. (2000). The Challenges of Sustainable Community Heritage Tourism. Heritage Management and Tourism Conference. Bhaktapur, Nepal: UNESCO Workshop on Culture.

Janes, P. (2006). *Marketing in Leisure and Tourism: Reaching New Heights*. State College, PA: Venture Publishing.

Jang, S., Bai, B., Hong, G., and O'Leary, J. (2004). Understanding Travel Expenditure Patterns: A Study of Japanese Pleasure Travellers to the Unites States by Income Level. *Tourism Management,* 25, 331–341.

Jansen-Verbeke, M. (1990). From Leisure Shopping to Shopping Tourism. In *Proceedings of the ISA Congress*, Madrid (pp. 1–17). Madrid: ISA.

Jansen-Verbeke, M. (1998). The Synergism between Shopping and Tourism: The Japanese Experience. In W.F. Theobold (ed.) *Global Tourism: The Next Decade* (pp. 37–62). Oxford: Butterworth-Heinemann.

Jayakar, P. (1973). Report on The Development Review Committee Jammu and Kashmir. Part III, Development of Handicrafts and Handlooms. Jammu and Kashmir.

Jeong, G. (1998). The Appraisal of Kumsan Ginseng Festival – A Longitudinal Study (94–96–97): As a Case of Cultural Festival Tourism. *Journal of Tourism Sciences*, 22(2): 57–63.

Jewell, B. and Crotts, J. (2001). Adding Psychological Value to Heritage Tourism Experiences. *Journal of Travel and Tourism Marketing*, 11(4): 13–28.

Jewell, B. and Crotts, J. (2009). Adding Psychological Value to Heritage Tourism Experiences Revisited. *Journal of Travel and Tourism Marketing*, 26, 244–263.

Johnson, H. and Wilson, G. (2000). Biting the Bullet: Civil Society, Social Earning and the Transformation of Local Governance. *World Development*, 28(11): 1891–1906.

Johnson, P. and Thomas, B. (1995). Heritage as Business. In D.T. Herbert (ed.) *Heritage, Tourism and Society* (pp. 170–190). London: Mansell.

Johnson, S. and Howard, E. (1990). The Leisure Market: Consumer Choice and Consumer Activity. In E. Howard (ed.) *Leisure and Retailing* (pp. 25–42). Harlow: Longman.

Jones, M. (1993). *Why Fakes Matter: Essays on Problems of Authenticity*. London: The Trustees of the British Museum.

Jones, P., Clarke-Hill, C., and Comfort, D. (2008). Marketing and Sustainability. *Marketing Intelligence and Planning*, 26(2): 123–130.

Josiam, B., Mattson, M., and Sullivan, P. (2004). The Historaunt: Heritage Tourism ate Mickey's Dining Car. *Tourism Management*, 25, 453–461.

Kamakura, W. and Russell, G. (1993). Measuring Brand Value with Scanner Data. *International Journal of Research*, 10(1): 9–22.

Kamara, M., Coff, C., and Wynne, B. (2006). *GMOs and Sustainability: Contested Visions, Routes and Drivers*. ESRC Center for Economic and Social Aspects of Genomics, Lancaster University, UK. Report prepared for the Danish Council of Ethics, Copenhagen.

Kanawati, D. (2006). *Founding or Funding: Are Historic House Museums in Trouble?* Theses, University of Pennsylvania.

Kaul, H. and Gupta, S. (2009). Sustainable Tourism in India. *Worldwide Hospitality and Tourism Themes*, 1(1): 12–18.

Keitumetse, S. (2001). The Eco-tourism of Cultural Heritage Management (ECT-CHM): Linking Heritage and Environment in the Okavango Delta Regions of Botswana. *International Journal of Heritage Studies*, 15(2–3): 223–244.

Keller, K. (2003). *Strategic Brand Management: Building, Measuring, and Managing Brand Equity*, 2nd edn. Sydney: Prentice Hall.

Kent, W., Shock, P., and Snow, R. (1983). Shopping: Tourism's Unsung Hero(ine). *Journal of Travel Research*, 21(4): 2–4.

Keowin, C. (1989). A Model of Tourists' Propensity to Buy: The Case of Japanese Visitors to Hawaii. *Journal of Travel Research*, 27(3): 31–4.

Kerstetter, D., Confer, J., and Bricker, K. (1998). Industrial Heritage Attractions: Types and Tourists. *Journal of Travel and Tourism Marketing*, 7(2): 91–104.

Kerstetter, D., Confer, J., and Graefe, A. (2001). An Exploration of the Specialization Concept within the Context of Heritage Tourism. *Journal of Travel Research*, 39(3): 267–274.

Khan, F. and Kilian, D. (1996). Tourism Beyond Apartheid: Black Empowerment and Identity in the 'New' South Africa. In W. Wells (ed.) *Keys to the Marketplace: Problems and Issues in Cultural and Heritage Tourism* (pp. 43–64). Middlesex, UK: Hisarlik Press.

Kim, C., Scott, D., Thigpen, J., and Kim, S. (1998). Economic Impact of a Birding Festival. *Festival Management and Event Tourism*, 5(1/2): 51–58.

Klein N. (2001). *No Logo*. London: Flamingo.

Klenosky, D. (2002). The Pull of Tourism Destinations: A Means-end Investigation. *Journal of Travel Research*, 40(4): 385–395.

Klumbis, D. and Munsters, W. (2005). Developments in the Hotel Industry: Design Meets Historic Properties. In *International Cultural Tourism*, Sigala, M. and Leslie, D. (eds.) London: Elsevier Butterworth Heinemann.

Knudson, D., Cable, T., and Beck, L. (1995). *Interpretation of Cultural and Natural Resources*. State College, PA: Venture.

Kohli, A. and Jaworski, B. (1990). Market Orientation: The Construct, Research Propositions, and Managerial Implications. *Journal of Marketing*, 54, 1–18.

Kopytoff, I. (1986). The Cultural Biography of Things: Commodification as Process. In A. Apadurai (ed.) *The Social Life of Things: Commodities in Cultural Perspective* (pp. 64–91). Cambridge: Cambridge University Press.

Koschnick, W. (1995). *Dictionary of Marketing*. Aldershot: Gower.

Kotler, P. (1982). *Marketing for Nonprofit Organizations*. Upper Saddle River, NJ: Prentice Hall.

Kotler, P. (2000). *Marketing Management*, the millennium edition: Upper Saddle River, NJ: Prentice Hall.

Kotler, P. and Andreasen, A. (1987). *Strategic Marketing of Nonprofit Organizations*. Upper Saddle River, NJ: Prentice Hall.

Kotler, P. and Levy, S. (1969a). Broadening the Concept of Marketing. *Journal of Marketing*, 35, 3–12.

Kotler, P. and Levy, S. (1969b). Beyond Marketing: The Furthering Concept. *California Management Review*, xii (Winter): 67–73.

Kotler, K., Bowen, J., and Makens, J. (2006). *Marketing for Hospitality and Tourism*. Upper Saddle River, NJ: Prentice Hall.

Kotler, N. and Kotler, P. (2000). Can Museums be All Things to All People? Missions, Goals, and Marketing's Role. *Museum Management and Curatorship*, 18(3): 271–289.

Kozinets, R. (1999). The Field Behind the Screen: Using Netnography for Marketing Research in Online Communities. *Journal of Marketing Research*, 36, 61–72.

Kozinets, R. (2002). The Field Behind the Screen: Using Netnography Research in Online Communities. *Journal of Marketing Research*, 39, 61–72.

Krippendorf, E. (1987). The Dominance of American Approaches in International Relations. *Journal of International Studies*, 16(2): 207–214.

Kumbh Mela Report (2009). *MahaKumbh*. India: UP Tourism Office.

Laarman, J. and Gregersen, H. (1996). Pricing Policy in Nature-based Tourism. *Tourism Management*, 17(4): 247–254.

Labrador, R. (2002). Performing Identity: The Public Presentation of Culture and Ethnicity among Filipinos in Hawaii. *Cultural Values*, 6(3): 287–307.

Laczniak, G. and Murphy, P. (2006). Normative Perspectives for Ethical and Socially Responsible Marketing. *Journal of Macromarketing*, 12(56): 154–177.

Lade, C. and Jackson, J. (2000). Key Success Factors in Regional Festivals: Some Australian Experiences. *Event Management*, 9(1/2): 1–11.

Langer, E. (1989). *Mindfulness*. Reading, MA: Addison-Wesley.

Law, R. and Au, N. (2000). Relationship Modeling in Tourism Shopping: A Decision Rules Induction Approach. *Tourism Management*, 21(3): 241–9.

Lazer, W. and Kelly, E. (1962). *Managerial Marketing: Perspectives and Viewpoints*, revised edition. Homewood, IL: Richard D. Irwin, Inc.

Lee, C., Lee, Y., and Wicks, B. (2004). Segmentation of Festival Motivation by Nationality and Satisfaction. *Tourism Management*, 25(1): 61–70.

LeMenestrel, S. (1999). *Constructions Identitaires et Contexte Touristique: L'exemple Des Cadiens du Sud-Ouest Du La Louisiane*. Ph.D. dissertation. Nanterre, France: Université de Paris.

Leones, J., Colby, B., and Crandall, K. (1998). Tracking Expenditures of Elusive Nature Tourists of Southeastern Arizona. *Journal of Travel Research*, 36, 56–64.

Lesser, J. and Hughes, M. (1986). Towards a Typology of Shoppers. *Business Horizons*, 29(6): 56–62.

Li, M., Wu, B., and Cai, L. (2008). Tourism Development of World Heritage Sites in China: A Geographic Perspective. *Tourism Management*, 29(2): 308–319.

Li, X. and Petrick, J. (2006). A Review of Festival and Event Motivation Studies. *Event Management*, 9, 239–245.

Li, Y. and Bong, L. (2004). Applicability of Market Appeal and Robusticity Matrix: A Case Study of Heritage Tourism. *Tourism Management*, 25(6): 789–800.

Lib, A. (2007). *Definition of Marketing*. ELMAR: Electronic Marketing.

Liechty, M. (2002). *Suitably Modern; Making Middle-Class Culture in a New Consumer Society*. Princeton: Princeton University Press.

Light, D. (1992). Bilingual Heritage Interpretation in Wales. *Scottish Geographical Magazine*, 108(3): 179–83.

Light, D. (1995). Visitors' Use of Interpretive Media at Heritage Sites. *Leisure Studies*, 14, 133–49.

Light, D. (1996). Characteristics of the Audience for Events at a Heritage Site. *Tourism Management*, 17(3): 183–190.

Littrell, M. (1990). Shopping Experiences and Marketing of Culture to Tourists. In M. Robinson, N. E. Evans and P. Callaghan (eds.) T*ourism and Culture: Image, Identity and Marketing* (pp. 107–20). Newcastle: University of Northumbria.

Littrell, M., Andersen, L., and Brown, P. (1993). What Makes a Craft Souvenir Authentic? *Annals of Tourism Research*, 20, 197–215.

Littrell, M., Baizerman, S., Kean, R., Gahring, S., Niemeyer, S., Reilly, R., and Stout, J. (1994). Souvenirs and Tourism Styles. *Journal of Travel Research*, 32(3): 3–11.

Liu, J., Sheldon, T., and Var, T. (1987). Resident Perceptions of the Environmental Impacts of Tourism. *Annals of Tourism Research*, 14(1): 17–37.

Liu, Z. (2003). Sustainable Tourism Development: A Critique. *Journal of Sustainable Tourism*, 11(6): 459–475.

Lovelock, C. and Weinberg, C. (1989). *Public and Nonprofit Marketing*. San Francisco: The Scientific Press.

Lowenthal, D. (1985). *Past is a Foreign Country*. Cambridge: Cambridge University Press.

Lowenthal, D. (2000). *Past is a Foreign Country*. Cambridge: Cambridge University Press.

Lyon, S. (2007). Balancing Values of Outstanding Universality with Conservation and Management at three United Kingdom Cultural World Heritage Sites. *Journal of Heritage Tourism*, 2(1): 53–63.

MacAloon, J. (1984). Introduction: Cultural Performances, Culture Theory. In J.A. MacAloon (ed.) *Rite, Drama, Festival, Spectacle: Rehearsals Towards a Theory of Cultural Performance* (pp. 1–15). Philadelphia: Institute for the Study of Human Issues.

MacCannell, D. (1973). Staged Authenticity: Arrangements of Social Space in Tourist Settings: *American Journal of Sociology*, 79, 589–603.

MacCannell, D. (1992). *Empty Meeting Grounds: The Tourist Papers*. London: Routledge.

MacDonald, S. (1992). Cultural Imagining among Museum Visitors. *Museum Management and Curatorship*, 12, 367–380.

MacInnis, D. and Price, L. (1987). The Role of Imagery in Information Processing: Review and Extensions. *Journal of Consumer Research*, 13, 473–491.

Maclaran, P. and Catterall, M. (2002). Researching the Social Web: Marketing Information from Virtual Communities. *Marketing Intelligence and Planning*, 20(6): 319–326.

Maffesoli, M. (1996). *The Time of the Tribes: The Decline of Individualism in Mass Society*. London: Sage.

Maffesoli, M. (2000). *L'Instant Eternal. Le Retour du Tragique dans les Societes Postmodernes*. Paris: Denoel.

Magrath, A. (1992). *The Six Imperatives of Marketing: Lessons from the World's Best Companies*. New York: AMACOM.

Manfredo, M., Bright, A., and Haas, G. (1992). Research in tourism advertising. In M. Manfredo and I.L. Champaign (ed.) *Influencing Human Behavior*. Champaign, IL: Sagamore.

Manning, E. and Dougherty, T. (1995). Sustainable Tourism: Preserving the Golden Goose. *Cornell Hotel and Restaurant Quarterly*, 36(2): 29–42.

Manning, F. (1983). Cosmos and Chaos: Celebration in the Modern World. In F.E. Manning (ed.) *The Celebration of Society: Perspectives on Contemporary Cultural Performance* (pp. 3–30). Bowling Green: Bowling Green University Popular Press.

Manning, F. (1992). Spectacle. In Bauman, R. (ed.) *Folklore, Cultural Performances, and Popular Entertainments* (pp. 291–299). Oxford: Oxford University Press.

Manning, T. (1996). Tourism: What are the Limits. *Ecodecision*, Spring, 36, 35–39.

Manning, T. (1999). Indicators of Tourism Sustainability. *Tourism Management*, 20(1): 179–181.

Marjanen, H. (1995). Longitudnal Study on Consumer Spatial Shopping Behavior with Special Reference to Out-of-town Shopping. *Journal of Retailing and Consumer Service*, 2(3): 163–74.

Markwell, S., Bennett, M., and Ravenscroft, N. (1997). The Changing Market for Heritage Tourism: A Case Study of Visits to Historic Houses in England. *International Journal of Heritage Studies*, 3(2): 95–108.

Marsh, J. (1993). An Index of Tourism Sustainability. In J. Nelson, R. Butler, and G. Wall (eds.) *Tourism and Sustainable Development: Guide for Local Planners*. Madrid: WTO.

Maslow, A. (1970). *Motivation and Personality*, 2nd edn. New York: Harper and Row.

Matheson, C. (2005). Festivity and Sociability: Study of Celtic Music Festival. *Tourism Culture and Communication*, 5, 149–163.

Mayfield, T. and Crompton, J. (1995). Development of an Instrument for Identifying Community Reason for Staging a Festival. *Journal of Travel Research*, 33, 37–44.

McCarthy, J. (1960). *Basic Marketing: A Managerial Approach*, 7th edn. Homewood, IL: Richard D. Irwin, Inc.

McCloskey, M. (1996). The Limits of Collaboration. *Harper's Magazine*, November: 34–36.

McDonnell, I., Allen, J., and O'Toole, W. (1999). *Festivals and Special Events Management*. Sydney: Wiley & Sons Australia.

McGehee, N. and Santos, C. (2005). Social Change, Discourse and Volunteer Tourism. *Annals of Tourism Research*, 32, 760–779.

McIntosh, A. (1999). Into the Tourist's Mind: Understanding the Value of the Heritage Experience. *Journal of Travel and Tourism Marketing*, 8(1): 41–64.

McIntosh, A. and Prentice, R. (1999). Affirming Authenticity: Consuming Cultural Heritage. *Annals of Tourism Research*, 26, 589–612.

McKercher, B. and du Cros, H. (2002). *Cultural Tourism: The Partnership between Tourism and Cultural Heritage Management*. New York: Haworth.

McKercher, B., Ho, P., and du Cros, H. (2004). Relationship between tourism and cultural heritage management: Evidence from Hong Kong. *Tourism Management,* 25(4): 539–548.

McKenzie-Mohr, D. (2000). Fostering Sustainable Behavior through Community-based Social Marketing. *American Psychologist*, 55(5): 531–537.

McLean, F. (1994). Services Marketing: The Case of Museums. *Service Industry Journal*, 14(2): 190–203.

McLean, F. (1995). A Marketing Revolution in Museums? *Journal of Marketing Management*, 11(6): 601–616.

McLean, F. (1997). *Marketing the Museum*. London: Routledge.

McLean, F. (2002). *Marketing the Museum*. London: Routledge.

McMaster, G. (1990). Problems of Representation: Our Home, But the Natives' Land. *Muse*, Autumn, 35–8.

Medina, L. (2003). Commoditizing Culture: Tourism and Maya Identity. *Annals of Tourism Research*, 30, 353–368.

Medway, D. and Warnaby, G. (2008). Alternative Perspective on Marketing and the Place Brand. *European Journal of Marketing*, 42(5/6): 641–653.

Mehmetoglu, M. and Ellingsen, K. (2005). Do Small-Scale Festivals Adopt "Market Orientation" as a Management Philosophy? *Event Management*, 9(3): 119–132.

Mercer, D. (1996). Native Peoples and Tourism: Conflict and Compromise. In W. Theobald (ed.) *Global Tourism: The Next Decade* (pp. 124–146). Melbourne: Butterworth-Heinemann.

Merriman, N. (1991). *Beyond the Glass Case: The Past, the Heritage and the Public in Britain*. Leicester: Leicester University Press.

Miller, D. (1999). Social Justice and Environmental Goods. *Fairness and Futurity*, Oxford Scholarship Online Monographs, 151–173.

Miller, G. (2001). The Development of Indicators for Sustainable Tourism: Results of a Delphi Survey of Tourism Researchers. *Tourism Management*, 22, 351–362.

Misiura, S. (2006). *Heritage Marketing*. Boston: Elsevier.

Mitra, A. and Lankford, S. (1999). *Research Methods in Parks, Recreation and Leisure Services*. Champaign, IL: Sagamore.

Mitsche, N., Reino, S., Knox, D., and Bauernfeind, U. (2008). Enhancing Cultural Tourism e-Services through Heritage Interpretation. Information and Communication Technologies in Tourism 2008 Proceedings of the International Conference, Innsbruck, Austria.

Modlin, A. (2008). Tales Told on the Tour. *Southeastern Geographer*, 48(3): 265–287.

Mok, C. and Iverson, T. (2000). Expenditure-based Segmentation: Taiwanese Tourists to Guam. *Tourism Management*, 21(3): 299–305.

Mohr, K., Backman, K., Gahan, L., and Backman, S. (1993). An Investigation of Festival Motivations and Event Satisfaction by Visitor Type. *Festival Management and Event Tourism*, 1(3): 89–97.

Moorman, C., Deshpande, R. and Zaltman, G. (1993). *Relationships between Providers and Users of Market Research: The Role of Personal Trust*. Working Paper No. 93–111, Cambridge, MA: Marketing Science Institute.

Morrison, A. (2002). *Hospitality and Travel Marketing*. 3rd edn. Albany, NY: Delmar.

Mortner, S. and Ford, J. (2005). Measuring Nonprofit Marketing Strategy Performance: The Case of Museum Stores. *Journal of Business Research*, 58, 829–840.

Moscardo, G. (1999). *Making Visitors Mindful*. Champaign, IL: Sagamore.

Moscardo, G. (2001). Cultural and Heritage Tourism: The Great Debates. In B. Faulkner, G. Moscardo and E. Laws (eds.): *Laws Tourism in the 21st Century*, (pp. 3–17). London: Continuum.

Moscardo, G. (2008). Sustainable Tourism Innovation: Challenging Basic Assumptions. *Tourism and Hospitality Research*, 8(1): 4–13.

Moscardo, G. and Pearce, P. (1999). Understanding Ethnic Tourists. *Annals of Tourism Research,* 26(2): 416–434.

Moscardo, G. and Woods, B. (1998). Managing Tourism in the Wet Tropics World Heritage Area: Interpretation and the Experience of Visitors on Skyrail. In E. Laws, B. Faulkner, and G. Moscardo (eds), *Embracing and Managing Change in Tourism* (pp. 307–323). London: Routledge.

Mules, T. and Faulkner, B. (1996). An Economic Perspective on Special Events. *Tourism Economics*, 2(2): 107–117.

Murphy, P. (1985). *Tourism: A Community Approach*. New York: Methuen.

Murphy, P., Lacinak, G., Bowie, N., and Klein, T. (2005). Ethical Marketing. Upper Saddle River, NJ: Pearson Prentice Hall.

Musée d'art et d'histoire (1998). *The Maison Tavel: History of a City and Its Day-to-day Life*. Geneva: Musée d'art et d'histoire.

Museums Association, UK (1984). Other Code of Ethics. Retrieved from http://icom. museum/other-codes_eng.html.

Museums Association (2009). Ethics. Retreived June 12, 2008 from http://www.museum-sassociation.org/ethics

Mustonen, P. (2006). Volunteer Tourism: Postmodern Pilgrimage. *Journal of Tourism and Cultural Change*, 3(3): 160 – 177

NAIA (1980). *North American Indian Museum By-laws*. Niagara Falls: North American Indian Museums Association.

Naisbitt, J. and Aburdene P. (1990).*Megatrends 2000*. New York: Morrow.

National Trust of Australia (2009). Facts. Retrieved 15 July, 2009 from http://www. nationaltrust.org.au/?pageid=2

Nicholson, R. and Pearce, D. (2000). Who Goes to Events: A Comparative Analysis of the Profile Characteristics of Visitors to Four South Island Events. *Journal of Vacation Marketing*, 6(3): 236–253.

Nicholson, R. and Pearce, D. (2001). Why do People Attend Events: A Comparative Analysis of Visitor Motivations at Four South Island Events. *Journal of Travel Research*, 39: 449–460.

Nill, A. and Schibrowsky, J. (2007). Research on Marketing Ethics: A Systematic Review of the Literature. *Journal of Macromarketing*, 27, 256–273.

Notarstefano, C. (2008). European Sustainable Tourism: Context, Concepts, and Guidelines for Action. *International Journal of Sustainable Economy*, 1(1): 44–59.

Nuryunti, W. (1996). Heritage and Postmodern Tourism. *Annals of Tourism Research*, 23, 249–60.

Nutini, H. (1988). Pre-Hispanic Component of the Syncretic Cult of the Dead in Mesoamerica. *Ethnology*, 27, 57–78.

Olsen, L. (2002). Authenticity as a Concept in Tourism Research. *Tourism Studies*, 2(2): 159–182.

Opperman, M. (1993). Regional Market Segmentation Analysis in Australia. *Journal of Travel and Tourism Marketing*, 2(4): 59–74.

O'Sullivan, D. and Jackson, M. (2002). Festival Tourism: A Contributor to Sustainable Economic Development? *Journal of Sustainable Tourism*, 10(4): 325–342.

Page, S. (1992). Managing Tourism in a Small Historic City. *Town and Country Planning*, 61(7/8): 208–211.

Painter, M. (1992). Participation in Power. In M. Munro-Clark (Ed.) *Citizen Participation in Government*. Sydney: Hale and Iremonger.

Parsons, E. and Maclaran, P. (2009). *Contemporary Issues in Marketing and Consumer Behavior*. San Francisco: Butterworth Heinemann.

Pavoni, R. and Selvafolta, O. (1998). La Diversita Delle Dimoremuseo: Opportunita Di Una Riflessione. In L. Leoncini and F. Simonett (eds.) *Abitare La Storia*, pp. 32–36. Turin: Umberto Allemandi.

Peacock, P. (1998). Data Mining in Marketing: Part I. *Marketing Management*, Winter, 8–19.

Pearce, D. (1992). Green Economics. *Environmental Issues*, 1(1): 3–13.

Pearce, D. (1997). The Role of the Public Sector in Conservation and Tourism Planning, In W. Nuryunti (ed.) *Tourism and Heritage Management* (pp. 88–100). Yogyakarta: Gadjah Mada University Press.

Pearce, P. (1995). From Culture Shock and Culture Arrogance to Cultural Exchange: Ideas Towards Sustainable Cultural Tourism. *Journal of Sustainable Tourism*, 3(3): 143–153.

Pearson, M. and Sullivan, S. (1995). *Looking after Heritage Places: The Basics of Heritage Planning for Managers, Landowners and Administrators*. Carlton: Melbourne University Press.

Peleggi, M. (2005). Consuming Colonial Nostalgia: The Monumentalization of Historic Hotels in Urban South-East Asia. *Asia Pacific Viewpoint*, 46(3): 255–265.

Petford, J. (1996). Pushed to the Limits – The Dynamics of Internal Neocolonialism in Peripheral Tourism Developments: Case Studies in Egypt and South Wales. In P. Atkinson-Wells (ed.) *Keys to the Marketplace: Problems and Issues in Cultural and Heritage Tourism* (pp. 87–100). Middlesex, UK: Hisarlik Press.

Phaswana-Mafuya, N. and Haydam, N. (2005). Tourists' expectations and perceptions of the Robben Island Museum – A World Heritage Site. *Museum Management and Curatorship*, 20, 149–169.

Phillips, R. and Steiner, C. (1999). *Unpacking Culture: Art and Commodity in Colonial and Postcolonial Worlds*. Berkeley: University of California Press.

Pigram, J. (1990). Sustainable Tourism Policy Considerations. *The Journal of Tourism Studies*, 1(2): 3–9.

Pine, B. and Gilmore, J. (1998). Welcome to the Experience Economy. *Harvard Business Review*, 76(4): 97–105.

Pine, B. and Gilmore, J. (1999). *The Experience Economy: Work's Theatre and Every Business a Stage*. Boston: Harvard Business School Press.

Pine II, J. and Gilmore, J. (2008). The Eight Principles of Strategic Authenticity. *Strategy and Leadership*, 36(3): 35–40.

Pinna, G. (2001). Introduction to Historic House Museums. *Museum International*, 53(2): 4–9.

Popelka, C. and Littrell, M. (1991). Influence of Tourism on Handicraft Evolution. *Annals of Tourism Research*, 18(3): 392–413.

Poria, Y., Butler, R., and Airey, D. (2001). Clarifying Heritage Tourism. *Annals of Tourism Research*, 28, 1047–49.

Poria, Y., Butler, R., and Airey, D. (2003). The core of heritage tourism. *Annals of Tourism Research,* 30(1): 238–254.

Prentice, R. (1989). Visitors to Heritage Sites. In D. Herbert, R. Prentice and C. Thomas (eds.) *Heritage Sites: Strategies for Marketing and Development* (pp. 15–61). Aldershot: Avebury.

Prentice, R. (1993). *Tourism and Heritage Attractions.* London: Routledge.

Prentice, R. (2001). Experiential Cultural Tourism: Museums and the Marketing of the New Romanticism of Evoked Authenticity. *Museum Management and Curatorship,* 19(1): 5–26.

Pretes, M. (2003). Tourism and Nationalism. *Annals of Tourism Research,* 30(1): 125–142.

Pretty, J. (1995). The Many Interpretations of Participation. *Focus,* 16: 4–5.

Price, S. (1999). *Primitive Art in Civilized Places.* Chicago: University of Chicago Press.

Prosser, R. (1994). Societal Change and the Growth in Alternative Tourism. In E. Cater and G. Lowman (eds.) *Ecotourism: A Sustainable Option?* (pp. 19–37). Chichester: John Wiley.

Quemuel, C. (1996). Filipino Student Apathy or Activism? In J. Okamura and R. Labarador (eds.) *Pagdiriwang: Legacy and Vision of Hawaii's Filipino Americans* (pp. 17–19). Honolulu: University of Hawaii, Student Equity, Excellence, and Diversity, and Center for Southeast Asian Studies.

Ralston, L. and Crompton, L. (1988). The Application of Systematic Survey Methods at Open Access Special Events and Festivals. *Visions in Leisure and Business,* 11(3): 18–24.

Rappaport, R. (1992). Ritual. In R. Bauman (ed.) *Folklore, Cultural Performances, and Popular Entertainments* (pp. 249–260). Oxford: Oxford University Press.

Reid, L. and Reid, S. (1993). Communicating Tourism Supplier Services: Building Repeat Visitor Relationships. *Journal of Travel and Tourism Marketing,* 2(2/3): 3–20.

Reisinger, Y. and Steiner, C. (2006). Reconceptualizing Object Authenticity. *Annals of Tourism Research,* 33(1): 65–86.

Revilla, G. and Dodd, T. (2003). Authenticity Perceptions of Talavera Pottery. *Journal of Travel Research,* 42, 94–99.

Rheingold, H. (1991). *Virtual Reality*: London: Secker and Warburg.

Richards, G. (1996). Production and Consumption of European Cultural Tourism. *Annals of Tourism Research,* 23, 261–283.

Richards, G. (2002). The Festivalization of Society or the Socialization of Festivals? The Case of Catalunya. In G. Richards (ed.) *Cultural Tourism? Global and Local Perspectives* (pp. 257–280). London: The Haworth Hospitality Press.

Ritchie, J. (1984). Assessing the Impact of Hallmark Events: Conceptual and Research Issues. *Journal of Travel Research,* 23: 2–11.

Ritchie, J. and Goeldner, C. (1989). *Travel and Tourism Research: A Handbook for Managers.* New York: John Wiley.

Rogers, D. and Whetten, D. (1982). *Interorganizational Coordination: Theory, Research, and Implementation.* Ames: Iowa State University Press.

Rogers, R. (1995). *The Oceans are Emptying: Fish Wars and Sustainability.* Institute of Policy Alternatives. Montreal: Black Rose Books.

Rosenzweig, R. and Thelen, D. (1998). *The Presence of the Past: Popular Uses of History in American Life.* New York: Columbia University Press.

Rowan, Y. and Baram, U. (eds.) (2004). *Marketing Heritage. Archaeology and the Consumption of Past.* Walnut Creek, CA: Altamira Press.

Saarinen, J. (2006). Traditions of Sustainability Studies. *Annals of Tourism Research,* 33(4): 1121–1140.

Saayman, M. and Saayman, A. (2006). Sociodemographics and Visiting Patterns of Arts Festivals in South Africa. *Tourism Management*, 9, 221–222.

Sampson, G. (2001). *The WTO and Sustainable Development*. New York: United Nations University Press.

Sangpikul, A. (2008). Travel Motivations of Japanese Senior Travellers to Thailand. *International Journal of Travel Research*, 10, 81–94.

Schiffman, L. and Kanuk, L. (1991). *Consumer Behavior*. Englewood Cliffs, NJ: Prentice Hall.

Schneider, I. and Backman, S. (1996). Cross-cultural Equivalence of Festival Motivations: A Study in Jordon. *Festival Management and Event Tourism*, 4, 139–144.

Schulz, D. (2001). It is now Time to Change Marketing's Name. *Marketing News*, 35(22): 8.

Scott, D. (1996). A Comparison of Visitor's Motivations to Attend Three Urban Festivals. *Festival Management and Event Tourism*, 3, 121–128.

Selin, S. (1999). Developing a Typology of Sustainable Tourism Partnerships. *Journal of Sustainable Tourism*, 7(3 and 4): 260–273.

Selin, S. and Chavez, D. (1995). Developing an Evolutionary Partnership Model. *Annals of Tourism Research,* 22(4): 844–866.

Selin, W. (1993). Collaborative Alliances: New Interorganizational Forms in Tourism. *Journal of Travel and Tourism Marketing*, 2, 217–227.

Selwyn, T. (1996). Introduction. In T. Selwyn (ed.). *The Tourist Image: Myths and Myth Making in Tourism* (pp. 1–33). Chichester: John Wiley and Sons.

Sheraton Wild Horse Pass Resort (2009). *Press Room*. Retrieved, June 15, 2009 from http://www.wildhorsepassresort.com/medialounge/login.php

Shoemaker, S., Lewis, R., and Yesawich, P. (2000). *Marketing Leadership in Hospitality and Tourism*. 4th edn. Upper Saddle River, NJ: Pearson Prentice Hall.

Shone, A. and Parry, B. (2001). *Successful Event Management: A Practical Handbook*. London: Continuum Books.

Sigala, M. (2005). Integrating Customer Relationship Management in Hotel Operations: Managerial and Operational Implications. *International Journal of Hospitality Management,* 24(3): 391–413

Silberberg, T. (1995). Cultural Tourism and Business Opportunities for Museums and Heritage Sites. *Tourism Management*, 16, 361–5.

Simmons, D. (1994). Community Participation in Tourism Planning. *Tourism Management*, 15, 98–108.

Simpson, M. (1996). *Making Representations: Museums in the Post-Colonial Era*. London: Routledge.

Simpson, M. (2008). Community Benefit Tourism Indicators: A Conceptual Oxymoron. *Tourism Management,* 29(1): 1–18.

Sinclair, M. and Stabler, M. (1997). *The Economics of Tourism*. London: Routledge.

Sirakaya, E. and Sonmez, S. (2000). Gender Images in State Tourism Bochures: An Overlooked Area in Socially Responsible Tourism Marketing. *Journal of Travel Research*, 38: 353–362.

Sirakaya, E., Jamal, T., and Choi, H. (2002). Developing Indicators for Destination Sustainability. In D. Weaver (ed.) *The Encyclopedia of Ecotourism*. Oxford: Cabi Publishing.

Sitarez, D. (ed.) (1998). *Sustainable America*. Carbondale, IL: Earthpress.

Slater, S. and Narver, J. (1995). Market Orientation and the Learning Organization. *Journal of Marketing*, 59, 63–74.

Smith, M. and MacKay, K. (2001). The Organization of Information in Memory for Pictures of Tourist Destinations: Are there Age-related Differences? *Journal of Travel Research,* 39(3): 261–266.

Smith, S. (1989). Funding our Heritage. In D.L. Uzzell (ed.) *Heritage Interpretation, vol. 2 The Visitor Experience* (pp. 23–28). London: Belhaven.

Spiropoulos, S., Gargalianos, D., and Sotiriadou, K. (2006). The 20th Greek Festival of Sydney: A Stakeholder Analysis. *Event Management*, 9, 169–183.

Spitz, J. and Thorn, M. (2003). Introduction. In J. Spitz, and M. Thorn (eds.) *Urban Network: Museums Embracing Communities* (pp. 3–7): Chicago: The Field Museum.

Stamboulis, Y. and Pantoleon Skayannis, P. (2003). Innovation Strategies and Technology for Experience-based Tourism. *Tourism Management,* 24(1): 35–43.

Stebbins, R. (1996). Cultural Tourism as Serious Leisure. *Annals of Tourism Research*, 23 (4): 948–950.

Steiner, Y. and Reisinger, C. (2006). Reconceptualizing Object Authenticity. *Annals of Tourism Research*, 33 (1): 65–86.

Stern, H. (1962). The Significance of Impulsive Buying Today. *Journal of Marketing*, 26(2): 59–62.

Stone, G. (1954). City Shoppers and Urban Identification: Observations on the Social Psychology of City Life. *American Journal of Sociology*, 60(1): 36–45.

Stynes, D. and Mahoney, E. (1986). *1984 Michigan Commercial Campground Marketing Study*. Department paper. Department of Park and Recreation Resources, Michigan State University.

Suarez, A. and N. Tsutu (2004). The Value of Museum Collections for Research. *Bioscience* 54(1): 66–74.

Sung, H. (2004). *Predicting the Likelihood of Selecting Different Adventure Trip Types: A Product Driven Approach for Segmenting the U.S. Adventure Travel Market*. Retrieved March 21, 2005, from www.ttra.com/pub/uplads/017.pdf

Swanson, K. (2004). Tourists and Retailer's Perceptions of Souvenirs. *Journal of Vacation Marketing*, 10(4): 363–377.

Swanson, K. and Horridge, P. (2006). Travel Motivations as Souvenir Purchase Decisions. *Tourism Management*, 27, 671–683.

Tartans of Scotland (2009). *Scottish Tartans*. Retrieved June 2009 from http://www. scotland.com/culture/tartans/

Taylor, G.D. (1991). "Tourism and Sustainability—Impossible Dream or Essential Objective?" In *Proceedings, Tourism—Environment—Sustainable Development: An Agenda for Research* (pp. 27–29). Hull, Quebec: Tourism Canada.

Taylor, J. (2001). Authenticity and Sincerity in Tourism. *Annals of Tourism Research*, 28(1): 7–26.

Teo, P. and Huang, S. (1995). Tourism and Heritage Conservation in Singapore. *Annals of Tourism Research*, 22(1): 589–615.

Theobald, W. (1998). *Global Tourism*. 2nd edn. Oxford: Butterworth-Heinemann.

The Imperial (2009a). *History and Art*. New Delhi: The Imperial.

The Imperial (2009b). *The Imperial Experience*. Summer. New Delhi: The Imperial.

Thrane, C. (2002). Jazz Festival Visitors and Their Expenditures: Linking Spending Patterns to Musical Interest. *Journal of Travel Research*, 40, 281–286.

Tibet House (2006). *Tibet House: Mission and Activities*. New Delhi: Tibet House.

Tiesdell, D., Oc, T., and Heath, T. (1996). *Revitalizing Historic Urban Quarters*. Oxford: Architectural Press.

Tilden, F. (1957). *Interpreting Our Heritage*. Chapel Hill, NC: University of North Carolina Press.

Tilden, F. (1977). *Interpreting Our Heritage.* Chapel Hill, NC: University of North Carolina Press.

Timothy, D. (2000). Building Community Awareness of Tourism in a Developing Country Destination. *Tourism Recreation Research*, 25(2): 111–16.

Timothy, D. (2002). Tourism and Community Development Issues. In R. Sharpely and D. Telfer (eds.) *Tourism and Development: Concepts and Issues* (pp. 149–74). Clevedon: Channel View Publications.

Timothy, D. (2005). *Shopping Tourism, Retailing and Leisure.* Clevedon: Channel View Publications.

Timothy, D. and Boyd, S. (2003). *Heritage Tourism.* New York: Prentice Hall.

Timothy, D. and Boyd, S. (2006). Heritage Tourism in the 21st Century: Valued Traditions and New Perspectives. *Journal of Heritage Tourism*, 1(1): 1–16.

Timothy, D. and Wall, G. (1997). Tourism and Built Heritage: Critical Issues. *Estudios Y Perspectivas En Turismo*, 6(3): 193–208.

Timur, S. and Getz, D. (2009). Sustainable Tourism Development: How Do Destination Stakeholders Perceive Sustainable Urban Tourism? *Sustainable Development*, 17, 220–232.

Tobelem, J. (1998). The Marketing Approach in Museums. *Museum Management and Curatorship*, 16(4): 337–354.

Tosun, C. (1999). Towards a Typology of Community Participation in the Tourism Development Process. *International Journal of Tourism and Hospitality*, 10, 113–134.

Tosun, C. (2006). Expected Nature of Community Participation in Tourism Development. *Tourism Management*, 27, 493–504.

Tourism Research Australia (2006). *International Market Tourism Facts.* Belconnen, Canberra, Australia: Tourism Australia.

Travel Industry Association of America (2001). *The Shopping Traveler.* Washington DC: Travel Industry Association of America.

Travel Industry Association of America (2008a). *Domestic Travel Fast Facts.* Washington DC: Travel Industry Association of America.

Travel Industry Association of America (2008b). *The Benefits Are Everywhere.* Washington DC: Travel Industry Association of America.

Travel Industry Association of America (2009). *TIA Fast Travel Facts.* Press Release, July 10.

Trilling, L. (1972). *Sincerity and Authenticity.* Cambridge, MA: Harvard University Press.

Trist, E. (1977). A Concept of Organizational Ecology. *Australian Journal of Management*, 2, 162–175.

Truettner, W. (ed.) (1991). *The West as America: Reinterpreting Images of the Frontier.* Washington and London: Smithsonian Press.

Tsiotsou, R. and Vasaioti, E. (2006). Satisfaction: A segmentation criterion for "short term" visitors of mountainous destinations. *Journal of Travel and Tourism Marketing*, 20(1): 61–73.

Tunbridge, J. and Ashworth, G. (1996). *Dissonant Heritage: The Management of the Past as a Resource in Conflict.* Chichester: John Wiley and Sons.

Turner, R., Pearce, D., and Bateman, I. (1994). *Environmental Economics: An Elementary Introduction.* Norfolk, UK: Harvester Wheatsheaf.

Uberlaker, D. and Grant, L. (1989). *Human Skeletal Remains: Preservation or Reburial? Yearbook of Physical Anthropology*, 32, 249–87.

UNESCO World Heritage Center (2000). *World Heritage Convention.* Retrieved October 2006 from http://www.unesco.org/whc/

UN-WTO (2004). *Tourism Congestion Management t Natural and Cultural Sites*. Madrid: World Tourism Organization.

Upitis, A. (1989). Interpreting Cross-cultural Sites. In D. Uzzell (ed.) *Heritage Interpretation, vol. 1: The Natural and Built Environment* (pp. 153–60). London: Belhaven.

Uriely, N. (2005). The Tourist Experience: Conceptual Developments. *Annals of Tourism Research*, 32(1): 199–216.

Urry, J. (1990). *The Tourist Gaze: Leisure and Travel in Contemporary Societies*. London: Sage.

Uysal, M., Gahan, L., and Martin, M. (1993). An Examination of Event Motivations: A Case Study. *Festival Management and Event Tourism*, 1(1): 5–10.

Var, T., Chon, J. and Doh, M. (2002). Acceptance of Technology by Texas Museums: An Application of Learning Curve. *Information Technology and Tourism*, 4, 123–130.

VisitBritain (2009). *Regional Intelligence and Research*. London: VisitBritain

Waitt, G. (2000). Consuming Heritage: Perceived Historical Authenticity. *Annals of Tourism Research*, 27, 835–862.

Walker, C., Scott-Melnyk, S., and Sherwood, K. (2002). *Reggae to Rachmaninoff: How and Why People Participate in Arts and Culture*. Washington DC: Urban Institute.

Wall, G. (1989). Cycles and Capacity: Incipient Theory or Conceptual Contradiction? Tourism Management, 3, 188–92.

Wall, G. (1989). An International Perspective on Historic Sites, Recreation, and Tourism. *Recreation Research Review*, 14(4): 10–14.

Wallace, G. (1993). Visitor Management: Lessons from Galapagos National Park. In Lindberg, K. and Hawkins, D. (eds.) *Ecotourism: A Guide for Planners and Managers* (pp. 55–82). North Bennington, VA: Ecotourism Society.

Walle, A. (2004). Building a Diverse Attendance at Cultural Festivals: Embracing Oral History and Folklore in Strategic Ways. *Event Management*, 8, 73–82.

Walle, G. (1997). Sustainable Tourism – Unsustainable Development. In S. Wahab and J. Pigram (eds.) *Tourism Development and Growth* (pp. 33–49). London: Routledge.

Wallendorf, M. and Arnould, E. (1988). My Favourite Things: A Cross-cultural Inquiry into Object Attachment, Possessiveness, and Social Linkage. *Journal of Consumer Research*, 14, 531–47.

Walo, M., Bull, A., and Green, H. (1996). Achieving Economic Benefits at Local Events: A Case Study of a Local Sport Event. *Festival Management and Event Tourism*, 3(3/4): 96–106.

Walters, G., Sparks, B., and Herington, C. (2007). The effectiveness of print advertising stimuli in evoking consumption visitors for potential visitors. *Journal of Travel Research*, 46(1): 24–34.

Wang, N. (1999). Rethinking Authenticity in Tourism Experience. *Annals of Tourism Research*, 26(2): 349–370.

Watt, D. (1998). *Event Management in Leisure and Tourism*. New York: Addison Wesley Longman.

Wearing, S. (2001). *Volunteer Tourism: Experiences that Make a Difference*. Wallingford: CABI.

Webster, C. (1995). Marketing Culture and Marketing Effectiveness in Service Firms. *Journal of Services Marketing*, 9(2): 6–21.

Weeden, C. (2005). *Niche Tourism: Contemporary Issues, Trends and Cases*. London: Butterworth-Heniemann.

Wells, P. (1989). Fiddle Music from Alabama, Wyoming, and Montana. *The Journal of American Folklore*, 102(406): 460–463.

Wheeller, D. (1993). Sustaining the Ego. *Journal of Sustainable Tourism*, 1(2): 121–129.

Wicks, B. and Fesenmaier, D. (1993). A Comparison of Visitor and Vendor Perceptions of Service Quality at a Special Event. *Festival Management and Event Tourism*, 1, 19–26.

Wilmott, M. (2003). *Citizen Brands*. Chichester: Wiley.

Wilmott, M. and Nelson, W. (2003). *Complicated Lives: Sophisticated Consumers, Intricate Lifestyles and Simple Solutions*. Chichester: Wiley.

Wilson, G. and Jones, R. (1984). Marketing and Museums. *European Journal of Marketing*, 18(2): 90–9.

Witt, S. and Moutinho, L. (1989). *Tourism Marketing and Management Handbook*. New York: Prentice-Hall.

Wood, E. (2004). Marketing Information for the Event Industry. In I. Yeoman, M. Robertson, J. Ali-Knight, S. Drummond and U. McMahon-Beattie (eds.) *Festival and Events Management: An International Arts and Culture Perspective* (pp. 130–157). New York: Elsevier.

World Commission for Environment and Development (1987). *Our Common Future*. New York: Oxford University Press.

WTTC, WTO and the Earth Council (1995). *Agenda 21 for the Travel and Tourism Industry*. WTTC, WTO and the Earth Council.

Xiao, H. and Mair, H. (2006). A Paradox of Images: Representation of China as a Tourist Destination. *Journal of Travel and Tourism Marketing,* 20(2): 1–14.

Xie, P. and Wall, G. (2002). "Visitors" Perceptions of Authenticity at Cultural Attractions in Hainan, China. *International Journal of Tourism Research*, 4, 353–366.

Yale, P. (1991). *From Tourist Attractions to Heritage Tourism*. Huntingdon: Elm Publications.

Yeoman, I., Brass, D., and McMahon-Beattie, U. (2007). Current Issue in Tourism: The Authentic Tourist. *Tourism Management*, 28, 1128–1138.

Yoo, B. and Donthu, N. (2000). Developing a Scale to Measure the Perceived Quality of an Internet Shopping Site (SITEQUAL). *Quarterly Journal of Electronic Commerce*, 2(1): 31–47.

Yu, J. (1990). Looking Backwards into the future. *Gao Ban*, 7(1): 1–5.

Zeppal, H. and Hall, C. (1992). Arts and Heritage Tourism. In B. Weiler and C. Hall (eds.) *Special Interest Tourism* (pp. 47–68). London: Belhaven.

Index